ANATOMY OF AN ESSAY

INSTRUCTIONS AND READINGS

Tina D. Eliopulos and Todd Moffett

Kendall Hunt
publishing company

Cover images © Sandra C. Schultz, (deceased) by Anne C. Schultz

www.kendallhunt.com
Send all inquiries to:
4050 Westmark Drive
Dubuque, IA 52004-1840

Copyright © 2019 by Kendall Hunt Publishing Company

ISBN 978-1-5249-7604-0

Published in the United States of America

To our mothers, Goldie Kris Eliopulos and Jacquelynne Wray Moffett, who taught us that words matter.

Sandy Christy Schultz's artwork appears with the permission of her daughter Anne. In addition to her work as an artist, Sandy traveled many roads, devoured literature, wrote nonfiction and fiction, supported environmental projects, and gave friendship to all, including the editors of this text. A graduation gift from her father, the 1954 Olivetti Lettera 22 typewriter featured on the back cover and in the chapter headings of *Anatomy of an Essay* was Sandy's companion for over fifty years. On it, she crafted numerous creative pieces, including, in January of 1997, "Ode to the Olivetti," where she calls her companion her "true friend" and expresses her gratitude: "[T]hank you for not giving suggestions, advice, / where to go for help; / I could just let you put it down like I thought it."

Contents

A Note about Spelling

Some of the readings in this book were originally produced or published in the United Kingdom, which has spelling rules different from those in the United States. Please note that you will see British spellings in those readings.

Chapter 1
The Act of Writing

The act of writing conjures different emotions in each of us. For some, writing provides a primal outlet to express one's convictions and ideas; for others, it induces the same fear felt when stalling their car in the middle lane of a six-lane interstate; and yet for others, writing is the pesky fly interrupting the perfect picnic—if they deal with it, they can return to the fun stuff. Our relationship with writing is connected to our early educational experience with it—we loved our fifth-grade English teacher, who made all assignments FUN, so we love to write—or we hated our fifth-grade English teacher, who made every assignment a time-sucking, tedious, tormenting task right before recess, so we hate it. But whether you love it, hate it, or are just bothered by it, you still have to write. And you already are doing it—probably multiple times a day like when you are writing an e-mail to a coworker; blogging about your Disneyland trip; reviewing a restaurant on Yelp; texting about home designs you repinned on Pinterest; documenting a lab experiment in organic biology; tweeting about tweeting (no idea what happens there); or penning (yes, with an actual ink pen) a letter to a loved one serving in the military. Humans write. We have to. We have a desire to communicate, and writing has been the medium we have used to do so for centuries. If you cannot communicate, you cannot survive—the Sumerians knew this, and *thousands* of years later, we still do too.

While in college, most of you will endure (and live to tell about it on Rate My Professors) at least one composition course—others, depending on your major, will navigate two or three. But every college student will have to *write* in 80% of *all* of their classes (thank you, math class, for that 20% of fun). So, it is time to take a deep breath, steady yourself, and commit to the writing process, especially the creation of the essay, your academic ally.

Freshman and sophomore composition courses are intended to sharpen the writing skills that you developed throughout your middle and high school experience, regardless of how many years removed from them you are or how you feel about those experiences. The emphasis in college is placed squarely on your ability to present your thoughts cogently. The primary vehicle of thought in composition courses is the essay, defined by twentieth-century critic and theorist Northrop Frye as "a literary composition on a single subject; usually short, in prose, and nonexhaustive." Tack onto Frye's definition that our word *essay* is derived from the French word *essai*, meaning "an attempt," and beginning writers should understand what their purpose in writing an essay is: to make an *attempt* at teaching, persuading, or informing their readers (their audience) of *their stance* on an issue—the topic of their essay—while at the same time providing some level of entertainment. The essay is sometimes ranked with poetry, fiction, and drama as a fourth literary genre. It is important. But it distinguishes itself from those other forms because it is a work of nonfiction—it is not a short story, although it may contain *real-life* anecdotes and narrative moments—and it is rooted in fact and TRUTH. Do not refer to your essays as short stories; they are not. Take a creative writing course if you want to write fiction. In composition courses, you are writing about your own truth and about the truths of others.

In order to write the essay, you will need to understand the components of the essay itself: **thesis, development and support, organization**, and **mechanics**. As you work with each of these tools, your essay writing will improve and grow. This textbook instructs you how to use them, and offers writing samples from professional and student writers that effectively—not necessarily perfectly—represent them. The components of an essay can also be considered a rubric—not sure who likes this word more, Millennials or academics—to evaluate writing. In other words, as you write, build your essay with these four components in mind because your instructor will evaluate your work based upon your competency in using them.

The Grammarly Web site credits Albert Einstein as saying, "A person who never made a mistake never tried anything new." As you read through this textbook's selections and work through its exercises, remember the famous physicist's words. These writers are exploring and experimenting with language and ideas in an attempt to enrich their own lives and those of their readers. Their work may be the product of two or two hundred drafts. They may have given up on an idea only to dig it out of the trash and redo it. They persisted because they value writing. You too will write and rewrite and rewrite again. You too will learn from your mistakes and your successes. You too will write with purpose. Now go do it.

Excerpts from *The Poet's Companion*
by Kim Addonizio and Dorianne Laux
From "Writing and Knowing"

This is where we begin, by looking over our own shoulder, down our own arms, into our own hands at what we are holding, what we know. Few of us begin to write a poem about "death" or "desire." In fact, most of us begin by either looking outward: that blue bowl, those shoes, these three white clouds. Or inward: I remember, I imagine, I wish, I wonder, I want. [. . .]

The trick is to find out what we know, challenge what we know, own what we know, and then give it away in language: I love my brother, I hate winter, I always lose my keys. You have to know and describe your brother so well he becomes everyone's brother, to evoke the hatred of winter so passionately that we all begin to feel the chill, to lose your keys so memorably we begin to connect that action to all our losses, to our desires, to our fears of death. Good writing works from a simple premise: your experience is not yours alone, but in some sense a metaphor for everyone's. Poems that fail to understand this are what a writer once parodied in a three-line illustration:

> Here I stand
> looking out my window
> and I am important.

Of course our lives are important, meaningful. But our daily experiences, our dreams and loves and passionate convictions about the world, won't be important to others—to potential readers of our poems—unless we're able to transform the raw material of our experiences into language that reaches beyond the self-involvement of that person standing at the window, so that what we know becomes shared knowledge, part of who we are as individuals, a culture, a species.

What do we all know? We know our lives. We all go through childhood, adolescence, adulthood and old age. We can write about it. Some of us go through marriage, childbirth, parenthood, divorce. We work, we go to school, we form bonds of friendship and love, we break dishes in anger, we daydream, we follow the news or turn from it in despair, we forget. These are all subjects for our poems, the moments in our own personal lives that need telling, that are worth our attention and preservation.

Poetry is an intimate act. It's about bringing forth something that's inside you—whether it is a memory, a philosophical idea, a deep love for another person or for the world, or an apprehension of the spiritual. It's about making something, in language, which can be transmitted to others—not as information, or polemic, but as irreducible art.

From "The Shadow"

According to the psychologist Carl Jung, each of us has a daily, more pleasant self with which we identify—our ego—and a hidden self which we tend to reject and deny—what is known as our shadow. While the division into ego and shadow comes from Jung, it's an idea that humankind has recognized for centuries and that we all immediately understand: that the self is both light and dark, that the world contains both good and evil.

Our personal shadow lies in the unconscious and is formed when we are young, when we learn to identify with what our culture tells us are acceptable behaviors, thoughts, emotions. Poet Robert Bly calls the shadow "the long bag we drag behind us," explaining that as we learn what others don't like or accept in us we start "bag-stuffing." By the time we reach adulthood, Bly says, there is only a "thin slice" of us left—the rest is in that long bag. [. . .]

How can you gain access to the shadow, and mine it for poetry? It's important to get past the voices that tell you what you "should" write, the voices that say you want people to like you, to think you are a good person—the "writing as seduction" school. It means going into territory that may be labeled "forbidden," or that may be personally difficult. It's important not to censor yourself. Give yourself permission to explore wherever the writing takes you. Of course, this kind of writing—going towards what is hardest to speak of, whether that's the suffering in the world or your own personal obsessions— takes a certain amount of courage. Your normal, denying self doesn't want to deal with those things. But sometimes, writing may be the only place you can express them. There's a great feeling of relief and catharsis when you manage to get something that's been buried or hidden out onto the page. And such a process, whether or not it eventually results in a poem, helps to integrate that part of the self. [. . .]

We think that, for poets, integrating the shadow side also means training yourself to *see*. We once gave an assignment in which we were focusing on the making of images—creating vivid, evocative, sensual descriptions of things in the world. It was suggested that everyone describe a homeless man or woman and render him or her in such graphic detail that each of us could conjure up this person before us in the classroom. One woman had difficulty with the assignment because, she said, "I never really looked at a homeless person closely." Poets need to train themselves to look closely at the world, to observe it carefully and continuously.

From "Writer's Block"

All of us have felt this way at one time or another, as if we had been banished from the kingdom of our own feelings, thoughts, words. It helps to know that we aren't alone in this. But here's the good news: We don't believe in writer's block. We believe there are times when you are empty and times when you are full. When you're full to overflowing you write poems until you're empty, then you wait around while you get filled up again. You can help fill yourself up with stuff: books of poetry, novels, movies, new kinds of food, travel, relationships, art, gardening, TV, school, music . . . basically, experiences. And while you're doing that, your life will fill you up with all that you can't control: the death of a friend, unexpected moments of intense joy, car accidents, births, natural disasters, spring, war, dental surgery, phone calls from old lovers. Once you have enough of those under your belt you can write again. In the meantime, relax and write whatever you can, even if it has that empty feeling, and wait until your head clears and you're full. When you are, the passion will be back, and the poems.

Discussion Questions for Chapter One

1. Although Addonizio and Laux are skilled poets, their insights about writing poetry speak to all worthy writing endeavors. In this piece, they speak of truth in writing. What truths— yours and those of others—would you like to explore in your essays for this course or for your own edification?

2. Addonizio and Laux mention the poet who could not describe a homeless person because she had not observed one for long enough to concretely do so. Her inability may stem from her own fear, shame, distraction, or environment. Study someone or something that you have not fully observed—willingly or unwillingly—and describe that individual or thing.

3. Consider Robert Bly's description of "bag-stuffing." What have you placed in your bag? Describe one or two of these qualities and behaviors. Should you take it out of the bag? If so, why? If not, why not?

4. Addonizio and Laux offer a long list of life events and emotions that interrupt or delay the writing process. What steps do you take (or would you like to take) to put yourself in the state of being able to write without distraction? Describe your perfect writer's room—your mental and physical landscapes.

Chapter 2
Thesis

An explicit **thesis** is a single (that means ONE) sentence that appears in the introductory paragraph of the essay. Its placement in the paragraph is entirely up to the writer. It does not need to be the first or last sentence of the paragraph, but it certainly can be. Its placement must be meaningful—it controls what comes before and after it. The thesis sets forth a purpose by naming the essay's issue, conveying the writer's stance about the issue, and implying the work's intended audience. The thesis thus establishes the relationship between writer, issue, and audience, the most meaningful relationship in communication.

If implicit, the thesis still connects the issue to the audience, but it is not presented in a single sentence; often, the thesis will be conveyed with a rhetorical device such as posing a question at the start of the essay and using the essay's content to answer it. In the majority of lower-division college course writing assignments, the thesis should be explicit unless the assignment dictates otherwise.

Whatever form it takes, the thesis is the brain center of all communication. Without one, your audience is lost. And if your audience is lost, it will abandon you. Your audience wants to learn from you, so your goal as a communicator is to demonstrate purpose. Writing is all about purpose—you must construct each essay with the intent of teaching, informing, entertaining, or persuading your audience. Consequently, developing a clear thesis is the writer's first task because when it is done correctly, you have taken a major step toward your goal.

To create a thesis, you must understand the assignment. For example, if your English instructor asks you to write a two-page informative essay about nutrition, you know three essential things: your **purpose**—to *inform* your audience—the **length** by which you have to achieve this task—*two pages*—and your assigned **topic**—*nutrition*.

9

You must then narrow the assigned topic to a suitable issue, one that you can cover completely in the given length. To do so, you must employ a prewriting device. You CANNOT create a thesis if you have not completed one or more of the many types of prewriting (invention) techniques. Many of you already have a toolbox of prewriting skills. Some of you are comfortable with mapping, brainstorming, clustering, free writing, listing, or other methods. Each of these has its own merits. Typically, the best choice is the one that allows you to get the most ideas freely onto the page—to purge your brain of any information that you possess about the assigned topic. Remember, when you are prewriting, there are really no wrong answers. You do not need to tinker with mechanics, organization, development and support, or anything else. If you feel comfortable prewriting on the computer that is fine, but prewriting is intended to be a doodling mess, so why not take pen or pencil to paper and see what you can create? To illustrate, here is a brainstorm about nutrition:

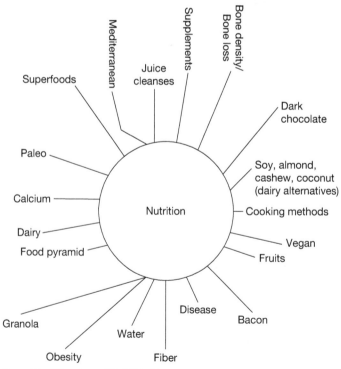

Source: Tina Eliopulos and Todd Moffett

Once you complete your prewriting, you may want to let it sit for a bit—study it and think about what it has generated. Look at what you have created and determine your level of comfort with the information in front of you. Such reflection may cause you to redo the prewriting or to plunge right into the next step, writing out a "working" thesis. Yes, your thesis is going to start doing the heavy lifting and earning its title as the essay's brain. Calling the thesis "working" means that you can revise it as you move through the drafting process. For example, if the topic calls upon you to complete research, then you may need to modify the thesis to accommodate the research that you ultimately gather. Another reason that you may change your thesis may have to do with changing your intended audience or rethinking your own stance for the essay. Whatever the reason, do not feel the need to marry yourself to your thesis until you are in the final stages of the drafting process—building paragraphs, reorganizing ideas, and so on.

But before we see the bigger picture, let's set our sights on creating the working thesis. One instrument to create a working thesis is through a device called the thesis triangle, also called a communication situation graphic, also called several other names, but all with the same intent of visually showing you the relationship between the writer, the issue, and the audience. With this in mind, we return to our brainstorm to sort through the many ideas that appear on it and consider which ones are appropriate for a two-page informative essay. After thinking about how miserable you were on your last juice cleanse and how tired you grew of eating fish on the Mediterranean diet, you decide you would like to write about granola. Who doesn't like granola? But what do you really know about granola other than you like it? When you have asked yourself this basic set of questions, then you realize your assignment is calling upon you to research your topic. Later in this book, you will learn about more concrete and specific college-level approaches to research. After spending an hour or so learning about granola so you can answer your questions, you feel ready to craft a thesis triangle—an advanced prewriting tool that is still a bit messy but provides a more organized approach to your topic. Here it goes:

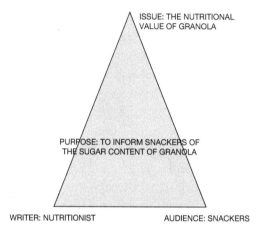

Working Thesis: The ingredients found in store-bought granola bars and mixes include many processed sugars.

Source: Tina Eliopulos and Todd Moffett

Now, with this working thesis in hand, you can begin drafting your two-page informative essay on granola. Even though you have identified your writer persona as a nutritionist, that does not mean you have actually become one in the writing of the thesis triangle. The *writer*, obviously, is You. But You as the writer can adopt any number of personas, serious or not, in order to present yourself to your audience. You have many roles to fill in your life, and you can work as one of them when you become the writer. With this example in mind—the writer as nutritionist—you will use research from experts in food science to develop and support your thesis.

Likewise, your eventual audience may reach beyond snackers—but really, who doesn't like to snack?—and benefit them. All essays should have a wider audience, well defined and interested in what you have to say about the issue, but you always write with a specific audience in mind. You want your essay content to address an audience that has a clear stake in what you have to say—a specific need for the information that you provide in the essay. Keep in mind that the wider audience is **never** the "general public"—that is, everyone. You **never** want to be considered the general writer. You want to be considered a writer with a unique and informed voice—and you want to extend the same courtesy to your reader.

Thesis Writing Exercises

Consider the two alternative thesis triangles below. One presents an instructive thesis, and the other a persuasive thesis, on the topic of granola. After studying both triangles, take another look at our original brainstorm—or create a completely new one—and craft three of your own thesis triangles, each representing one of the three distinct essay purposes: to inform, to teach, and to persuade.

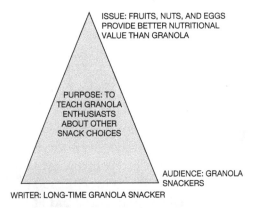

Working Thesis: Oranges, almonds, and eggs make better snack choices than granola bars.

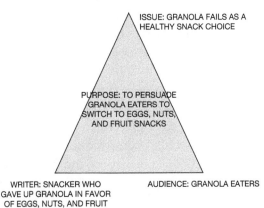

Working Thesis: Because of granola's processed sugars and empty calories, it fails to provide the necessary nutrients of other snacks such as oranges, almonds, and eggs.

Source: Tina Eliopulos and Todd Moffett

The Declaration of Independence
by Thomas Jefferson

WHEN in the Course of human events, it becomes necessary for one people to dissolve the political bands which have connected them with another, and to assume among the Powers of the earth, the separate and equal station to which the Laws of Nature and of Nature's God entitle them, a decent respect to the opinions of mankind requires that they should declare the causes which impel them to the separation.

We hold these truths to be self-evident, that all men are created equal, that they are endowed by their Creator with certain unalienable Rights, that among these are Life, Liberty and the pursuit of Happiness.—That to secure these rights, Governments are instituted among Men, deriving their just powers from the consent of the governed.—That whenever any Form of Government becomes destructive of these ends, it is the Right of the People to alter or to abolish it, and to institute new Government, laying its foundation on such principles and organizing its powers in such form, as to them shall seem most likely to effect their Safety and Happiness. Prudence, indeed, will dictate that Governments long established should not be changed for light and transient causes; and accordingly all experience hath shewn, that mankind are more disposed to suffer, while evils are sufferable, than to right themselves by abolishing the forms to which they are accustomed. But when a long train of abuses and usurpations, pursuing invariably the same Object evinces a design to reduce them under absolute Despotism, it is their right, it is their duty, to throw off such Government, and to provide new Guards for their future security.—Such has been the patient sufferance of these Colonies; and such is now the necessity which constrains them to alter their former Systems of Government. The history of the present King of Great Britain is a history of repeated injuries and usurpations, all having

The Declaration of Independence by Thomas Jefferson, 1776.

in direct object the establishment of an absolute Tyranny over these States. To prove this, let Facts be submitted to a candid world.

He has refused his Assent to Laws, the most wholesome and necessary for the public good.

He has forbidden his Governors to pass Laws of immediate and pressing importance, unless suspended in their operation till his Assent should be obtained; and when so suspended, he has utterly neglected to attend to them.

He has refused to pass other Laws for the accommodation of large districts of people, unless those people would relinquish the right of Representation in the Legislature, a right inestimable to them and formidable to tyrants only.

He has called together legislative bodies at places unusual, uncomfortable, and distant from the depository of their Public Records, for the sole purpose of fatiguing them into compliance with his measures.

He has dissolved Representative Houses repeatedly, for opposing with manly firmness his invasions on the rights of the people.

He has refused for a long time, after such dissolutions, to cause others to be elected; whereby the Legislative Powers, incapable of Annihilation, have returned to the People at large for their exercise; the State remaining in the mean time exposed to all the dangers of invasion from without, and convulsions within.

He has endeavored to prevent the population of these States; for that purpose obstructing the Laws for Naturalization of Foreigners; refusing to pass others to encourage their migrations hither, and raising the conditions of new Appropriations of Lands.

He has obstructed the Administration of Justice, by refusing his Assent to Laws for establishing Judiciary Powers.

He has made Judges dependent on his Will alone, for the tenure of their offices, and the amount and payment of their salaries.

He has erected a multitude of New Offices, and sent hither swarms of Officers to harass our People, and eat out their substance.

He has kept among us, in times of peace, Standing Armies without the Consent of our legislatures.

He has affected to render the Military independent of and superior to the Civil Power.

He has combined with others to subject us to a jurisdiction foreign to our constitution, and unacknowledged by our laws; giving his Assent to their Acts of pretended Legislation:

For quartering large bodies of armed troops among us:

For protecting them, by a mock Trial, from Punishment for any Murders which they should commit on the Inhabitants of these States:

For cutting off our Trade with all parts of the world:

For imposing Taxes on us without our Consent:

For depriving us in many cases, of the benefits of Trial by Jury:

For transporting us beyond Seas to be tried for pretended offenses:

For abolishing the free System of English Laws in a neighboring Province, establishing therein an Arbitrary government, and enlarging its Boundaries so as to render it at once an example and fit instrument for introducing the same absolute rule into these Colonies:

For taking away our Charters, abolishing our most valuable Laws, and altering fundamentally the Forms of our Governments:

For suspending our own Legislatures, and declaring themselves invested with Power to legislate for us in all cases whatsoever.

He has abdicated Government here, by declaring us out of his Protection and waging War against us.

He has plundered our seas, ravaged our Coasts, burnt our towns, and destroyed the lives of our people.

He is at this time transporting large Armies of foreign Mercenaries to complete the works of death, desolation, and tyranny, already begun with circumstances of Cruelty & perfidy scarcely paralleled in the most barbarous ages, and totally unworthy the Head of a civilized nation.

He has constrained our fellow Citizens taken Captive on the high Seas to bear Arms against their Country, to become the executioners of their friends and Brethren, or to fall themselves by their Hands.

He has excited domestic insurrections amongst us, and has endeavored to bring on the inhabitants of our frontiers, the merciless Indian Savages, whose known rule of warfare, is an undistinguished destruction of all ages, sexes and conditions.

In every stage of these Oppressions We have Petitioned for Redress in the most humble terms: Our repeated Petitions have been answered only by repeated injury. A Prince, whose character is thus marked by every act which may define a Tyrant, is unfit to be the ruler of a free People.

Nor have We been wanting in attentions to our British brethren. We have warned them from time to time of attempts by their legislature to extend an unwarrantable jurisdiction over us. We have reminded them of the circumstances of our emigration and settlement here. We have appealed to their native justice and magnanimity, and we have conjured them by the ties of our common kindred to disavow these usurpations, which, would inevitably interrupt our connections and correspondence. They too have been deaf to the voice of justice and of consanguinity. We must, therefore, acquiesce in the necessity, which denounces our Separation, and hold them, as we hold the rest of mankind, Enemies in War, in Peace Friends.

We, THEREFORE, the Representatives of the UNITED STATES OF AMERICA, in General Congress, Assembled, appealing to the Supreme Judge of the world for the rectitude of our intentions, do, in the Name, and by Authority of the good People of these Colonies, solemnly publish and declare, That these United Colonies are, and of Right ought to be FREE AND INDEPENDENT STATES; that they are Absolved from all Allegiance to the British Crown, and that all political connection between them and the State of Great Britain, is and ought to be totally dissolved; and that as Free and Independent States, they have full Power to levy War, conclude Peace, contract Alliances, establish Commerce, and to do all other Acts and Things which Independent States may of right do. And for the support of this Declaration, with a firm reliance on the Protection of Divine Providence, we mutually pledge to each other our Lives, our Fortunes and our sacred Honor.

Is Sushi "Healthy"? What about Granola? Where Americans and Nutritionists Disagree

by Kevin Quealy and Margot Sanger-Katz

Is popcorn good for you? What about pizza, orange juice or sushi? Or frozen yogurt, pork chops or quinoa?

Which foods are healthy? In principle, it's a simple enough question, and a person who wishes to eat more healthily should reasonably expect to know which foods to choose at the supermarket and which to avoid.

Unfortunately, the answer is anything but simple.

The Food and Drug Administration recently agreed to review its standards for what foods can be called "healthy," a move that highlights how much of our nutritional knowledge has changed in recent years—and how much remains unknown.

With the Morning Consult, a media and polling firm, we surveyed hundreds of nutritionists—members of the American Society for Nutrition—asking them whether they thought certain food items (about fifty) were healthy. The Morning Consult also surveyed a representative sample of the American electorate, asking the same thing.

The results suggest a surprising diversity of opinion, even among experts. Yes, some foods, like kale, apples and oatmeal, are considered "healthy" by nearly everyone. And some, like soda, french fries and chocolate chip cookies, are not. But in between, some foods appear to benefit from a positive public perception, while others befuddle the public and experts alike. (We're looking at you, butter.)

"Twenty years ago, I think we knew about ten percent of what we need to know" about nutrition, said Dariush Mozaffarian, the dean of the Tufts Friedman School of Nutrition Science and Policy. "And now we know about forty to fifty percent."

Here's what we found.

Of the fifty-two common foods that we asked experts and the public to rate, none had a wider gap than granola bars. More than seventy percent of ordinary Americans we surveyed described them as healthy, but less than a third of nutritional experts did. A similar gap existed for granola, which less than half of nutritionists we surveyed described as healthy.

Several of the foods considered more healthful by everyday Americans than by experts—including frozen yogurt, a SlimFast shake and granola bars—have something in common: They can contain a lot of added sugar. In May [of 2016], the Food and Drug Administration announced a new template for nutrition labels, and one priority was to clearly distinguish between sugars that naturally occur in food and sugars that are added later to heighten flavors. (You'd be surprised how many foods contain added sugar.) It's possible nutritionists know this, but the public still does not.

On the other end of the spectrum, several foods received a seal of approval from our expert panel but left nonexperts uncertain. Most surprising was the reaction to quinoa, a "superfood" grain so often praised as healthful that it has become the subject of satire. (At the moment, *The New York Times* cooking site offers 167 recipes for quinoa, roughly a third of which are explicitly tagged "healthy.")

In addition, tofu, sushi, hummus, wine and shrimp were all rated as significantly more healthful by nutritionists than by the public. Why?

One reason may be that many of them are new foods in the mainstream American diet. Our colleague Neil Irwin measured mentions of trendy foods in *Times* coverage over the years, and found that quinoa had only recently picked up steam. Others may reflect mixed messages in press coverage of the healthfulness of foods. Shrimp was long maligned for its high rate of dietary cholesterol, though recent guidelines have changed. And public messages about the healthfulness of alcohol are conflicting: While moderate drinking appears to have some health benefits, more consumption can obviously have real health costs.

We weren't surprised to find areas in which ordinary Americans and experts disagreed.

We expect researchers to be better informed about current research, and everyday consumers to be more susceptible to the health claims of food marketers, even if the claims are somewhat dubious.

But some of the foods in our survey split both the public *and* our panel of experts. Four foods—steak, cheddar cheese, whole milk and pork chops—tend to have a lot of fat. And fat is a topic few experts can agree on. Years ago, the nutritional consensus was that fat, and particularly the saturated fat found in dairy and red meat, was bad for your heart. Newer studies are less clear, and many of the fights among nutritionists tend to be about the right amount of protein and fat in a healthy diet.

The uncertainty about these foods, as expressed both by experts and ordinary Americans, reflects the haziness of the nutritional evidence about them. (If you're a steak lover and you find this news discouraging, our colleague Aaron Carroll has written that red meat is probably fine in moderation.)

It's clear that many shoppers *do* want to eat healthful foods but are unsure what to choose. To gain some perspective on this, we asked Google which foods were most commonly part of a simple search: "Is [blank] healthy?" The food people were likeliest to ask about was also one nutritionists generally approve of: sushi.

There are some areas of nutritional consensus. Nearly everyone agreed that oranges, apples, oatmeal and chicken could safely be described as healthy, and also agreed that chocolate chip cookies, bacon, white bread and soda could not.

Where does this leave a well-meaning but occasionally confused shopper? Reassured, perhaps: Nutrition science is sometimes murky even to experts.

Your overall diet probably matters a lot more than whether you follow rigid rules or eat just one "good" or "bad" food.

We also asked our experts whether they considered their own diet healthful, and how they described it. Ninety-nine percent of nutritionists said their diet was very or somewhat healthy. The most popular special diet type was "Mediterranean"; twenty-five percent of our nutritionists picked it. But the most common answer, even for experts, was "no special rules or restrictions."

I Was Young, Had Hair, and Went to War
by H. Lee Barnes

I read too many stories of small lives in search of understanding something so vague it hardly seems a problem, if indeed it exists at all, and I wonder why these writers don't have messier lives or at least messier minds. Are their lives and minds as sterile as their prose is clean? What experience do they hit the water with when the fire is at their backs? The fact of experience may not stir a smooth, easy psycho-fictive drama that leads to a nice, neat epiphany, but experiences, especially those worth having, are rarely smooth and rarely internal. They are rather internalized, become perhaps obsessions.

I was young, had hair, and went to war. No experience since has been as forceful or as immediate or genuine. Thirty years later it is an after ring, an irritant, a vibration that gives tone to everything I write, but there is one moment that slips irresistibly into my consciousness. The moment lives by itself, forms and recasts itself in the fiction, non-fiction, and poetry I've written. In part, this is it:

> I stand on a mound atop my camp, Tra Bong, a bare swell of red earth, cut by trenches and surrounded by three barriers of barbed wire. Monsoon clouds stalk landward up the fertile valley, which in sunlight is emerald and shimmering with rice paddies where water lies so still you can walk the berms and see trees and sky reflected precisely on the surface. But now everything is leaden, and colorless except the red clay, which slurries in the trenches like molten rust. I watch one hundred Vietnamese soldiers march away from the camp led by four Americans, one my captain, two my friends, Brownie and Jacobson, and the last Riffschnelder, who is due to rotate out of the country in weeks. Him I barely know. There are reasons I cannot write this image out of my life, try though I may. First, all of the Americans died. Second, I was supposed to go on the operation and Brown died in my place. Third, it was an

ill-advised mission. Fourth, I saw a beetle crawl out of a bullet hole in Jacobson's forehead. Fifth, Captain Fewell's body was never recovered, but his head was discovered months later in a Buddhist pagoda where he'd been decapitated. I along with a handful of others survived to try and make sense of our buddies' deaths and to speculate, I especially, on that most profound and most dreadful of questions: Why me? (Or, if you prefer: Why not me?)

All experience orders up opposing questions, and roughly the same lame answers, and despite the impact of this particular experience, more than fifteen years lapsed before I began writing about Vietnam. The first manuscript, a novel, went through a round of rejections, some complimentary, most standard, before I wrote away from that subject. Twelve years would pass before Vietnam again found space in my writing. When it did, it became the force behind a novel manuscript, a novella, seven short stories and an ongoing string of poems, all written in two years. Obsession.

Of course I didn't realize it was an obsession until Alberto Ríos, who teaches graduate writing at ASU, told me of a seminar he conducts called "Obsessions." The concept is to take a particular image, work it and rework it for an entire semester, following whatever direction it takes. The method, even as he described it to me, resounded with truth, for as a way to develop an honest dialogue with experience, the writer must, I think, be a bit obsessed. This, it seems, is approximately what I've experienced in writing about Vietnam. It isn't the fact or the truth of the experience I wish to capture, but the intensity and effect. Poe was right on this count: The writer should write toward effect. Roderick Usher, crushed under the weight of his house, took the full force of it in front of his friend's eyes. In my story "Gunning for Ho" Bruce Stoner used explosives and a television camera to negate the problem of distance. The narrators (survivors) are compelled to tell the story. The plots are (quite by accident) parallel but the experiences that impel the stories are dissimilar and thus the details are quite different. Each experience has its own frequency.

I don't know what inspired Poe, but I drew upon the experience of climbing mountains into Laos, of being in the Tra Bong Valley, of seeing friends die, of witnessing and engaging in youthful macho behavior. Plot limits stories; experience limits the writer but creates a uniqueness of vision.

In both "Gunning for Ho" and "Cat in the Cage" I use the image of a prisoner carried in a bamboo cage. This was an actual condition some captured Americans, particularly pilots and Special Forces troopers, endured. Though I never experienced it, I was indoctrinated to the possibility of suffering such mistreatment if captured. I, by being in proximity to where such things happened, experienced the fright. I best relate this to a woman I know who suffers nightmares about rape, all manner of violations. I'll not venture into the psychology of her phobia, but I know with certainty she has experienced the terror of rape. Must a woman be raped to feel the fear or imagine the indignities involved?

Along with the actual and imagined experience, my writing includes use of the collective experience, which includes history and social setting. This is the hard part of writing stories about Vietnam; here is where gender and age, where bias and assumption, where "other" experiences and myths and stereotypes emerge. I know from rejections that accompany my Vietnam stories (and there are many) that women generally, particularly young women, can't enter into the narratives. The stories, simply put, meter out too high on the testosterone scale—men, Vietnam, death. The collective experience of women readers from my generation seems rooted in antiwar marches or loss of family or friends and the women's movement (and those are their stories); the younger ones' reactions are likely linked to *Rambo* and bad-movie dates with pimply-cheeked kids who were raised watching cartoon warriors (and those are their stories). Women and men alike associate Vietnam with My Lai, napalm, heroin addiction and racism. It's so easy to view it from these perspectives, to give it your own slant. (In fact My Lai was an aberration, but atrocities committed by the Viet Cong and North Vietnamese on Montagnard and South Vietnamese were commonplace and part of a political strategy).

Recently I read of a Navy corpsman who served with the Marines at Hue. He'd crawled out into enemy fire to carry wounded Marines to safety or to administer aid and gather ammunition. Though wounded several times, he'd continued to go out and had saved several Marines. He was so badly shot up that he was thought to be dead and was set aside with the dead while the wounded were evacuated. Somehow he lived through his wounds and drifted into obscurity. Over twenty-five years later he was recognized by one of the Marines who'd witnessed his courage on that violent day. Others came forward to testify to this man's selfless acts of courage. Thirty years after the battle, he was awarded the Congressional Medal of Honor. This speaks of old-fashioned heroism, but in a way speaks also of the collective experience I mentioned, the one that is somehow counter to the greater consciousness of the literary establishment. The corpsman's story isn't one day at Hue or a ceremony during which the president of the United States drapes a medal over a hero's neck; it is the thousands of days in between and the tomorrow he faces.

I like the splash and the ripples that move the boat, the sudden surprise when a fish jumps unexpectedly. I feed off what is incomprehensible. I want a continuing dialogue with the boy who stood atop that mound of red clay and watched his friends march down a valley to their deaths. He raises the questions that start the process (for these are my stories).

Discussion Questions for Chapter Two

1. Create a thesis triangle for each essay in this chapter. Clearly, the writer of each is the author(s) of the piece, but see if you can discern something about the writer's stance, background, or persona. Identify the issue and three details about that issue. Identify the audience and determine the audience's stake in and opinion toward the issue. Write down each author's purpose and thesis sentence. If the thesis sentence is implied, then write one using your own words. Once you have completed the thesis triangle, determine if you feel the writers achieved their purposes.

2. Thomas Jefferson and H. Lee Barnes seem to address audiences who may be hostile toward or at least ignorant of the issues they have raised. What strategies do the authors use to engage with these audiences? Write out your own stance on the issues the authors address.

3. In chapter 1, Addonizio and Laux discuss the idea of obsession and how it relates to the shadow. Two of the readings in this chapter, those by Quealy and Sanger-Katz and by Barnes, address this idea. Quealy and Sanger-Katz report on a topic— diet and nutrition—that seems to be an obsession among the American public, while Barnes describes an image from his time in Vietnam that haunts him to this day. How do we as Americans express our obsession with diet? Compare how we express it to how Barnes has expressed his obsession in his essay. How do these expressions follow what Addonizio and Laux say about the shadow?

Chapter 3
Development and Support

Writing is much like growing up. As we age, we learn from our mistakes—we repeat what works well for us and we eliminate what fails us. Likewise, as writers, we turn to patterns of writing that have proven to help us communicate our ideas to others.

We call these patterns *development and support*. The composition instructor defines development and support as the means used by a writer to elaborate, explain, or prove the essay's thesis. Development and support is as important to a writer as evidence is to an attorney. Imagine a lawyer attempting to win over a jury without proof. It just does not happen. Similarly, once a writer has crafted a working thesis, she must begin to gather the necessary development and support. Sometimes in the prewriting or invention stage, you will brainstorm ideas that will actually be part of the development and support you will use within the essay. So look closely at that cluster or that triangle or that free write again. Now you will use those ideas with intent.

There are several ways of developing a thesis:

Description
Narration
Example
Process
Comparison and contrast
Cause and effect
Classification and division
Definition
Argumentation

We start with *description*, perhaps the most important, because the other modes named above rely on this skill, and all types of

27

writing—personal, academic, creative, vocational, professional—require it. Description allows readers to understand a subject through their senses: sight, sound, taste, touch, and smell. For example, if you are eating at a sushi restaurant for the first time, you may need some assistance to navigate the menu. You have never tried unagi before, but your friends have, so you ask them, "What does it taste like?" You probably will not agree to try it just because they reply, "It's good." *Good* is one of those abstract words that means something different to each of us. You need concrete details. So when your friends say, "It has a strong salty flavor and firm flesh that is balanced very nicely by the sweet sauce in which it's prepared," the description now appeals to your senses, and you are more willing to try this new food even when you find out that unagi is eel. (Another treatment of concrete versus abstract language appears in the discussion of poetry in chapter 7.)

Whereas descriptive writing can make time stand still as it gathers its sensory impressions, sometimes for several paragraphs, *narrative* writing relies on a moving chronological sequence of events. For example, your experience with unagi could evolve into a series of episodes setting out how your friends took you to the bar, how you saw unagi on the menu, how you first tasted it, and how it became your favorite food. Your introduction to such an essay might be as follows: "Many twenty-one-year-olds mark their legal age with a drink at the bar, but I chose a different path. I went to a sushi bar and met unagi. Now, I spend each year celebrating my birthday with an eel." Sometimes the flow of events is leisurely, sometimes rapid; sometimes the normal sequence is changed, as when the writer uses a flashback—an earlier scene that illuminates the main action. Although many writers may experiment with stories that are held together more by association than by strict chronology, a traditional narrative is almost always dominated in its organization by the ceaseless flow of time.

An essay using description or narration will contain multiple *examples*, which in their own right are an essential method of development. An example is an illustration used to clarify a general statement and is usually signaled by a transitional phrase such as *for example, for instance*, or *to illustrate*. Say your essay's purpose is to explore historic vacation spots. You may want to illustrate them according to their geographic locations: "Each region in the United States has several historic landmarks to visit. For example, in the west, tourists flock to California's gold country to recall the riches discovered there in 1848 and reflect on the grit and ingenuity of the early western settlers. Similarly, while visiting Pennsylvania, many gather to view the Liberty Bell and marvel at the Founding Fathers' role in securing America's freedom." Examples can be stacked or isolated within the essay's body paragraphs. What's important is to make sure the examples support the thesis/paragraph idea and are interpreted accordingly.

Another form of development, *process*, has inundated our society, in which creating, assimilating, and distributing information is a major activity. Think about the thousands of instructional videos found on the Internet. Many of these are **directional processes** such as how to tune a car's engine, how to make a meringue, how to install an air filter in a fish tank, or how to apply mascara. Similarly, self-help books continue to top best-seller charts by telling us how to win through a particular behavioral method, how to improve our class standing, how to make friends, and how to find the perfect partner. The subject matter is as diverse as the shoppers who seek them out. On the other hand, an **informational process** tells us not how to do something but how something came about. Thus, accounts relating how the West was won, how the earth was formed, how a baby develops in the womb and is born, how a bill is passed through Congress, how a medication affects the body, and how the Vegas Golden Knights won the Western Conference of the NHL in 2018 are informational processes. Either type of process needs to be enriched by examples that underscore the concise steps. If telling your audience how to schedule a trip, for example, you might list a process such as this one: "When planning your vacation to New York City, the first thing you must do is consider which of the city's landmarks fit your interests, then you must save money to enjoy each of them, and then you must contact your travel agent to secure the most budget-friendly rates for airfare and hotel."

Comparison and contrast, like process, is a thinking strategy that we do every day. Should I wear slacks or shorts? Should I travel surface roads or the freeway? Should I splurge on dinner out or make a peanut butter and jelly sandwich? Underlying questions like these are comparisons of how one might look in pants versus shorts, how long it might take to travel one route or the other, or how much better a pie from Metro Pizza might taste than the sandwich. Developing our ideas with comparison and contrast comes quite naturally, but we still need to identify some points of distinction when we attempt to do the same task in writing.

First, we need to distinguish comparison from contrast. When we compare, we point out similarities between two things. Thus, in comparing cats with dogs, we notice that they both have a strong affinity for human beings, a tendency to defend their territory against intruders, a carnivorous diet, and a habit of taking over a household if given half a chance. When we contrast, on the other hand, we look for differences. Thus, in a contrast of cats and dogs, we can point out that while cats largely care for themselves, demanding only food, water, and a clean litter box, dogs require a great deal more, including a daily walk and frequent bathing; that while both cats and dogs will fight off animals intruding into their territory, only dogs will attack human intruders; and that while cats do most of the their damage to our furniture with their claws, dogs do most of theirs with their teeth. Frequently, our goal when comparing or contrasting two or more items is to make a choice. Our reason for comparing cats and dogs thus might be to choose one or the other as our next pet: "Though dogs require more care, they also offer more protection from human intruders; thus, they make better pets than cats."

Cause and effect is a pattern which students encounter frequently. In sociology class, for instance, we may have been asked to consider why we may hold certain beliefs. In our history class, we may have studied the causes behind the suffrage movement. In political science class, we may have studied the effect of the United States Supreme Court's ruling on corporations being viewed as individuals. When we speak of causes, we are looking for sources of a certain behavior, act, relationship, or phenomenon. When we focus upon effects, we are looking for consequences or results. For example, in his article "What Are the Repercussions of One Lost Night's Sleep?" journalist Paul Kelley presents the effects of sleep loss on work performance. Kelley relates the famous case of Arianna Huffington: "Her appalling self-inflicted sleep deprivation led her to pass out and collapse. To her credit, she didn't just change her life so that she had time to sleep, she made sure that her employees had time to sleep too, even when this meant having sleep pods in the office."

Classification and division is a pattern of development that examines the classes or categories of an issue or subject. Whereas classification requires us to break a group of things into two or more subgroups, division requires us to break one thing into its component parts. For instance, after my thousands of experiences eating sushi in the Las Vegas Valley, I can classify the many restaurants as traditional, contemporary, or fusion. Or I can focus on one restaurant—say, Osaka—and divide the unagi roll into its component parts: eel, rice, nori, cucumber, and unagi sauce.

Definition, like division, isolates a subject and describes its unique characteristics. However, in your essay, you should not go to a dictionary to find a definition. Instructors will want you to create your own. To do so, use this frame: A ____ is a ____ that ____. In the first blank, put the **term** to be defined. In the second, put the **class** to which the term belongs. In the third, put the **differentiation**: what makes the term different from other items in its class. A definition based on this model might look like this: "A <u>bicycle</u> is a <u>mode of transportation</u> that <u>requires human propulsion</u>." In many courses, you may be asked to write an extended definition, which will require that you create a simple definition based on the frame above but then lengthen your answer with other methods of development. Extending the bicycle example above, a student may go on to describe a certain style of bike, or classify types of bikes, or compare racing bikes to commuter bikes, or determine the health effects of bike riding.

An *argument* (or an appeal to *logos*) is a chain of reasoning such as is found in **induction** or **deduction**, or is a **body of proofs** gathered from research. Induction studies a pattern of similar events which leads to a general hypothesis:

1. When I drove my first Ford Mustang, it had great acceleration.
2. When I drove my second Ford Mustang, it, too, had great acceleration.
3. When I drove my third Ford Mustang, yet again it had great acceleration.
4. Therefore, it is likely that if I drive another Ford Mustang, it will have great acceleration.

Deduction moves from general truths to specific examples and often takes the form of a **syllogism**, with a major premise, a minor premise, and a conclusion:

Major premise: All dogs are mammals.
Minor premise: Winnie is a dog.
Conclusion: Therefore, Winnie is a mammal.

The syllogism follows a formula: Members of group A (dogs) are assigned a quality B (mammals); individual C (Winnie) is a member of group A (dogs); therefore, individual C (Winnie) also has quality B (mammal).

If you are writing an assignment that calls for research, then you must provide a body of proofs, many of which may come in the form of statistics, research data, and quotations. These proofs must present evidence from experts in the field or from other credible sources whose authority will bolster your own standing as a writer and add strength to your voice. Statistics, research data, and quotations will require that you investigate outside sources, preferably your course textbooks or materials available in your school library. More information on how to incorporate and document materials taken from primary and secondary sources appears in chapters 4, 6, and 7. Here's an example of an argument supported by quotations/ expert knowledge and data: "Research done by the Psychology Institute of Harvard University reveals that four out of five adult Americans take vacations to relieve stress. This data rings true to Gina, a AAA travel agent in Las Vegas, who recently made plans for the following clients: Stephanie booked a week-long stay in Sun Valley, Idaho, to escape her chaotic job as a receptionist at a major law firm; Rowdy sought hiking information for Estes Park in Colorado to recover from a family death; and Blossom booked a flight to Cannes, France, to attend the film festival and get away from her sixty-hour work weeks."

Development and support should be tailored to meet the needs of the audience to whom you are writing. For example, if your audience is a group of businessmen and you want to convince them that a different managerial strategy will save their corporation money, then you will probably want to rely on a statistical analysis of the effects your proposed change will cause. Personal experiences in the form of a narrative may not have the information your audience needs. On the other hand, if you are speaking to some ten-year-olds at a summer camp about drug abuse, you will want to keep your ideas and explanations simple. You will not want to cite hard statistics to support a cause-and-effect analysis but rather tell them what happened to your nine-year-old brother when the police found him carrying a joint in his back pocket. A narrative of personal experiences in this case would work better.

Development and support can help you if you are stuck for an idea. Consider trying a type of development and support you have not used yet in the paper. If you have been using several personal examples and have exhausted your knowledge about the topic, you might think about doing some research in the library or maybe looking at the chain of causes and effects that is connected with your issue. Each new means of development and support that you use can add a paragraph (or even more) to your paper.

When you make a point or state an argument in your paper, you should always ask yourself, "Why?"—Why is this so? Why is this important? Why does this have an effect on my issue? Asking yourself "Why?" will force you to answer "Because," and this answer will in turn force you to rethink your issue using the types of development and support you have at your disposal. The writers of the essays that follow incorporate a variety of patterns of development, each hoping to prove a point.

Being Good
by Frankie Mac

"Are you *good* at anything?"

" . . . What?"

The question startled me. I was sitting at my desk in my sixth-grade classroom hovering over a disgruntled-looking art project. My knuckles whitened as I nervously gripped the glue stick in my hand. Where did this come from? The poser of the question was Daphne, a girl whom I'd known since kindergarten, and who'd since then been my personal Regina George. A cloud of frustration filled my lungs and stomach. What I couldn't admit to myself in that moment was that I didn't have an answer.

"I'm good at school."

Daphne and her posse began snickering and muttering to themselves. *How pathetic.* Daphne had the singing pipes of Celine Dion. Her right-hand girl Shelly was a star soccer player who invited people over to her house just so they could see her medals. Lisa drew sketches that were so detailed and beautiful that our art teacher constantly accused her of tracing. Everybody in my grade had a *thing.* What was I good at?

And so, the odyssey began.

That year, I joined a Greek dance troupe upon the strict wishes of my well-meaning, but overbearing mother. I enjoyed going to practice. I made good friends of a similar cultural background. But when it came time for choosing someone to do a spotlight performance, or sing a solo during a folksong for one of the more complicated dances, I was always overlooked, even though I was one of only two girls in the troupe. After one amongst my plethora of rejections, my dance instructor pulled me aside and told me that maybe I should settle for the background.

Then, in eighth grade, I tried out for the school track team. My PE coach told me that I was fast, and that I should consider giving one of the long-distance runs a shot, despite the fact that the only sport I'd ever participated in was witty banter. By some Christmas miracle, I actually made the team, which, to me, was a success in itself. However, when it came down to our first and only meet, I came in last in my race. I'll never forget the look of disappointment on my teammates' faces, and the slimy feeling of my hand as I was given a participation ribbon.

Amidst all of this mediocrity and failure, part of me started to wonder what the point of all this was. Why was the need for the knowledge of being good at something, especially as a middle schooler, so dire? But my other half, the stronger of the two, told the first one to shut up.

Finally, high school arrived, as well as a world of possibility. As orientation came to a close, I had a lot to consider. I didn't want my high school experience to mimic the one I'd had in junior high: go to school, go home, do schoolwork, sleep, repeat. That monotonous routine wasn't going to prove that bitch from sixth grade wrong. It was time to let go.

I looked over all my options. I figured sports were totally off the table, since I couldn't go through that condescending humiliation again. My conservative Catholic high school clearly wouldn't offer Greek Orthodox folk dancing. But I figured I'd stick to the arts. In my mind, they felt like the safest bet. That narrowed my search down to two potential fates: ceramics and theater. But since I wasn't one who enjoyed getting my hands dirty in a literal sense, the latter it was.

Theater came to me as a surprisingly exciting prospect. In the fifth grade, my parents and I had gone to see the musical *Wicked* in LA, and afterwards, I had demanded that we play the original Broadway soundtrack in our car for months. The idea that I could be the next Elphaba—strong and free and the center of attention—or any other character I could imagine, was too seductive for me to handle.

And so, during the second week of school, I signed up for the Fall Farce. The audition would take place on my fifteenth birthday.

Upon arrival, a dark-haired girl with a nervous smile and a stick up her ass handed me an audition side.

"You'll be waiting in the blackbox," she said.

"Cool."

When I entered the cramped, cluttered space, I thought there'd been some sort of mistake. It was absolute hormonal mayhem. Guys were rolling around doing acrobatics hindered by gravity. Girls were in the corner talking and singing to themselves, occasionally getting aggressive in a Jekyll/Hyde manner. The volume in the room reached an all-time high, and my nerves kicked in. Preparing for the worst, I popped a squat in isolation.

"Frankie," I heard above the chaos, twenty minutes later. It was the dark-haired girl poking her head in the door.

"Yeah?"

"They're ready for you."

The dimly lit theater had a welcoming blue and brown color scheme. I thought I was alone standing on the stage until I squinted out into the audience. Three people were sitting in the front row. One was a student—a tall dude with a big nose and glasses who I was almost certain was in my math class. The second was a serious, elegant woman in her mid-twenties donning all black. Then, there was the third, Yvonna Francisco-Enriquez. She had a figure and a face as imposing as her name. Although she seemed a little kooky in a brightly patterned paisley dress and clogs, there was something terrifyingly omniscient behind her gaze.

"Frankie Mac . . ." she pondered, looking at a sheet in front of her, "What a fantastic name."

I gulped. "Thank you."

"Freshman, huh?"

"Yeah."

"Well . . . let's see what you've got."

I read. The whole time, all three observers roared with a laughter harder than a canned audience in a sitcom. At first, I thought they were laughing out of cruelty, the sort of enjoyment I'd been so used to. I finished.

"Was that okay?"

They looked at each other.

" . . . Get the others in here."

Like a trained dog, the boy with the glasses ran out of his seat and exited the theatre. When he returned, all the other auditioners who had been in the blackbox were at his heels.

"All right, people," boomed Yvonna, "This is Frankie Mac. Watch and learn."

With a smug grin that only someone who knows show business can give, she turned to me.

"Do it again."

I obeyed. It was the same response. With every line I spoke, chuckles burst through the house. The something—the feeling I'd sensed squirming in the pit of my stomach since my entry into high school—suddenly morphed into a fuzzy ball of light. I was trying to stay in character, but I soon found myself beaming with joy.

The same ball of light later led me to participate in South Coast Repertory Theatre's Acting Intensive Program. When the program began, I didn't feel anxiety. Proving myself was no longer a concern because I knew what I was good at. Then, one day, I was sitting in my Training for the Audition class, where we were adding "special skills" to our theatrical résumés.

I stared at mine blankly.

"Joy," I asked my instructor, "what constitutes as a special skill?"

She chuckled. "Anything that isn't acting, obviously."

Silence fell between us. As I wracked my brain, desperate for an idea, Joy said five words that branded into my memory.

"What are you good at?"

In that moment, something clicked. Unlike what Daphne tried to teach me many years ago, life isn't for the one-trick ponies. It's for the people who take a leap of faith—for those who go out for the track team or the dance troupe, despite the awareness that they might fail. But those people don't stop trying once their niche is found. That's why I won't be good at something. I will be good at many things for the rest of my life.

So This Is Freedom
by S. L. Kelly

When I decided to learn to ride a motorcycle, I had two goals in mind: learn to ride and ride as far as you can! I did not make the connection between riding and freedom until I found myself in the middle of the Nevada desert.

My riding story began in September of 2016 when I purchased a 1999 Honda Nighthawk from Craigslist. It was the first step in my journey towards achieving a long-forgotten dream. When I was about ten years old, one afternoon, my older sister and I were busy creating our futures. While she opted for two kids, an economy car and a house, I announced, "When I grow up, I'm gonna buy a motorcycle and ride all over the world!" That memory suddenly came flooding back thirty years later, when I found myself in the middle of an MSF course in the parking lot of a community college.

I rode my starter bike for ten months, practicing the skills I learned in the MSF course on the streets of Sin City. In July 2017, I purchased my first "big" bike, a 2016 Kawasaki Versys 650LT in candy metallic orange. I named her Virginia. She spoke to me about her ability to go anywhere—freedom. I liked that.

To me, freedom means the ability to "come and go as you please" or to "live without limits" or restrictions of any kind. These definitions barely scratch the surface of the concept, a notion I would come to realize once I got Virginia up to highway speed on my first ride through the desert.

The Nevada desert is both stunning and mesmerizing. While visually beautiful and frightening, there are many stories about strange things that happen in the desert, alien landings, holes filled with the bodies of wily gangsters and spiritual awakenings. The desert is certainly alive. Amid the tall rocks, black mountains, and cacti, though, I had my first real experience with freedom.

At 65 miles an hour, I was cruising along relishing the fact that I had made a great choice in a motorcycle for my riding style and my

---

"So This is Freedom," first appeared in the anthology, *Women Who Ride: Rebel Souls, Golden Hearts, and Iron Horses*, edited by Sarah Andreas, 2018. Reprinted with permission of the author.

future riding aspirations. I felt blessed. Virginia and I were becoming fast friends. She was eating up the curves. The windscreen was doing its job, and although I had begun to feel a little numbness in my throttle hand, I felt good. While taking in the scenery, my mind was busy taking in road conditions, my speed, fuel consumption, and the 70-degree weather. In short, I was doing the "work" of riding and doing my best to "enjoy the ride."

A strange feeling overwhelmed me. This was new. As a rider, I understand the danger that is ever-present on a motorcycle. I understand that few people accept the risk that comes with riding. I had accepted that risk with full knowledge of what could happen. I do this every time I get on my bike. This wasn't a feeling of fear or anxiety. I was no longer worried about my being able to "keep up," maneuvering curves, my speed or the amount of fuel left in my tank. As I glanced around me at the scenery, I suddenly realized that what I was feeling was free.

Riding through the desert among the rocks, I was not afraid. I did not feel lonely, abandoned, or near the brink of certain death. I felt a connection to my bike; it is so much more than just a means of conveyance. I felt a sense of camaraderie with my fellow riders, those in my small group and those I happily waved the lowered "peace" sign to as they passed on the other side of the road. We were all in this together, having the same experience. For a few moments, the world existed, but it existed of my will. I felt that I could change the trajectory of my future with a simple turn down a new road or byway. I could see the road ahead, with its ups and downs, lying straight and curved before me, and on that bike, I felt that I could handle any situation that came my way. Optimism. Freedom.

My thoughts were transported back in time. While the future was ahead of me, I thought about my past and the pasts of women like me. I thought about the trepidation with which I had accepted the challenge of learning to ride a motorcycle. I thought about the many women who were not allowed the privilege of living their dreams. Riding through the desert that day was transcendent. I embodied the spirit of my ancestors, and they were pushing me forward. What did they dream as enslaved Negro women? Would they have accepted the same challenge that I had? What might they have achieved if they had been given the opportunity? Everything. Freedom.

That Saturday afternoon in the desert, I learned a new definition of freedom. Freedom is following your passion. Having the desire and determination to follow your dreams at all costs. The *feeling* of freedom is riding a motorcycle. I get it now. Fifteen months ago, I bought a motorcycle and learned to ride it. Because I can.

Black and White and Blue All Over
by Lisa Bailey

Not everyone learns about their legendary mistakes while standing in line at the grocery store, but if a piano is going to land on a community newspaper publisher, that's exactly where it will happen.

"Can you believe they put that photo in there?"

The guy in front of me slapped a copy of my newspaper against the checkstand. It was fairly early in the morning; after delivering all my newsstand, I'd just dropped the kids off at school—and I'd come back to the grocery store to pick up a couple of gallons of milk.

"Oh, I know," the checker said, her hands busy swiping the guy's beef jerky over her scanner. "Nobody can believe it."

I didn't recognize the guy. The checker fussed over bagging his half-case of Bud Light and potato chips. *Probably a hunter*, I thought.

"What's wrong with the photo?" I asked the guy, quickly, before the checker noticed me and could tell him who I was. I tried not to wince as he angrily jammed the copy of my newspaper back onto the checkstand. He left the paper hanging, cockeyed, over the edge of the counter.

"I mean, there's just common decency, isn't there?" he muttered. "Who else but a newspaper would put a picture of a dismembered hand on the friggin' front page?"

Who else but a newspaper, indeed? By the time the infamous hand photo was printed, I *was* the newspaper. Equal parts honest and nosy, I sported such an abysmal level of self-esteem that I was convinced that working eighty hours a week—*every* week—was exactly what I deserved. I was also just stupid enough to believe that I had a shot at redemption every week, too—which shackled me so firmly to my black-and-white mistress that the two of us became indistinguishable.

The schizophrenic ability of a good journalist to remain invisible in public but fearless in print might have served me well on an anonymous big-city beat, but in a small town . . . well, people cannot be blamed for thinking that I was completely crazy.

Those people showed up to holler at me on my front porch, since the newspaper office was in our house. I knew all of them. I knew the tearful ones who showed up clutching notebook-paper obituaries. I knew the city councilmember who sent me drunken emails every Saturday night—he'd cruelly point out all the mistakes I'd made in the paper that week before hinting that he wanted to sleep with me.

"I've never seen anyone with such an easily-triggered sense of justice, Goldilocks," he sneered in one email.

Since the business was continually strapped for cash, I had to take accident pictures. (A front-page wreck photo in a small town is a guaranteed sellout.) I became a wizard at finding access to blocked scenes—plowing my old Taurus through the weeds on canal roads if necessary. It wasn't uncommon for me to beat the ambulance.

But the hand photo was taken at a double fatality that featured easy parking. The victims had ended up in the parking lot of an ag chemical company just east of Royal City, and I felt like I was cheating when I pulled up—it was almost too easy, like going to the mall.

I remember shooting a little mangled red and white Coleman cooler that was lying next to the car as the blanket-covered bodies of the two women were loaded.

The women's lunch—tinfoil-wrapped tamales—had spilled out of the cooler and onto the gravel of the parking lot. Everything was splattered with blood. I couldn't stop thinking about how they'd probably grabbed a few things from the fridge right before they'd left for work—in a hurry, laughing maybe—never knowing it would be one of the last things they ever did.

Although I was used to cops making inappropriate jokes at fatalities, when a trooper rolled his eyes about the "whole famdamily" (while nodding toward the silent relatives of the dead women), I barely managed a polite smile.

Over a dozen people stood and watched the bloody sedan—not wailing, not crying, just staring. They rimmed the edge of the WSP-required fifty-foot fatality buffer like a guardrail. The EMTs had half-heartedly flung disposable blue sheeting over the back door of the mangled sedan for privacy as they had worked to remove the bodies of the two women. I noticed they'd even left their discarded nitrile gloves lying around: a sign of frustration they'd lost both the victims.

I came home, still thinking about the tamales on the bloodstained gravel, and threw up in the utility sink in my laundry room. Then I Photoshopped the pictures of the crushed car, sharpening the focus, and—as advised by our press—I changed the photos into black and white so they would "dot up" better.

And that was how a bright blue nitrile glove thrown on the shattered back window of a Honda became a dismembered hand.

The newspaper went under last year, after the Recession choked off the last of our dying ad revenue. All I have is a stack of silent morgue books now, big, awkward library-bound things stacked in my downstairs pantry along with cans of kidney beans and extra paper towels. I used to pay the bindery in Walla Walla every year to make us a tidy book of our back issues, and I always wondered what the binders thought as they lined up a whole year of our news to sew together. Not that it matters now.

It doesn't seem like those silent morgue books should be able to contain my raucous eight years of being a newspaper. But isn't the past always muffled by the ash of history as it sifts down on all of us? Sifting and sifting, until even someone who had to know everything can forget, until even the most high-contrast black and white memories start to gray and blur, until even a rubber glove in the back of a wrecked car can look like it's waving goodbye.

Drowning
by Violet E. Baldwin

Nobody really remembers what life was like when they were a toddler. All memories before age five seem to fuse into one grand flashback. Like shifting shadows, the slightest details of my childhood vacations are vague; however, when I was no more than three years old I experienced an unforgettable sensation that was forever etched into my memory. It was the day I almost drowned in the radiant blue sea.

My great-grandfather grew up on the white sand beaches of Puerto Rico, with the sun beating down on his face and the cool water rushing over his feet as he trotted his Paso Fino horses along the bright blue shoreline. For his eightieth birthday, he wanted us to go back to that place he once loved. He wanted my family to experience the beauty of the chrysanthemum sunset over the pastel blue waters. He wanted to show us how the colors mixed and made an alluring portrait on the waterfront.

That part, however, I do not remember. I do not remember the smell of sea salt every morning as we woke up on the beach, nor the color of the ripe bananas growing outside the creaking white house we had rented for the week. I don't remember the sweet taste of water from a fuzzy green coconut as it trickled down my throat or the chirp of the coqui singing outside my window. I was only three.

It was a quiet morning in the hefty white building in which the many hallways and the doors seemed never ending to the miniscule toddler roaming about. The birds would sing just outside the towering, cream-colored door housing a brass oblong handle. I sat with my family at breakfast eager to play in the froth of the waves and feel the beads of sand between my petite toes. I scarfed down the unimportant breakfast and chugged my Ovaltine chocolate milk concoction patiently yearning for the moment I could feel the cool ocean breeze on my face and the warmth of the sand on my feet.

That moment finally arrived. We made our way down to the shore. I was fidgety and impatient throughout the lengthy walk among the trees reminding me of green army men preparing for battle. I felt the crisp breeze on the tips of my ears. My nose tickled as the salty sea air hit me directly in the face. My father picked me up and proceeded to hoist me into the air. My mother, aunts, and grandparents settled in on the sand.

My mother set my then-infant brother on the sand beside her. He gleefully shoveled piles of the golden, honeysuckle-colored sand into his mouth. My aunts took to the waves on their surfboards, tackling each tower of water head on. My dad's warm hand held mine as we raced towards the waves crashing on shore. He held me by my waist and hurled me over the blueberry waves which crashed and produced a foam colored like the moon. I laughed as the tomfoolery seemed to last forever. I was having the time of my life.

Without warning everything seemed to shift. My father was no longer waist deep in the water. His legs kicked frantically as he treaded the water. The waves seemed to grow; they were trying to swallow us whole. Soon all that was above the waterline was our heads bobbing in the waves. My dad held me up and kept me afloat; he tried not to panic so as to keep me calm. I knew something was wrong.

On the shore my mother was in a frantic state of emergency, signaling to my aunts who were too far away to hear the screams over the crashing of the waves. My grandparents joined in, but their efforts were not effective. It was at that moment my grandfather made the choice to swim out in an attempt to save us. He powered out there with all his adrenalin pumping, but when his toes no longer gripped the sand on the bottom, he was stuck as well. We all swam there, treading water, my grandpa now holding me so my father could focus his energy on keeping himself alive.

There is a feeling that a three-year-old should never have to feel, the feeling of helplessness. I saw it in my grandfather's eyes as he held me above the waves. I turned to my dad who was slowly giving in to the hateful deep waters. I then realized that this was it; as a three-year-old I had to understand that we were all about to give in to the greedy tide that had pulled us out to sea.

In this moment we saw my aunt paddling her long surfboard toward us; she reached us just before we let go. With the last bit of strength my grandpa had, he lifted me onto the board, then himself. My dad held onto the board, his energy drained. She pulled us back to shore. We crawled along the sand which had never felt so pleasant before. That day the ocean was not able to defeat me. I didn't give in to the harsh forces that attempted to drag us down.

A three-year-old child's life is brimming with hope and possibility. When something takes place to shift that paradigm, the effects can be devastating. Nearly losing my life in the ocean was one of those moments. The vivid memories would pursue me for years, never allowing me to forget the day I could have lost my life to the harsh reality of ignorance in an unknown environment.

Body Ritual among the Nacirema
by Horace Miner

The anthropologist has become so familiar with the diversity of ways in which different peoples behave in similar situations that he is not apt to be surprised by even the most exotic customs. In fact, if all of the logically possible combinations of behavior have not been found somewhere in the world, he is apt to suspect that they must be present in some yet undescribed tribe. This point has, in fact, been expressed with respect to clan organization by Murdock (1949:71). In this light, the magical beliefs and practices of the Nacirema present such unusual aspects that it seems desirable to describe them as an example of the extremes to which human behavior can go.

Professor Linton first brought the ritual of the Nacirema to the attention of anthropologists twenty years ago (1936:326), but the culture of this people is still very poorly understood. They are a North American group living in the territory between the Canadian Cree, the Yaqui and Tarahumare of Mexico, and the Carib and Arawak of the Antilles. Little is known of their origin, although tradition states that they came from the east. According to Nacirema mythology, their nation was originated by a culture hero, Notgnihsaw, who is otherwise known for two great feats of strength—the throwing of a piece of wampum across the river Pa-To-Mac and the chopping down of a cherry tree in which the Spirit of Truth resided.

Nacirema culture is characterized by a highly developed market economy which has evolved in a rich natural habitat. While much of the people's time is devoted to economic pursuits, a large part of the fruits of these labors and a considerable portion of the day are spent in ritual activity. The focus of this activity is the human body, the appearance and health of which loom as a dominant concern in the ethos of the people. While such a concern is certainly not unusual, its ceremonial aspects and associated philosophy are unique.

The fundamental belief underlying the whole system appears to be that the human body is ugly and that its natural tendency is to

---

"Body Ritual among the Nacirema" by Horace Miner, originally published in *American Anthropologist*, June 1956, pp. 503–507.

debility and disease. Incarcerated in such a body, man's only hope is to avert these characteristics through the use of the powerful influences of ritual and ceremony. Every household has one or more shrines devoted to this purpose. The more powerful individuals in the society have several shrines in their houses and, in fact, the opulence of a house is often referred to in terms of the number of such ritual centers it possesses. Most houses are of wattle and daub construction, but the shrine rooms of the more wealthy are walled with stone. Poorer families imitate the rich by applying pottery plaques to their shrine walls.

While each family has at least one such shrine, the rituals associated with it are not family ceremonies but are private and secret. The rites are normally only discussed with children, and then only during the period when they are being initiated into these mysteries. I was able, however, to establish sufficient rapport with the natives to examine these shrines and to have the rituals described to me.

The focal point of the shrine is a box or chest which is built into the wall. In this chest are kept the many charms and magical potions without which no native believes he could live. These preparations are secured from a variety of specialized practitioners. The most powerful of these are the medicine men, whose assistance must be rewarded with substantial gifts. However, the medicine men do not provide the curative potions for their clients, but decide what the ingredients should be and then write them down in an ancient and secret language. This writing is understood only by the medicine men and by the herbalists who, for another gift, provide the required charm.

The charm is not disposed of after it has served its purpose, but is placed in the charm-box of the household shrine. As these magical materials are specific for certain ills, and the real or imagined maladies of the people are many, the charm-box is usually full to overflowing. The magical packets are so numerous that people forget what their purposes were and fear to use them again. While the natives are very vague on this point, we can only assume that the idea in retaining all the old magical materials is that their presence in the charm-box, before which the body rituals are conducted, will in some way protect the worshipper.

Beneath the charm-box is a small font. Each day every member of the family, in succession, enters the shrine room, bows his head before the charm-box, mingles different sorts of holy water in the font, and proceeds with a brief rite of ablution. The holy waters are secured from the Water Temple of the community, where the priests conduct elaborate ceremonies to make the liquid ritually pure.

In the hierarchy of magical practitioners, and below the medicine men in prestige, are specialists whose designation is best translated "holy-mouth-men." The Nacirema have an almost pathological horror of and fascination with the mouth, the condition of which is believed to have a supernatural influence on all social relationships. Were it not for the rituals of the mouth, they believe that their teeth would fall out, their gums bleed, their jaws shrink, their friends desert them, and their lovers reject them. They also believe that a strong relationship exists between oral and moral characteristics. For example, there is a ritual ablution of the mouth for children which is supposed to improve their moral fiber.

The daily body ritual performed by everyone includes a mouth-rite. Despite the fact that these people are so punctilious about care of the mouth, this rite involves a practice which strikes the uninitiated stranger as revolting. It was reported to me that the ritual consists of inserting a small bundle of hog hairs into the mouth, along with certain magical powders, and then moving the bundle in a highly formalized series of gestures.

In addition to the private mouth-rite, the people seek out a holy-mouth-man once or twice a year. These practitioners have an impressive set of paraphernalia, consisting of a variety of augers, awls, probes, and prods. The use of these objects in the exorcism of the evils of the mouth involves almost unbelievable ritual torture of the client. The holy-mouth-man opens the client's mouth and, using the above mentioned tools, enlarges any holes which decay may have created in the teeth. Magical materials are put into these holes. If there are no naturally occurring holes in the teeth, large sections of one or more teeth are gouged out so that the supernatural substance can be applied. In the client's view, the purpose of these ministrations is to arrest decay and to draw friends. The extremely sacred and traditional character of the rite is evident in the fact that the natives return to the holy-mouth-men year after year, despite the fact that their teeth continue to decay.

It is to be hoped that, when a thorough study of the Nacirema is made, there will be careful inquiry into the personality structure of these people. One has but to watch the gleam in the eye of a holy-mouth-man, as he jabs an awl into an exposed nerve, to suspect that a certain amount of sadism is involved. If this can be established, a very interesting pattern emerges, for most of the population shows definite masochistic tendencies. It was to these that Professor Linton referred in discussing a distinctive part of the daily body ritual which is per-formed only by men. This part of the rite involves scraping and lacer-ating the surface of the face with a sharp instrument. Special women's rites are performed only four times during each lunar month, but what they lack in frequency is made up in barbarity. As part of this ceremony, women bake their heads in small ovens for about an hour. The theoretically interesting point is that what seems to be a prepon-derantly masochistic people have developed sadistic specialists.

The medicine men have an imposing temple, or *latipso*, in every community of any size. The more elaborate ceremonies required to treat very sick patients can only be performed at this temple. These ceremonies involve not only the thaumaturge but a permanent group of vestal maidens who move sedately about the temple chambers in distinctive costume and headdress.

The *latipso* ceremonies are so harsh that it is phenomenal that a fair proportion of the really sick natives who enter the temple ever recover. Small children whose indoctrination is still incomplete have been known to resist attempts to take them to the temple because "that is where you go to die." Despite this fact, sick adults are not only willing but eager to undergo the protracted ritual purification, if they can afford to do so. No matter how ill the supplicant or how grave the emergency, the guardians of many temples will not admit a client if he cannot give a rich gift to the custodian. Even after one has gained admission and survived the ceremonies, the guardians will not permit the neophyte to leave until he makes still another gift.

The supplicant entering the temple is first stripped of all his or her clothes. In every-day life the Nacirema avoids exposure of his body and its natural functions. Bathing and excretory acts are performed only in the secrecy of the household shrine, where they are ritualized as part of the body-rites. Psychological shock results from the fact that body secrecy is suddenly lost upon entry into the *latipso*. A man, whose own wife has never seen him in an excretory act, suddenly finds himself naked and assisted by a vestal maiden while he performs his natural functions into a sacred vessel. This sort of ceremonial treatment is necessitated by the fact that the excreta are used by a diviner to ascertain the course and nature of the client's sickness. Female clients, on the other hand, find their naked bodies are subjected to the scrutiny, manipulation and prodding of the medicine men.

Few supplicants in the temple are well enough to do anything but lie on their hard beds. The daily ceremonies, like the rites of the holy-mouth-men, involve discomfort and torture. With ritual precision, the vestals awaken their miserable charges each dawn and roll them about on their beds of pain while performing ablutions, in the formal movements of which the maidens are highly trained. At other times they insert magic wands in the supplicant's mouth or force him to eat substances which are supposed to be healing. From time to time the medicine men come to their clients and jab magically treated needles into their flesh. The fact that these temple ceremonies may not cure, and may even kill the neophyte, in no way decreases the people's faith in the medicine men.

There remains one other kind of practitioner, known as a "listener." This witch-doctor has the power to exorcise the devils that lodge in the heads of people who have been bewitched. The Nacirema believe that parents bewitch their own children. Mothers are particularly suspected of putting a curse on children while teaching them the secret body rituals. The counter-magic of the witch-doctor is unusual in its lack of ritual. The patient simply tells the "listener" all his troubles and fears, beginning with the earliest difficulties he can remember. The memory displayed by the Nacirema in these exorcism sessions is truly remarkable. It is not uncommon for the patient to bemoan the rejection he felt upon being weaned as a babe, and a few individuals even see their troubles going back to the traumatic effects of their own birth.

In conclusion, mention must be made of certain practices which have their base in native esthetics but which depend upon the pervasive aversion to the natural body and its functions. There are ritual fasts to make fat people thin and ceremonial feasts to make thin people fat. Still other rites are used to make women's breasts larger if they are small, and smaller if they are large. General dissatisfaction with breast shape is symbolized in the fact that the ideal form is virtually outside the range of human variation. A few women afflicted with almost inhuman hypermammary development are so idolized that they make a handsome living by simply going from village to village and permitting the natives to stare at them for a fee.

Reference has already been made to the fact that excretory functions are ritualized, routinized, and relegated to secrecy. Natural reproductive functions are similarly distorted. Intercourse is taboo as a topic and scheduled as an act. Efforts are made to avoid pregnancy by the use of magical materials or by limiting intercourse to certain phases of the moon. Conception is actually very infrequent. When pregnant, women dress so as to hide their condition. Parturition takes place in secret, without friends or relatives to assist, and the majority of women do not nurse their infants.

Our review of the ritual life of the Nacirema has certainly shown them to be a magic-ridden people. It is hard to understand how they have managed to exist so long under the burdens which they have imposed upon themselves. But even such exotic customs as these take on real meaning when they are viewed with the insight provided by Malinowski when he wrote (1948:70):

> Looking from far and above, from our high places of safety in the developed civilization, it is easy to see all the crudity and irrelevance of magic. But without its power and guidance early man could not have mastered his practical difficulties as he has done, nor could man have advanced to the higher stages of civilization.

References Cited

Linton, Ralph. *The Study of Man*. New York: D. Appleton-Century Co. 1936.

Malinowski, Bronislaw. *Magic, Science, and Religion*. Glencoe: The Free Press. 1948.

Murdock, George P. *Social Structure*. New York: The Macmillan Co. 1949.

Excerpt from *The Secret Knowledge of Water*

by Craig Childs

From Chapter 1, "Maps of Water Holes"

Cabeza Prieta, Arizona
February-March

The desert breathed and then went silent at the first mention of nightfall, a kind of quiet that comes only at the edge of the earth. The last small winds broke apart, rolling down unrelated washes like pearls off a snapped necklace. Then came stars. And a crescent moon. And a desert strung in every direction, iridescent indigo in the west where the sun had just set, black in the east.

I walked west, toward an escarpment on the horizon barely into Arizona from the Mexican border. In evening silhouettes, these sere, isolated mountains had the look of tall ships strewn about the desert. Between were gulfs of open land furrowed with slight washes. Within the washes were the dimpled tracks of black-tailed jackrabbits and kangaroo rats, and within them the curled parchment of bursage leaves left by a wind gone somewhere else.

Across the flats I heard only the hushing sound of my boots through sand, then the sharper sound of my boots through the broken granite above the washes. The hum of one of the stray breezes through thousands of saguaro cactus needles. The sound of creosote leaves scratching the brim of my hat. At night it is best to walk through the desert with a hat held in the hand, pushed forward to block the thorns and sharp spines of occasional unseen plants. Almost everything alive out here is armored with some barb, spike, or poison quill. From the years that I did not carry my hat, the back of my right hand is scarred as if it had been offered to a furious cat.

Tonight the moon, a waxing crescent thin as an eyelash, would not give enough light for shadows. I used it as a reference, walking directly toward it, carrying on my back all of the gear needed to resupply a base camp fifteen miles out, and the gear to supply the lesser camps beyond that. I had come to map water holes, working on a project for the U.S. Fish and Wildlife Service. The agency wanted to know what kind of water hid among these mountains, in some of the driest land in the Western Hemisphere. There are years when rain never falls, and sometimes the water holes contain nothing but rainwater that is twelve or sixteen months old, if they hold anything at all.

To find the water, I took thirty-seven days to traverse a single mountain range, hunting in its cracks and canyons. I carried simple measuring tools along with a device that communicates with satellites to record latitude and longitude of whatever water I found, perhaps a quart of evaporating rainwater in a rock depression. With my coordinates recorded, I placed small red marks on the map, showing one water hole, then the next.

This survey area was chosen not for any special characteristics, or a promise of water, but because it looked as arid and embattled as any of the mountains out here. Now and then I would return to my truck, which was parked beside a wash, off a long-winded road made of sand. There I would refill my supplies and cache them in the desert beyond. As I found water from the outlying natural cisterns, I was able to drink and extend deeper into the range, until I had recorded lifelines of water holes leading from my base camp into nowhere.

The final product of this work would go to the files of Cabeza Prieta National Wildlife Refuge. The refuge is managed primarily for desert bighorn sheep that supposedly thrive on these quarts. There are those people who worry for the sheep, who believe water should be shipped into the desert during early-summer droughts so that the sheep can maintain an "optimum" population, so that they can fill their range. There are also those who believe that after ten thousand years of seeking water, sheep do not require our aid.

While out walking through these canyons, below summits sharp as ice picks, I have heard sheep clattering among rocks but have rarely been able to get close enough to see their eyes. I have lifted their discarded bones and horns, turned them in my hand, and studied their tracks near water holes. One morning I watched a group of four rams carefully pick through steep talus. I waited above, crouched shirtless in shade, observing their choices, how their hooves negotiated each small rock. I tried to decipher their boldness and indecision, learning how an animal must behave in this landscape. The fourth ram, the youngest, waited until the others were out of sight before making its own mistakes, then backtracking. This made me smile, made me rest easier.

My personal reasons for mapping water holes here had little to do with bighorn sheep. I came to put a story back together and recover parts that had been lost. The story, when it was complete, would have told of secret water in a desperately ragged place, would have shown the route to safely cross from one end of Cabeza Prieta to the other. I wanted to understand water in a land this dry. Within the 860,000 acres of this refuge, only one spring exists. It is a bare, dripping spring, yet is enough to have bestowed the entire mountain range in which it sits with the name *Agua Dulce*. Sweet Water.

The desert cities have their cement aqueducts to siphon distant rivers, and holes are drilled into ten-thousand-year-old banks of groundwater. Familiarity with scattered water holes has become obsolete, left only for the bighorn sheep. Words are now missing from the story of ephemeral waters, severing critical pieces of information. Many people have died while crossing this desert, regardless of their reasons for being here. They died because the story was forgotten.

This country is not idle. The mountains are bitterly seared. Rising a couple thousand feet off the floor, they are offset by swaths of bulged, rolling desert, called *bajadas*, that take days to cross. As I walked on this night of the crescent moon, the bajada unfurled to the horizons to the north and south. Here and there it was intercepted by farther mountains, each an island, or a chain, or a misshapen monstrosity bursting straight from the ground.

On long night walks like this, brushing through plants and walking up and down against the grain of dry, north-flowing washes, I told myself stories, recounting whatever I remembered about the place. Stories gave the land definition at night, as the mountains vanished around me. Sometimes I would speak the stories out loud to break the loneliness. A particular one came from a site about eight miles straight ahead of me. An archaeologist making a sweep of the area found among assemblages of prehistoric potsherds two .45-caliber Colt cartridges, manufactured by the Winchester Repeating Arms Company. They had probably been discharged onto the ground in the early 1900s. The two cartridges had been rammed together, making a small, enclosed capsule. Inside this capsule was a note that read, "Was it worth it?"

So I invented scenarios, tried to imagine what the message meant. Death or desperation or gold that was never found or somebody like myself pushing the edges of the desert only to be confronted with this question in the end.

Just south of these two cartridges, in six hundred square miles of lava flows, cinder cones, and dune seas, ten forty-pound boulders were found butted against one another to form a perfect southeast-to-northwest line. It is not possible to tell if it was constructed hundreds or thousands of years ago, but it was done, for whatever reason, by strenuous human labor. I told myself stories about this. Perhaps they levered the boulders with wooden saguaro ribs tied together, rolling them from miles away. For what? To appease certain gods? To reinvent the mountains? To invite the rain with a signal that could be seen from the clouds?

In another place each small rock on the ground had been cleared, revealing the pale belly of earth in a line six feet wide and seven hundred feet long without deviation. There are other, more ornate sites: geometric designs hundreds of feet in length, with mazes and inner circles that can be seen as a whole only from an airplane. I have seen in one of these stone clearings the life-size and accurate image of a horse, probably a sixteenth-century Spanish horse as seen by an indigenous artist, while around it ran a web of exposed lines radiating into the landscape.

In the mountain range ahead of me, a Spanish missionary of the Franciscan order came through in the 1700s, querying local inhabitants about the mounds of horns and bones from bighorn sheep he found erected near the water holes. He was talking to the people called the Hia C'ed O'odham, known as the Sand People by the Spanish. Without offering further explanation, the people gave him a simple answer. The horns and bones had been placed to keep the wind from leaving the country.

Stories everywhere. This is the place where people came to hold on to the wind. It is where they brought expectations that were rammed into rifle shells. In the coming dark, the desert grew richer with stories. And I became more alone. I knew of a small group of archaeologists with a work site about a four- or five-day walk southwest of here. Probably a few illegal immigrants were coming up from the border, but not through here, where people die from exposure and thirst. So I figured I was the only person for thirty to eighty miles in any direction. This left a kind of openness and remoteness that made merely breathing feel obscene. A friend once traveled with me here and as we walked the perimeter of one of these ranges, he said the vastness reminded him of the Arctic, up by the Brooks Range where great basins of tundra lie between distant and imposing mountains, where there is no human artifact. I nodded at the time, realizing a sensation I had not yet been able to place.

Humans are absent here because they die. One document records the death of four hundred people here by 1900, many of whom were traveling from Mexico to the California goldfields. More have died since. Within view of several distant mountains, a family had been memorialized by black pieces of basalt arranged to form the numeral 8, telling how many family members perished. Sixty-five graves surround one of the better-known watering sites, presumably from the times that the holes went dry. Most victims died of dehydration and exposure, but occasional reports concerned those who drowned, too weak from thirst to climb out of the deep stone water holes into which they had plunged.

There are more recent deaths, those of illegal immigrants from Mexico, who come seeking jobs picking watermelons or cleaning houses. These people walk out in small groups, some of them from the tropics, never having seen the desert. They hire a person, a *coyote*, who deposits them across the border and points the way to Interstate 8. Each carries a gallon plastic milk jug filled with water, which in the summer lasts a few hours. The walk takes many days and they live maybe until the afternoon of the second or third day, their tracks of discarded belongings and empty milk jugs signaling insanity. Some of their milk jugs are, in fact, found half-full beside their bodies, skin taut to bursting. This story repeats itself every year.

As in stories I have heard from Mount Everest, where bodies of climbers are dispersed among glaciers, bodies here are turned to bones and spread across the sand and gravel and in the rocks. The bones are uncounted and unburied, scattered like offerings. It is perhaps these bones, rather than those of bighorns, that now prevent the wind from leaving the country.

Coming close to the horizon, the moon appeared to move quickly. As it fell into the mountains of Cabeza Prieta, it described ridges as splintered as dry wood broken over a knee. For a moment, all that remained in the sky was the watermark stain of the moon's dark side. Then it set, leaving this hysterical swarm of stars. I chose certain constellations and followed them, my hat still extended in my hand.

There were good places to sleep. There were open flats where the ground curved slightly, barren of most plants. I could lie on one of these flats with my eyes open, the earth presenting me to the sky as if I were a newborn or a sacrifice. I chose instead a narrow wash, one barely depressed so that the wind had to bend down to find me. I protected myself beneath a creosote bush on ripples of wash sand. This is where I slept, in a country littered with arcane rock symbols, and death, and rumors of water.

Heroes of Las Vegas: The Hospital Staff Called to Action after the Mass Shooting
by Dan Hernandez

When a festival became the scene of the worst mass shooting in modern America, Sunrise Hospital staff had only minutes to prepare. Here are their stories.

Sunrise Hospital's emergency room was already full at about 10 p.m. on 1 October [2017] when a police officer dropping off an accident victim received a call on his radio announcing: "Shots fired."

Doctor Kevin Menes and nurse Rhonda Davis looked up from their charts. "Is this for real?" Menes asked. A series of gunshots crackled through the officer's radio in automatic bursts. It sounded like a combat zone. As he ran out, the officer said, "That's the Route 91 concert."

Immediately, Menes realized there would be hundreds if not thousands of victims, and Sunrise—Las Vegas's largest trauma center and the hospital nearest to the site of the country music festival— would probably receive the most.

He and Davis started to prepare. Menes contacted house supervisor Kat Comanescu, who then summoned all available nurses to the ER to help move or discharge patients. Davis requested crash carts and gurneys.

With only four ER doctors and one trauma surgeon on shift at the time, a mass casualty incident alert went out to bring in day-shift doctors, nurses and support staff.

On a typical day, Sunrise receives 20 trauma patients, but in the coming hours they would see approximately 200, including 124 people with gunshot wounds, the first of which would arrive within 15 minutes.

The staff waited with a line of stretchers and wheelchairs in Sunrise's ambulance bay as the sirens grew closer and louder. The plan was to separate patients into triage zones based on whether each person had seconds, minutes or hours to live, then stabilize or resuscitate them in preparation for surgery.

Everyone who was there that night described the blood and chaos, but also shared oddly uplifting stories of teamwork, humanity and grit. *The Guardian* interviewed ten Sunrise staff members—here are their experiences.

Kevin Menes, ER doctor

The first thing Menes did was get a police radio from his car. As well as being an ER physician, he is a medic for the SWAT team, and listening to the Las Vegas Metropolitan police channel he began to grasp the scope of the tragedy. Menes gathered the four other ER doctors on shift, and they agreed that Menes would handle lead triage. That meant organizing patients for nurses and physicians who would focus on blood, intubation, chest tubes and everything else needed before surgery.

Menes told secretaries to prep all 24 operating rooms and call every surgeon and anesthesiologist. "The surgery department is really what's going to save people's lives," he told *The Guardian*. "As ER doctors we bring people back to life and keep them alive for a short time, but surgeons are the ones who work the miracles. They're the ones who get the bleeding to stop and continue to get them better over the next days and weeks, and eventually get them home."

All available gurneys and wheelchairs were taken out to the ambulance bay, where non-ER staff would wheel patients in. They set up and waited. "At about that time I was out on the driveway," Menes recalled. "You could hear it in the distance. You could hear the sirens coming soft initially, then getting louder and louder. The first cars that came were police cruisers. They can run red lights and had filled up with as many patients as they could."

There is a textbook way to handle a mass casualty surge. Patients are given colored tags based on whether they have seconds or minutes to live (red), an hour or so (yellow), are unlikely to die (green), or have died (black). But to save time, Menes designated the four trauma bays as red, orange, yellow and green, inventing an extra severity level and skipping black—those he believed to be dead would go to the red tag area so a second doctor could assess them in case Menes was wrong. Those who had died went to a temporary morgue in the endoscopy room.

It was a plan he had developed through studying the hospital's layout and the city's vulnerability. "It's an open secret that we have a lot of crowds here in Las Vegas and there is always the potential for something like this to happen. For years I'd been thinking about what I'd do. I never said anything to anyone though because I didn't want them thinking I was crazy."

After 150 people had been brought in, a nurse came out to the ambulance bay to say, "Menes, they need you inside; they're getting behind." He went to help stabilize or resuscitate people who were near death, while a trauma surgeon decided who would go into the operating room next. At one point Menes told nurses to take every unit of O-negative from the blood bank and fill their pockets with the intubation drugs to save the precious time it normally takes to fill out paperwork and use digital devices that track supplies. "These are complete no-nos in nursing—carrying drugs in pockets that aren't accounted for," Menes admitted. "But we had to do it to save patients' lives, and it worked."

After 30 minutes, more staff showed up, additional operating rooms were opened, and after an hour more surgeons and doctors arrived. "We were getting more and more patients out of the ER and into life-saving surgeries. This dance continued on for hours, and when everything was said and done, at 5 a.m., it was like a ghost town. Almost everybody had been taken care of."

Sixteen people of at least 200 patients seen that night died in their care, but during the first six hours the trauma team performed 28 surgeries to stop internal bleeding, and 67 operations in the first 24 hours.

More than 100 physicians and 200 nurses had come in.

"As a medical community we came together. But it wasn't just us. This happened all over the [Las Vegas] Valley, and in a smaller way this happens every night all over the world, 365 days a year."

Rhonda Davis, trauma nurse

"We actually got a few minutes' heads-up quicker than anyone else because that officer just happened to be standing in our ER," recalled Davis. "It kind of took a while to process what was really going on.

Hearing a barrage of bullets was shocking—I was stunned." After worrying about friends at the show her "nurse brain" kicked in. "I thought: oh my goodness, this is going to be huge."

She helped notify doctors and surgeons. They started getting the trauma bays ready, which required moving non-critical patients to other areas of the hospital. Emergency dispatchers for Clark County, which contains Las Vegas, usually estimate how many people each hospital will receive, but this time all they could do was stress: "You will get a lot of patients."

"Even then I didn't quite get the grand scale of what it would be," Davis recalled. "It's hard to imagine that you're going to get hundreds of patients in minutes."

This first wave arrived in police cars and private vehicles. She saw a young man with a gunshot wound to his leg, and seconds later the most critical patients started coming in, covered in blood. The most critical cases were gunshot wounds to the head, chest and stomach. Some of the patients did not have a pulse.

"We were trying to do CPR, putting chest tubes in, all of the life-saving measures that you would do," she said. "We get patients like this all the time, but maybe two at a time at most. You do all these steps to try to save their life. At this moment we had several who needed all these life-saving critical interventions at the same time. We went patient to patient as quickly as possible, trying to help save them. I wasn't thinking. You just kind of do. Quickly it turned into a sea of blood and patients."

Nurses usually get assigned patients to care for through their shifts, but in this case "you literally did whatever you could to whatever patient," she recalled. The four trauma bay rooms typically hold six patients in total, yet each one was being used for four or five people, and there were more in the halls.

She recalled receiving a young female who had been shot in the chest. With every square inch of the trauma bay taken, Davis and an anesthesiologist worked on her in the hall. He was trying to put a chest tube in, because she wasn't breathing, and when they could not detect a pulse Davis started doing CPR immediately. "I was leaning up on top of the gurney doing chest compressions, trying to save this poor girl's life, and there's just blood coming out of her chest from the wound."

At one point Davis looked up and saw three more patients being moved into the hallway. Doctors and nurses were doing the exact same things for them. There was blood all over the floor.

Unfortunately, the patient she was working on could not be saved. Davis had to move on very quickly to the next patient: another young female in the same situation.

Not a day goes by without Davis thinking about that night. "Some moments during the day I'm completely fine, then I'll hear something or see something and the memory of that scene in the ER will pop in my mind. It's very vivid still."

Dorita Sondereker, emergency department director

When she received the first Mass Casualty Incident alert, Sondereker turned on the news and saw nothing. She called her unit and was told: "There's blood everywhere. Get in here now."

While driving in she heard that 75 ambulances had been dispatched to the Strip, which was "beyond comprehension," she said. "That's never happened before."

Ambulances flew past as she drove in, and while turning into Sunrise, pickup trucks cut her off; she heard injured people crying in their flatbeds. "In 35 years in medicine I've worked in ambulance, EMS, trauma and helicopter crews. I've seen burn ward devastation, but nothing like this."

The victims arrived in cars, trucks, rideshares, police SUVs and of course ambulances, which instead of the usual one patient would transport six to eight at a time.

She too mentioned a "sea of blood": "I've never seen this amount of trauma in a few hours come through the door. The bullet wounds were the size of your nail bed, but the devastation those bullets caused in the human body was catastrophic. People could be talking with a small wound in their chest then be gone within seconds.

"The night flew so fast," she said. "You directed it, but it was surreal how things just happened; the flow was amazing. We'd call for more stretchers and recliners and they'd appear. The ER was full, so we moved people up and discharged from the top floors. In all the chaos was a calmness I can't describe because everyone was working their hearts out. That's one reason it was successful—a camaraderie and teamwork like I've never experienced in my life."

She added: "Hospitals have an option to divert [patients]. EMS kept asking me, 'how many more can you take?' I kept saying 10 more. It was an eyeball thing—like where are we at? How many have I moved to cardio, to ICU, to surgery?"

Within an hour, 100 physicians and 100 nurses had arrived to help. "I'm from small-town Iowa; I've seen camaraderie, but nothing like Las Vegas has put out in the past few weeks. The way they came together was heroic—concierges helping people in, nurses' assistants holding hands, even the patients who said "take care of those who are hurt worse. I'm good." It wasn't an ER of screaming. There was a calmness, because people were being taken care of."

Jennifer Sanguinet, director of infection prevention

Sanguinet had to wait for her mother to come to watch her kids before she could get to Sunrise at 4 a.m. The hospital was on lockdown and the halls were quiet. "The fear and anguish was palpable," she said. "Everyone had the same look of shock."

At that hour victims' families were also trickling in, some from out of state. Sanguinet went to the family resource center to help provide food, blankets and emotional support. Victims who had already been discharged from the ER were interspersed with families, holding each other's hands. "People swirled around us," she recalled, "because they saw a badge and saw us taking names. It definitely put my skills to a test. I tried to set aside my own emotions as a parent, but obviously I'm still human, so as I'm walking and doing my job, I'm also crying."

She and two colleagues took it upon themselves to search for people. They photographed images from the families' cellphones and walked floor to floor, in some cases scrutinizing victims' tattoos or piercings. "A lot of people unfortunately had issues where they weren't recognizable. You also look different in a hospital than when you're on the street smiling and happy."

If a victim was alive and could be touched, staff immediately ran to the family to bring them to their side. But if the person was in the morgue, it was more complicated. Sanguinet personally matched eight or nine fatally wounded victims to their family members, a bittersweet experience. She delivered the news with a team that included clergy, medical staff and a case manager. "I was there for the comforting part."

A couple of days later, one of those parents called to see if her late daughter's boots had been found—the family wanted to bury their daughter in her favorite outfit. Very few patients' belongings were at Sunrise—a lot of loose items fell off or were torn away at the site. But at the bottom of the ER's storage box were the young woman's boots in a bag.

"I went to package them," Sanguinet said. "I took them out of the bag and saw they were covered in blood, dirt, and filth from the event. I'm a mom. I have kids, and God forbid this would ever happen to me, I wouldn't want that to come back. I wouldn't want that reminder. I closed my door, I put something on the floor, and I sat there for two hours scrubbing those boots. A coworker brought me a tool to help clean the soles.

"It was really a cathartic time for me to sit and reflect on everything that had happened. It brings home the fact that Las Vegas is my home now, and Sunrise Hospital is my home now. I know that that mom is grateful that I took the time; for me it was a bit of closure to know that even out of tragedy you could do something to make a difference in an outcome that was so horrible."

Ecaterina "Kat" Comanescu, house supervisor

As a former trauma nurse, Comanescu knew exactly what was needed when Menes called saying: "Something has happened at the Mandalay Bay," the hotel from which the killer shot into the crowd. Her ER experience also allowed her to stay calm. "I was thinking we needed manpower, space and supplies if a lot of people are coming. Our hospital was almost full."

She broadcast to intensive care and telemetry units: "Send all your available nurses to the ER." Less critical patients needed to be moved out of trauma bays. Each department was also instructed to keep one "crash cart," or mobile cabinet, and these were rolled to the ER, their trays full of chest tubes, drugs and other life-saving supplies. They were in high demand when the ER became overrun with gunshot wound victims as patient after patient needed to be stabilized and intubated for emergency surgery.

"They were amazing," Comanescu says of her staff. "People were just coming to help, bringing all these supplies. The fact that people came from home and opened spaces that weren't open . . . That night will stay with me for the rest of my life."

Thea Parish, pharmacy technician

Parish ran full speed pushing crash carts to the ER. They are heavy machines, and to keep supplies flowing she would sprint back and forth between the pharmacy and the ER throughout the night. A nursing student, once the ER was stocked with drugs, she told the charge nurse: "There are limited things I can do, but I can help." So many patients were in danger of bleeding out that she helped assess wounds, apply tourniquets, place IVs and monitor vital signs to notify doctors when patients crashed, until on-call staff nurses arrived.

"Some of the nurses from upstairs were traumatized," she recalled. "They've seen patients pass before, but on a scale this size it's overwhelming."

She helped colleagues focus on a checklist: assess and if necessary pack the wounds—stopping the bleeding came first. And she helped victims call their families. "There were people who couldn't operate their phones because they had blood in their eyes, were in shock, or had lost their phones. I let them use mine, and it's been a little hard now. I have families contacting me to say thank you even though their people didn't make it."

By that time the staff was operating with mechanical efficiency, she said.

"Everybody was doing exactly what they needed to do to help as many people as they could. At that point I was in awe . . . Ever since I started nursing school, the human race has been declining and hating on each other. I was debating whether I wanted to be a nurse.

But when I looked around, I was like, this is what it's about: saving people. We were the helpers. That was the most memorable moment. Yeah, there was a lot of trauma happening, but at the same moment humanity was happening and it was amazing."

Chris Fisher, trauma surgeon

"A lot of mass casualty alerts end up not significant, or false alarms," said Fisher. "But when I first pulled in it was an unbelievable sight. I got a pit in my stomach walking up because I knew something huge happened. There were multiple Metro vehicles, ambulances pulling in, nurses bringing out multiple gurneys to take people in stretchers from private vehicles."

Two other surgeons were already in and three more were en route. Fisher went to the operating room where the first patient was on the table, prepped and draped. The anesthesiologist came in while Fisher located the wounds. He started operating. The key difference from a normal night, apart from the sheer volume of patients, was that the wounds were from a rifle, which is more serious because the rounds have a higher velocity than handgun bullets.

Their assembly-line approach worked "fantastically well," he said. "Patients didn't have to wait to be operated on. We used all 24 operating rooms. All the staff came in right away, and that made a huge difference."

Fisher operated on five people during a 24-hour shift. In between, he helped coordinate where patients would go and who would be next while performing triage. Everyone was in the zone, and the gravity of the mass shooting did not hit him until he went home the next night and his dogs smelled and licked the blood on his shoes. He put them in the trash.

Tracy Szymanski, guest services director

At first, Szymanski experienced the night's trauma as a concert-goer. She and her husband were about to leave the Route 91 festival when the gunfire started. They believed they were hearing the sound of firecrackers. Security officers screamed that people should turn around and take cover, so they ducked into a bar with a roof over-head. They ran out in between shots, and she called her hospital to tell them what was happening. As they got away, they passed injured people resting against dumpsters, and Szymanski asked them: "Are you OK?"

"Honestly, it felt very debilitating," she recalled, "because I'm a non-clinical member of our team." All she could do was help Sunrise prepare.

Showing up in her concert T-shirt and shorts, she turned the auditorium into a waiting room for victims' families. There, she gave people in blood- or dirt-stained clothes fresh outfits and handed cell-phone chargers out, got the cafe open to provide coffee, and began working with case managers to help find missing loved ones. "Going back and forth between the war zone was unlike anything I've ever seen, but the patients were so wonderful. Many of them laying on gurneys in the ER were saying, 'No I'm not that bad, go to work on them not me.'"

The next day she managed a massive influx of food and water donations and brought in therapy dogs. Between five and twelve golden retrievers would visit Sunrise over the next few weeks, inter-acting with families, patients and staff. "My phone was blowing up with names of people who needed fuzzy love. It made a big difference."

Heather Brown, intensive care unit nurse

Brown was part of the team that moved people upstairs from the ER, and then came back down to help triage the emergency cases. "It was difficult," she said. "We're not used to being the first line, per se. I had to revert back to training and try to think of basic things that needed to be done."

When she returned to the ICU at 7 a.m., she cared for patients whom she had helped stabilize downstairs who had now gone through life-saving surgeries. In the weeks that followed, she watched them further improve. "Some people we thought might not wake up, or talk or walk again were able to get up and move. From everything we saw that night to a week later the progress was amazing."

Her most vivid memory, though, was of a patient who had arrived at the ER before the shooting, an older blind woman who asked to leave. "She couldn't see what was going on in the ER at all, but she could sense it, and hear it obviously. She had a daughter in town who'd gladly take her home, she said. In the middle of everything that was going on, when she came up to ask me that, it was touching. She was realizing she didn't need to be in our busy ER for what she had at that exact moment. It kind of stuck. There were other victims who were the same way after that. You start to see all that good from people who've gone through something traumatic, and it keeps you going for all the ones who aren't able to do that."

Todd Sklamberg, hospital CEO

"As a level two trauma center we see all sorts of trauma, from stabbings to gunshots, to car accidents," said Sklamberg, speaking in front of signed placards from medical staff in Orlando, San Bernardino, Denver, Boston and Newtown. "We drill and we prepare on a very regular basis, but nothing could have prepared us for this event in terms of the quantity of patients that came. Over 120 gunshot victims came into Sunrise over a two-hour period of time—unprecedented numbers in the history of the US. But the preparation, the drilling we do, gave us the foundation upon which to provide that care to all the patients who came in.

"No patient was turned away."

Discussion Questions for Chapter Three

For Frankie Mac

1. Most of us have experienced a Daphne (or a Donald) in our lives. Describe yours. Did your Daphne make you strive to be better, or did she prevent you from achieving your goals? Describe a few specific moments from your experience with this individual. Looking back on them, how do you wish you could change those moments? If you feel you reacted in an effective way, explain why.

2. In addition to description, what other types of development does Mac employ? How do these types serve the thesis? Write out the essay's thesis first, and then list five examples that validate it.

3. What are you "good at"? Describe it. Do you share this ability with others? How has this ability shaped your sense of yourself?

4. Mac creates an arc between the essay's introduction and conclusion. What is this arc, and how does it help the essay and its reader?

For S. L. Kelly

1. Kelly creates a causal chain within her essay. It begins with her childhood conversation with her sister about their dreams and ends with the essay's final sentence. List the effects between those two declarations in her life. How does each connect to the other?

2. What assumptions do you make about those who participate in a particular hobby or vocation? Identify one or two hobbies or activities and write out your assumptions. What are these assumptions based on? How does Kelly challenge assumptions about riding a motorcycle?

3. Kelly's essay defines freedom. Paraphrase (that means use your own words) her definition. What does freedom mean to you? Identify a hobby, avocation, or activity that you enjoy that symbolizes your pursuit (and realization) of freedom.

For Lisa Bailey

1. Bailey divides the essay into four sections (the extra line spacing signals the sections). What is the main point raised by each of the four sections? Why do you think the section breaks occur where they do?

2. Bailey uses multiple types of development to validate her implied thesis. First, in your own words, write out the essay's purpose, and then identify four types of development used in the piece. How does each effectively serve the thesis? If you were Bailey's publisher when this piece went to print, what other details would you have encouraged her to add?

3. The image of the hand returns to frame the essay. What meaning does it have at the end? How does its meaning change from when it is first introduced in the essay?

4. In your own words, describe how Bailey feels about her profession versus how her community feels about it. How do these views counter and serve one another?

5. Identify a photo whose content you did not understand upon first looking at it. What did you initially see? Then describe its truth after you looked at it more fully. What meaning did it gain?

For Violet E. Baldwin

1. Compare and contrast the methods used by Baldwin and Mac to confront situations that once intimidated them. What tone does each writer take in her essay, and how do their tones affect your understanding of the significance of these situations for them?

2. Name something that once prompted or that still elicits fear in you. Describe the cause (if known) of this fear. What are some techniques that you employ to ease the fear?

3. Write out four sensory details that Baldwin uses to convey her subject matter. What important facts about her, her environment, and her family do these details convey to the reader?

4. Evaluate the manner in which Baldwin organizes her development and support. How does she frame her narration? What other techniques could she have chosen to present her material?

For Horace Miner

1. Miner's essay has long been considered a satire of American hygiene practices. What exactly is a satire? Which hygiene practices are being satirized?
2. Miner seems to say that the rituals of the Nacirema indicate "definite masochistic tendencies" (paragraph 12). Which rituals in particular reveal these tendencies? Is he right in his evaluation? Having experienced Nacirema rituals for yourself, are there others you could add to the list?
3. Since Miner's piece was written in 1956, how has the practice of going to a dentist's office changed? What new gadget or invention might Miner have enjoyed satirizing?
4. Even though the piece is intended to be humorous, Miner's essay still employs some techniques specific to his field of study: anthropology. What are some of those techniques? How do they add to the satire?

For Craig Childs

1. "Maps of Water Holes" is a piece with allusions to water management and water rights as well as to immigration. Are these issues important to your environment? If so, why?
2. Childs intersperses present-time action (things that he is doing) with recollections of historical events, past experiences, and stories from scientists and other explorers. Why does he do this? What would his writing be like if he had simply described what he himself was doing?
3. Identify a specific seemingly barren landscape. If any, what people once lived on it? Why did they leave? What intrigues you about this place? What truths does it hold?

4. To which senses does Childs appeal most strongly in his descriptions? Why did he choose to appeal to those senses and not to some others?

5. How do Childs and Miner compare and contrast in their treatment of conveying a people's history?

For Dan Hernandez

1. Hernandez offers the accounts of ten "heroes" at Sunrise Hospital who responded to the horrific event of October 1, 2017, in Las Vegas, Nevada. Offer your own example of a hero who has responded to an unexpected human-caused or natural disaster. What actions did this individual take to improve, restore, and/or secure the environment affected by the disaster?

2. How does Hernandez make use of division as an organizational pattern? Are the accounts randomly or purposefully put together? Explain.

3. Each of the individuals named in Hernandez's account is a trained professional in healthcare and must follow specific protocols. Consider a profession in another field and describe the importance of following its protocols. Name as many of the steps that you know. When is it ever appropriate to break that protocol—go above and beyond training—to better execute a task?

Chapter 4

Organization

"Get your stuff together!" Have you heard those words before? Typically, that command addresses some level of chaos in our midst. While some thrive in a less than organized environment, most do not. Hence, the many television programs geared to get you, your closet, your family, your pet, your garage, your spice rack, and your everything else, organized. And if you cannot do it on your own with the help of a show's advice, you can hire a life coach who may begin with a seemingly simple message—get rid of the clutter in your life: If you do, your mind and body will thank you. Well, consider your composition instructor your writing's life coach. And the first thing your instructor will advise you to do with your essay is to organize it. If the essay's content is not organized, it will read like an unwelcome word salad.

As we draft, rewrite, and revise, we must keep in mind the several levels of organization that operate within a paper at once:

Word by word
Sentence by sentence
Paragraph by paragraph
Overall for paper

Word-by-word organization is sometimes referred to as *syntax* and is usually covered when discussing mechanics. Word-by-word organization is important because the positions of the words can determine the meaning of a sentence. For instance:

I almost killed seventy people.
I killed almost seventy people.

These two sentences have the same words in them, but by shifting two of the words, we give them very different meanings.

Word-by-word organization is also affected by grammatical structures such as passive and active verb formations, questions, commands, and dependent and independent clauses. These structures can show the relative importance of the ideas in a sentence or establish a sequence. Look at these three sentences:

The ball was hit by Tom before it broke the window.
Tom hit the ball before it broke the window.
Before it broke the window, Tom hit the ball.

When you put something at the end of a sentence—or in the last slot of a clause—you are giving it a special stress, called **end focus**, that you want your readers to notice. These three sentences are saying the same thing, but each is stressing something different about what happens by placing end focus on a different pair of words. You can actually hear the stresses if you read the sentences aloud. The first sentence, written in passive voice, puts primary stress on *window* and secondary stress on *Tom*. The second sentence, written in active voice, puts primary stress on *window* and secondary stress on *ball*. The third sentence, written in active voice but with the dependent clause coming first, reverses the order of the events; also, the primary stress is on *ball* and secondary stress is on *window*.

There are other ways of altering word order to manipulate end focus. For example, if you have the sentence *A giant black dog is sitting on the doorstep*, the natural end focus is on *doorstep* since it comes at the end of the sentence. But the most interesting detail in the sentence is the dog, as signaled by the adjectives loaded in front of the word. To give the dog proper stress, we can move it to a place of more prominence with a ***there*-transformation**:

There is a giant black dog sitting on the doorstep.

Now when you read the sentence aloud, the stress falls on *giant black dog*. What we have done is removed that phrase from the subject position it held in the original sentence, stuck the word *There* (an expletive) in its place, and shifted it behind the verb *is*, thus giving it the final slot in the clause. We can also use a transformation called the ***it*-cleft**:

It's a giant black dog that is sitting on the doorstep.

Again, when you read the sentence aloud, the stress falls on *giant black dog*. We did the same thing here as we did in the *there*-transformation: moved the phrase out of the subject position, filled the subject slot with an expletive (*It*), and put the phrase into a slot behind the verb *is*. We might instead try a transformation called the ***what*-cleft**:

What's sitting on the doorstep is a giant black dog.

Here, the phrase *a giant black dog* falls at the very end of the sentence for maximum stress. We can do something similar with a transformation called the **participle shift**:

Sitting on the doorstep is a giant black dog.

Or with a **preposition shift**:

On the doorstep is sitting a giant black dog.

With these last three transformations, not only are you giving *giant black dog* extra stress by using end focus, you are also building anticipation. The shift in syntax alerts your reader that something special, or surprising, or shocking is coming at the end of the sentence, and the reader will expect a payoff to reward her patience. Consider these sentence pairs:

Hearing snarls and howls so loud that they could raise the dead, Tom opened the door. A giant black dog was sitting on the doorstep.

Hearing snarls and howls so loud that they could raise the dead, Tom opened the door. Sitting on the doorstep was a giant black dog.

We have changed the verb tenses, but still, the second sentence pair, by holding *a giant black dog* until the very end, should cause you more anticipation before you finally learn what is snarling and howling so loudly.

Sentence-by-sentence organization usually follows some sort of sequence, usually of either time or space. That means when we are telling a story, one event usually follows another event; when telling a friend how to change an oil filter, you tell her what steps she must take from first to last in order to do the job. Each sentence should set forth a step in that process.

Sentence-by-sentence organization can also be determined by the purpose of the sentences within a paragraph. You have probably been told that a paragraph in an essay should begin with some sort of topic sentence and end with a conclusion, with some sentences of explanation or development in between:

Topic sentence (with transition)
Narrow down
Quotation (or example, description, etc.)
Explanation
Conclusion

Two paragraphs based on that model might look like this:

A typical paragraph begins with a topic sentence that sets forward the point to be discussed. The point is narrowed down to a specific instance by means of development and support in the next sentence—or, if a quotation from an outside source will be used to support the point, then this sentence introduces the source of the quotation; as Maxine Hairston and John J. Ruszkiewicz tell their readers, "You have to select [quotations] purposefully, introduce them intelligently, and tailor them to fit your own language" (626). After using a quotation or providing an example, you might explain how the example supports the point you are making. If your point needs no further explanation, you can conclude the paragraph with this sentence and move on to your next point.

Often, the first sentence of a paragraph will serve as a transition. In that case, you need to signal your reader with one of the transition words or by repeating a key word or by using a synonym for a key word from a previous paragraph. The transition word does not have to appear at the front of the first sentence, but it needs to be present so that you establish the relationship between the paragraphs and signal to your reader whether you are continuing a previous idea or introducing a new idea. This transition shows the reader the direction of your paragraph and avoids confusion. Once the point of the second paragraph is explained adequately, then it too can be concluded, and you can move on to the next paragraph.

Scrambling the sentence order of these paragraphs would confuse their meaning because the sentences fulfill specific duties within the paragraphs: to introduce the main idea, to elaborate on the idea, and to finish with the idea while preparing the reader for the next paragraph. Sentence-by-sentence organization works in conjunction with the essay's purpose. The model above is especially important for presenting research and evidence. The chapters on the research essay and the literature essay will address how the model works for those types of essays.

Sentence-by-sentence organization is also strongly governed by a feature called the **known–new contract.** This feature works hand in hand with the end focus principle of word order and is important for establishing cohesion in a series of sentences. The contract is as follows: The writer puts information that is already known to the reader at the front of a sentence, and she puts information that is new to the reader at the end of the sentence, where it gains emphasis from end focus. The contract is the reason why, in the sentences above where Tom opens the door, *a giant black dog* works better at the end position, because the detail about the dog is new information and deserves special placement. The contract also brings cohesion to the two sample paragraphs illustrating the five-step model above. Let's look at the first of those paragraphs again, this time with the known information underlined and the new information boldfaced:

A typical <u>paragraph</u> begins with **a topic sentence that sets forward the point to be discussed.** The <u>point</u> is narrowed down **to a specific instance by means of development and support in the next sentence**—or, if a <u>quotation from an outside source</u> will be used **to support the point**, then <u>this sentence</u> introduces **the source of the quotation**; as Maxine Hairston and John J. Ruszkiewicz tell their readers, "You have to select [quotations] purposefully, introduce them intelligently, and tailor them to fit your own language" (626). After using a quotation or providing an example, <u>you</u> might explain **how the example supports**

the point you are making. If your <u>point</u> needs **no further explanation**, <u>you</u> can conclude **the paragraph with this sentence and move on to your next point**.

In the first sentence, the word *paragraph* is known information because it was introduced beforehand ("Two paragraphs based on that model . . ."). In the next sentence, the word *point* is known information because it was introduced in the previous one. The phrase *quotation from an outside source* is known information because quotations are a form of development and support, the idea introduced as new in the previous sentence. This pattern of placing information you have already covered in the subject slot of your following sentences is behind the idea of **cohesion** mentioned above. If you open a sentence with new information—information you have not yet made known—you will confuse your reader, who will wonder where this information is coming from. By starting your sentences with known information, you create a pleasing flow between them. Your sentences, however, must also be governed by **coherence**—one unifying principle—as emphasized in the next level of organization.

Paragraph-by-paragraph organization is also determined by purpose. Each paragraph should illuminate one idea, and you should move on to another paragraph when you introduce a new idea or change directions with the old one. For example, if your history instructor has asked you to discuss the causes of the Civil War, then each body paragraph should address a particular cause. Likewise, if your culinary professor has asked you to write the recipe for making meringue, then each paragraph should set out a step in the process. While in a psychology class, if you are tasked with classifying high school cliques, then each paragraph should describe a different group.

The paragraphs so far in this chapter have followed this thinking: After the paragraph introducing the four levels of organization, each paragraph since has focused on one of those levels; paragraph breaks have indicated each new level or a fresh idea about the current level. Sometimes an idea will take more than one paragraph to develop— an idea might take you in one direction, then another. But all of the paragraphs relating to the same central idea should link together to keep that idea unified.

One way to link paragraphs and sentences is to use *transitions*. Transitions are like road and street signs; they provide us with directions so that we can arrive at our proper destination. Imagine driving through an unfamiliar city with no street signs—At which corner do I turn? Am I traveling east or west? Where is the nearest freeway?—and you will understand the difficulty of reading a paper without clear transitions. There are two main ways of providing transitions. The first is by using transitional words and phrases. For this method, keep this list of transition words and phrases handy:

> **Time Order and Sequence**: first, first of all, for one thing, one way, second, the third reason, another, another way, also, next, and, in addition, moreover, furthermore, then, after, before, while, meanwhile, now, during, later (on).
>
> **Spatial**: above, across, after, around, behind, below, beside, in front (back) of, near, next (to), over, under(neath), toward the start (end) of, at the start (back) of, to the left (right) of, on top of, on the bottom of.
>
> **Change of Direction**: although, alternatively, but, however, yet, while, in contrast, despite, still, on the other hand, otherwise, on the contrary.
>
> **Illustration**: for example, for instance, as an illustration, to illustrate, particularly, specifically, such as, like.
>
> **Conclusion**: therefore, consequently, thus, then, as a result, in summary, to conclude, last (most) of all, in the end, finally.

By using one of the transitional words or phrases in the first sentence of your paragraphs, you signal to your reader the sequence of your thoughts and connect the ideas you are developing.

The second method of making transitions is to repeat a key word or idea (or a synonym or a pronoun substituting for that idea) from a previous paragraph in the first sentence of the new paragraph. The first sentence of this paragraph repeated the word *transitions*; the repetition signaled that this paragraph was related to the previous one because it was talking about the same topic. It also used the word *second* (a transitional word) to let you know that it was moving on to the next type of transition. You must remind your reader what direction you are taking and which of your ideas are related, or else your reader will feel as though you have left her stranded in that unfamiliar city. Clear transitions provide signs for your reader to follow.

Overall-for-paper organization incorporates all of the levels mentioned above, but one important consideration will guide how you order your ideas within a paper: Your ideas must make as much impact upon your reader as possible. Three common ways of organizing your paper for effect are by chronology, by relative importance, and by subordination/coordination.

Chronology

If you are reporting a series of events, describing a process, or writing about a topic that involves a sequence, then the most natural way to organize your paper would be by chronology. Violet E. Baldwin's essay "Drowning" follows this method to report on a near-tragic series of events that happened to her while vacationing with her relatives in Puerto Rico, from the moment she and her family went down to the shoreline, to the terrifying moments when she and her father were caught by the waves, to the final rescue by her aunt and their return to the safety of the beach.

Relative Importance

This method means saving "the best for last"; that is, saving your strongest argument or example or description for last and structuring your essay according to Aristotelian plot structure. Perhaps you have talked about the idea of plot and seen this picture:

This drawing might look like a mountain to you, and that might be a good way to remember it. The first, smaller peak is the *initial conflict*, which sets everything in motion. The long, gradual uphill toward the second peak is the *rise in tension* or the *complication*. The top of the second peak is the *climax*. Baldwin's essay "Drowning" makes use of this method as well: She establishes the initial conflict in the opening paragraphs by foreshadowing the accident and by listing the sensory impressions she can no longer remember because of the terror she experienced; the rise in tension comes as she describes how the waves pull her and her father into deeper water, how her father struggles to keep her afloat, how her aunts cannot hear her family's cries, and how her grandfather swims out to help them. Her most startling and provocative details come last as she describes the helplessness in her grandfather's eyes, her father's losing battle with the undertow, and her realization that they are about to die. The climax—and a release of the built-up tension—comes when her aunt paddles over and saves them all with her surfboard. Used correctly, this type of organization can pull a reader through an essay by arousing and maintaining her interest.

Subordination/Coordination

Subordination/Coordination is a method of grouping similar ideas. To use this method when writing your own papers, follow these four steps:

1. Make a complete list of the ideas, issues, topics, and/or arguments that you wish to discuss in your paper.
2. See if any items on the list are related. If they are, group them together (this is coordination) in a list. Above the list, write out the quality that relates the items in the list (this is subordination). Repeat this step until all of the items have been put into lists. For instance, if your list reads

   carrots bread pork
   cereal orange juice peas
   beef rice turnips milk

   you can align carrots, peas, and turnips under the heading *vegetables*; you can align pork and beef under the heading *meats*;

you can align bread, cereal, and rice under the heading *grains*;
you can align orange juice and milk under the heading *drinks*.

3. Find a "title" which describes the common feature(s) of all
the lists (this is subordination again). For the example used in
step two, you can align all of the lists under the title *foods* or
grocery list.

4. Now redraw your lists—with the headings and title included—
in an outline form:

> Foods
> I. Vegetables
>   A. Carrots
>   B. Peas
>   C. Turnips
> II. Meats
>   A. Pork
>   B. Beef
> III. Grains
>   A. Bread
>   B. Cereal
>   C. Rice
> IV. Drinks
>   A. Orange Juice
>   B. Milk

You now have a blueprint for your paper. Your title becomes a thesis
statement; your headings become sections within the paper; the items
under each heading become the topics of individual paragraphs.

The overall organization of a paper can also be influenced by
the type(s) of development and support you use to elaborate your
thesis. For example, if you are describing an object, you may want
to organize the details spatially: move from the top to the bottom of
the object, or from the left side to the right, or from front to back.
If a car is your object, that would mean starting with the roof and
finishing with the underside, or going from the driver's side to the
passenger's side, or going from the front bumper to the rear bumper.
A description can also be organized by sensory impression: first, by
how it looks; then, by how it sounds; then, by how it smells, and so on.

Here are some methods of development and support and the organization patterns that can be used with them:

Cause and Effect
Centered around key event
Chronological

Comparison and Contrast
Alternating
Continuous

Classification and Division
Subordination/Coordination
Best for last (Relative importance)

Description
Chronological
Spatial
Sensory impression
Best for last

Definition
Definition/example/definition/example
Definition/example/example . . .

Examples
Chronological
Subordination/Coordination
Best for last

Process
Chronological
Spatial
Simple to complex (start with easy steps and move toward more difficult ones)

Argument
Alternating (supporting argument/opposing argument/supporting/ opposing)
Continuous (supporting/supporting/opposing/opposing)
Specific to general (inductive)

General to specific (deductive)
Best for last
Background information/opposing view/supporting arguments

Quotations/Citing Authorities/Statistics
Best for last
Subordination/Coordination

If it better serves your paper's purpose, you may choose more than one method for organizing your paper; these strategies are not mutually exclusive. The key point to remember when selecting your method, as stated above, is making an impact upon your reader. At all times, you must consider the effect you are trying to create on the audience.

You should also remember that the four levels of organization build upon one another; all four levels must work together to create the greatest impact upon your reader. However, you should wait to consider your paper's organization until you have finished a rough draft and are about to begin another. The ideas presented above will be easier to use when you have a first draft on the page.

Finally, keep the lessons of your writing life coach with you as you move beyond the academic environment. You may not write a formally organized description or a cause and effect or a comparison essay while on the job. But your boss will likely ask you to inventory a warehouse, or the doctor on duty will ask you to evaluate a patient's symptoms and discuss when they began and how they have changed, or a prospective buyer will ask you to explain the difference between the Toyotas on your car lot versus the Hondas across the street. At that moment, you may need your coach to remind you of the organization patterns you have learned in this chapter.

Works Cited

Hairston, Maxine, and John J. Ruszkiewicz. *The Scott, Foresman Handbook for Writers*. Scott, Foresman, 1988.

Excerpt from *On Tyranny*
by Timothy Snyder

Chapter 11, "Investigate"

Figure things out for yourself. Spend more time with long articles. Subsidize investigative journalism by subscribing to print media. Realize that some of what is on the internet is there to harm you. Learn about sites that investigate propaganda campaigns (some of which come from abroad). Take responsibility for what you communicate with others.

"What is truth?" Sometimes people ask this question because they wish to do nothing. Generic cynicism makes us feel hip and alternative even as we slip along with our fellow citizens into a morass of indifference. It is your ability to discern facts that makes you an individual, and our collective trust in common knowledge that makes us a society. The individual who investigates is also the citizen who builds. The leader who dislikes the investigators is a potential tyrant.

During his campaign, the president claimed on a Russian propaganda outlet that American "media has been unbelievably dishonest." He banned many reporters from his rallies, and regularly elicited hatred of journalists from the public. Like the leaders of authoritarian regimes, he promised to suppress freedom of speech by laws that would prevent criticism. Like Hitler, the president used the word *lies* to mean statements of fact not to his liking, and presented journalism as a campaign against himself. The president was on friendlier terms with the internet, his source for erroneous information that he passed on to millions of people.

In 1971, contemplating the lies told in the United States about the Vietnam War, the political theorist Hannah Arendt took comfort in the inherent power of facts to overcome falsehoods in a free society: "Under normal circumstances the liar is defeated by reality, for which there is no substitute; no matter how large the tissue of falsehood that an experienced liar has to offer, it will never be large enough, even if he enlists the help of computers, to cover the immensity of factuality." The part about computers is no longer true. In the 2016 presidential election, the two-dimensional world of the internet was more important than the three-dimensional world of human contact. People going door-to-door to canvass encountered the surprised blinking of American citizens who realized that they would have to talk about politics with a flesh-and-blood human being rather than having their views affirmed by their Facebook feeds. Within the two-dimensional internet world, new collectivities have arisen, invisible by the light of day—tribes with distinct worldviews, beholden to manipulations. (And yes, there is a conspiracy that you can find online: It is the one to keep you online, looking for conspiracies.)

We need print journalists so that stories can develop on the page and in our minds. What does it mean, for example, that the president says that women belong "at home," that pregnancy is an "inconvenience," that mothers do not give "100 percent" at work, that women should be punished for having abortions, that women are "slobs," "pigs," or "dogs," and that it is permissible to sexually assault them? What does it mean that six of the president's companies have gone bankrupt, and that the president's enterprises have been financed by mysterious infusions of cash from entities in Russia and Kazakhstan? We can learn these things on various media. When we learn them from a screen, however, we tend to be drawn in by the logic of spectacle. When we learn of one scandal, it whets our appetite for the next. Once we subliminally accept that we are watching a reality show rather than thinking about real life, no image can actually hurt the president politically. Reality television must become more dramatic with each episode. If we found a video of the president performing Cossack dances while Vladimir Putin claps, we would probably just demand the same thing with the president wearing a bear suit and holding rubles in his mouth.

The better print journalists allow us to consider the meaning, for ourselves and our country, of what might otherwise seem to be isolated bits of information. But while anyone can repost an article, researching and writing is hard work that requires time and money. Before you deride the "mainstream media," note that it is no longer the mainstream. It is derision that is mainstream and easy, and actual journalism that is edgy and difficult. So try for yourself to write a proper article, involving work in the real world: traveling, interviewing, maintaining relationships with sources, researching in written records, verifying everything, writing and revising drafts, all on a tight and unforgiving schedule. If you find you like doing this, keep a blog. In the meantime, give credit to those who do all of that for a living. Journalists are not perfect, any more than people in other vocations are perfect. But the work of people who adhere to journalistic ethics is of a different quality than the work of those who do not.

We find it natural that we pay for a plumber or a mechanic, but demand our news for free. If we did not pay for plumbing or auto repair, we would not expect to drink water or drive cars. Why then should we form our political judgment on the basis of zero investment? We get what we pay for.

If we do pursue the facts, the internet gives us enviable power to convey them. The authorities cited here had nothing of the kind. Leszek Kolakowski, the great Polish philosopher and historian from whom this book takes its epigraph, lost his chair at Warsaw University for speaking out against the communist regime, and could not publish. The first quotation in this book, from Hannah Arendt, came from a pamphlet entitled "We Refugees," a miraculous achievement written by someone who had escaped a murderous Nazi regime. A brilliant mind like Victor Klemperer, much admired today, is remembered only because he stubbornly kept a hidden diary under Nazi rule. For him it was sustenance: "My diary was my balancing pole, without which I would have fallen down a thousand times." Václav Havel, the most important thinker among the communist dissidents of the 1970s, dedicated his most important essay, "The Power of the Powerless," to a philosopher who died shortly after interrogation by the Czechoslovak communist secret police. In communist Czechoslovakia, this pamphlet had to be circulated illegally, in a few copies, as what east Europeans at the time, following the Russian dissidents, called "samizdat."

"If the main pillar of the system is living a lie," wrote Havel, "then it is not surprising that the fundamental threat to it is living in truth." Since in the age of the internet we are all publishers, each of us bears some private responsibility for the public's sense of truth. If we are serious about seeking the facts, we can each make a small revolution in the way the internet works. If you are verifying information for yourself, you will not send on fake news to others. If you choose to follow reporters whom you have reason to trust, you can also transmit what they have learned to others. If you retweet only the work of humans who have followed journalistic protocols, you are less likely to debase your brain interacting with bots and trolls.

We do not see the minds that we hurt when we publish falsehoods, but that does not mean we do no harm. Think of driving a car. We may not see the other driver, but we know not to run into his car. We know that the damage will be mutual. We protect the other person without seeing him, dozens of times every day. Likewise, although we may not see the other person in front of his or her computer, we have our share of responsibility for what he or she is reading there. If we can avoid doing violence to the minds of unseen others on the internet, others will learn to do the same. And then perhaps our internet traffic will cease to look like one great, bloody accident.

Two Ways of Seeing a River
by Mark Twain

Now when I had mastered the language of this water and had come to know every trifling feature that bordered the great river as familiarly as I know the letters of the alphabet, I had made a valuable acquisition. But I had lost something, too. I had lost something which could never be restored to me while I lived. All the grace, the beauty, the poetry, had gone out of the majestic river! I still kept in mind a certain wonderful sunset which I witnessed when steamboating was new to me. A broad expanse of the river was turned to blood; in the middle distance the red hue brightened into gold, through which a solitary log came floating, black and conspicuous; in one place a long, slanting mark lay sparkling upon the water; in another the surface was broken by boiling, tumbling rings that were as many-tinted as an opal; where the ruddy flush was faintest was a smooth spot that was covered with graceful circles and radiating lines, ever so delicately traced; the shore on our left was densely wooded, and the somber shadow that fell from this forest was broken in one place by a long, ruffled trail that shone like silver; and high above the forest wall a clean-stemmed dead tree waved a single leafy bough that glowed like a flame in the unobstructed splendor that was flowing from the sun. There were graceful curves, reflected images, woody heights, soft distances, and over the whole scene, far and near, the dissolving lights drifted steadily, enriching it every passing moment with new marvels of coloring.

I stood like one bewitched. I drank it in, in a speechless rapture. The world was new to me and I had never seen anything like this at home. But as I have said, a day came when I began to cease from noting the glories and the charms which the moon and the sun and the twilight wrought upon the river's face; another day came when I ceased altogether to note them. Then, if that sunset scene had been repeated, I should have looked upon it without rapture and should have commented upon it inwardly after this fashion: "This sun means

---

"Two Ways of Seeing a River" by Mark Twain, 1883.

that we are going to have a wind tomorrow; that floating log means that the river is rising, small thanks to it; that slanting mark on the water refers to a bluff reef which is going to kill somebody's steamboat one of these nights, if it keeps on stretching out like that; those tumbling 'boils' show a dissolving bar and a changing channel there; the lines and circles in the slick water over yonder are a warning that the troublesome place is shoaling up dangerously; that silver streak in the shadow of the forest is the 'break' from a new snag and he has located himself in the very best place he could have found to fish for steamboats; that tall dead tree, with a single living branch, is not going to last long, and then how is a body ever going to get through this blind place at night without the friendly old landmark?"

No, the romance and beauty were all gone from the river. All the value any feature of it had for me was the amount of usefulness it could furnish toward compassing the safe piloting of a steamboat. Since those days, I have pitied doctors from my heart. What does the lovely flush in a beauty's cheek mean to a doctor but a "break" that ripples above some deadly disease? Are not all her visible charms sown thick with what are to him the signs and symbols of hidden decay? Does he ever see her beauty at all, or doesn't he simply view her professionally and comment upon her unwholesome condition all to himself? And doesn't he sometimes wonder whether he has gained most or lost most by learning his trade?

What Causes Knuckles to Crack? Scientists Now Think They Know
by Nicola Davis

New model explains how pressure changes in joint fluid air bubbles create the noise.

The sound of popping knuckles has long been a source of bafflement for scientists. Now researchers say they might have cracked its origins.

While previous research has shown that not all joints can make the sound, and that those that do can only be cracked once every 20 minutes or so, quite what is behind the auditory pop has been a topic of hot debate.

"The cavity in between the two knuckles is filled with a fluid that is called the synovial fluid, and when you suddenly change the pressure in that fluid as a result of increasing the spacing between the knuckles, some of the gases in that fluid can nucleate into a bubble," said Professor Abdul Barakat of the École Polytechnique's hydrodynamics laboratory, a coauthor of the new study.

Some researchers have suggested that it is the collapse of such bubbles, formed of carbon dioxide and other gases, that causes the well-known crack, but others have proposed another possibility. "As you form this bubble you can cause pressure changes, and that can produce sound," said Barakat.

In 2015 researchers in Canada appeared to have solved the puzzle, after one of the team had his knuckles cracked in an MRI scanner as images were taken. The verdict: the cracking sound was down to the rapid separation of the joint and bubble formation, not bubble collapse.

Barakat says the idea of delving deeper into the issue came from one of his students, a coauthor of the new research, who chose to study the phenomenon for a course project.

Noting that imaging techniques do not provide the necessary time resolution to capture the high-speed dynamics of knuckle-cracking, the pair developed a mathematical model to explore whether collapsing bubbles could be behind the sound after all.

The model, said Barakat, is based on three components: the change in pressure of the fluid as the knuckles move apart, the growth and collapse of the resulting bubble, and how changes in pressure from the bubble turn into sounds.

The team compared the sounds they would expect from collapsing bubbles produced from joint-popping, according to the model, with sound patterns recorded from a handful of knuckle-cracking participants, and found a good match between the two. By contrast, Barakat says formation of bubbles has not been shown to produce sounds of the observed magnitude or loudness.

But there is an extra nuance: some have argued that it takes longer for the bubble to collapse than for a crack to be heard, and that this makes it an unlikely source of the sound. Barakat has an answer.

"What we demonstrate here is you don't need full collapse," he said, pointing out that even if the bubble just partially collapsed to leave a micro-bubble, it would generate the sound on the necessary time scale. The discovery, the authors add, could explain why small bubbles have been observed in synovial fluid even after knuckle-cracking.

Dr. Greg Kawchuk from the University of Alberta, a coauthor of the 2015 study, welcomed the new research. "Their main finding, that theoretical bubble collapse can create sound, is not surprising," he said. "What makes this paper interesting is that it suggests that other phenomena may occur in between frames of the MRI video published in our prior study and that these phenomena may create sounds that are similar to those produced in knuckle-cracking."

But, he added, the case was not yet closed, noting that the latest research is a mathematical model that has yet to be verified by experiment.

While there has been some debate about whether knuckle-cracking increases the risk of osteoarthritis, studies do not appear to support a link.

Among those to study the phenomenon was Dr. Donald Unger, who won an IgNobel Prize in 2009 at the age of 83 for cracking only his left knuckles since his teenage years, while leaving his right knuckles uncracked. Unger reported no signs of arthritis in either hand.

Not everyone can produce a knuckle crack. "Some people cannot crack their knuckles because the spacing between their knuckles is too large for this to happen," said Barakat.

But, for those who can and enjoy the sensation, Barakat has a tip: "The more rapidly you pull on your knuckle, the faster you are changing the pressure and therefore the more likely you are to generate a knuckle crack."

What Are the Repercussions of One Lost Night's Sleep? Rudeness Is Just the Start
by Paul Kelley

Disturbed sleep can produce behaviour that has serious economic and social outcomes. As NHS doctors say, we need to change shift patterns.

We've all known people at work who are persistently rude, obstructive and selfish. It's estimated that these workers with counterproductive behaviours cost the US economy $200 billion a year. Now Laura Giurge at Erasmus University Rotterdam thinks she has discovered such negative behaviours can be caused by just one night's bad sleep.

Whatever the initial cause of counterproductive behaviours at work, "a night of poor sleep can make it harder for someone to stop doing it," Giurge has said. Poor sleep seems to trigger these behaviours again the next day, similar to addiction's negative feedback loop. Giurge found the day after a bad night's sleep workers showed negative workplace attitudes and lower self-regulation.

Lack of sleep can impact on work, social skills and performance. In other research, sleep deprivation has been shown to reduce cognitive and emotional functioning generally, leading to worse performance, decision-making, communication, and empathy with others. Emotionally, the sleep-deprived have increased feelings of tiredness, irritability, mood changes, frustration and risk-taking behaviours.

Giurge's research also shows these addictive counterproductive behaviours were found in workers with little power within the organisation rather than leaders—which is hardly surprising. But sleep deprivation is rife in CEOs too and, unlike counterproductive workers, they can take things to extremes.

Perhaps the best-known case of CEO sleep-related burnout is that of Arianna Huffington, creator of the *Huffington Post*. Her appalling self-inflicted sleep deprivation led her to pass out and collapse.

To her credit, she didn't just change her life so that she had time to sleep, she made sure that her employees had time to sleep too, even when this meant having sleep pods in the office.

Just one night's bad sleep can have fatal consequences in transportation, emergency services and war. A single night shift is enough to make even the most dedicated people sleep-deprived. Dr. Steven Lockley in the Harvard Work Hours, Health and Safety Group proved that good doctors become positively dangerous during night shifts.

Lockley suspected that even Harvard doctors—some of the best doctors in the world—would be deeply influenced by working night shifts. His team set up a random controlled trial to discover if this was true, and the results were truly shocking. Doctors on the 24-hour shifts (used in the US) made 36% more serious medical errors and five times as many serious misdiagnoses. Even their consultants showed an increased risk of burn-out and depression.

These doctors are not alone—night shifts can be dangerous for medical staff and patients in the NHS too. In a study of more than 50,000 NHS nurses, those working shifts at night had increased levels of obesity, caffeine intake, total calorie intake, they smoked more, and had overall less sleep. The underlying problem, as one nurse remarked, is that it is "almost impossible to get any sustained sleep during the day." Despite these problems in the NHS over half the staff work unpaid overtime.

Staff in the NHS are deeply aware of the negative impact on patients and staff of badly scheduled night shifts and 12-hour daytime shifts. Working hours became a major issue last year, and junior doctors in the NHS planned industrial action as a result. Currently NHS staff can experience excessive working hours, poorly organised night shifts and sleep deprivation, and two-thirds of doctors may be under serious stress. The NHS staff are rightly worried about the quality of care for patients, and they are not alone: in America, 24-hour shifts are still the norm in hospitals, despite Lockley's work.

Literally billions of workers are sleep-deprived because their working hours and commutes leave them too little time to sleep. More than 20% of all workers are in jobs with unsocial hours, and the number of jobs requiring night shifts is increasing.

There are solutions. Working hours should be kept to sensible limits and when this happens performance improves. Most workers and adolescents suffer from sleep deprivation because their work starts too early, so starting education and work at 10 a.m. could be implemented, which improves health and performance. There are better shift patterns that could be put in place for the emergency services and the NHS. Then maybe, just maybe, there would be fewer workers with counterproductive behaviours.

Morbid? No—*Coco* Is the Latest Children's Film with a Crucial Life Lesson
by Lucinda Everett

Some say we're forcing children to face issues beyond their years. But films can help make them resilient, self-aware adults.

At the weekend Disney Pixar's new film, *Coco*, hit cinemas. It topped the UK box office and has already won a Golden Globe, so you can probably guess what it's about. Princesses, right? Or dinosaurs, maybe.

Nope. It's death: actual send-the-12-year-old-hero-to-the-afterlife-to-meet-his-dead-relatives-type death. Set during the Mexican *Día de Muertos* (Day of the Dead), when people remember their departed loved ones, its core message is that those we lose live on in our memories. Speaking of memory, there's also a character with senile dementia. Really kid-friendly stuff.

Children's films have always had life lessons at their heart. And while most of them have traditionally sat in the positive platitudes category—work hard, be brave, do the right thing—there have been some home truths over the years, too: people are cruel (the *Dumbo* lesson); you'll outgrow your childhood and its trappings (thanks, *Toy Story 2*).

But in recent years, as young people's lives have become more complex and challenging than ever before, kids' movies have stepped up, tackling increasingly tricky subjects. If there's something you're loth to talk to a child about, chances are there's a film that will do it for you.

Death is one tough subject that has always been common—even if not quite as central as it is in *Coco*. Disney's first heroine, Snow White, was an orphan, and they were soon offing loved ones on screen, starting with Bambi's mum. In fact, a 2014 *British Medical Journal* study found that, proportionally, main characters die on screen in more children's animated films than dramatic films for adults.

By 1994, *The Lion King*'s Simba was experiencing real grief, and in *Toy Story 3* (2010) the heroes slid towards seemingly certain death, hand-in-hand, eyes closed, accepting. But they escaped: death was still a plot point. These days it *is* the plot.

If you're thinking life can be as painful as death, modern kids' films have got that covered too. Take the opening sequence of Pixar's *Up* (2009). You know, the one that shows you how dead you are inside by how long you can last without blubbing. It charts every punishing blow of adult life from losing a baby to money troubles to repeatedly putting your dreams on hold.

In the last decade, Disney films have also turned their gaze outwards, championing society's mistreated and marginalized. Disney's 2013 megahit *Frozen* was a feminist triumph, with two kick-ass female leads and a finale centered on sisterhood. It also briefly showed what many believe was Disney's first same-sex couple, complete with cute kids. And it opened a conversation about parental abuse. Not the overt torture of Disney's early wicked stepmothers, but a more insidious brand that saw Elsa's parents shame her for being different.

In 2015, Pixar's *Inside Out* tackled what is often the very trickiest subject for children to understand—their own feelings. Set inside the head of a young girl struggling with life, it personified her four key emotions, and concluded that it's actually totally fine to feel sad, something any child struggling with depression will find deeply reassuring.

And if that wasn't grown-up enough, 2016 saw Disney release *Zootropolis*, an anthropomorphic comedy with a hard-hitting message about racial inclusion—highly subversive given the xenophobic political rhetoric that was rife at the time.

Some may say we're forcing kids to face issues that are beyond their years—that we should go back to the old days where, aside from the odd bereavement, most troubles were solved with a little courage and a singsong. But times have changed, and the way children experience life has changed, too. There are new pressures, new fears, new opportunities, and the chance to mix with people whose identities and choices are, thankfully, being newly embraced by society.

Films are the perfect way for children to understand all this—not only via storylines that they can relate to but in a safe space where they can ask questions freely.

What's more, the common reference point that films provide means that answering those questions becomes easier for parents, and a more open and honest conversation can develop. Let's face it, most kids won't even bat an eyelid at the stuff adults worry will shock or confuse them. Kids accept the society we present to them, meaning films that normalize any and every expression of what it means to be human are a key tool in moving us towards a more inclusive society.

But perhaps most importantly of all, films can help kids cope better when life's struggles hit them for real. They've already experienced some of the associated emotions vicariously. They've seen how the characters handle the situation. Perhaps they've even thought about what they'd do in the same position. If modern kids' films can help the next generation grow into resilient, self-aware, inclusive adults, I say: keep them coming.

Why Are Americans Afraid of Dragons?
by Ursula K. Le Guin

This was to be a talk about fantasy. But I have not been feeling very fanciful lately, and could not decide what to say; so I have been going about picking people's brains for ideas. "What about fantasy? Tell me something about fantasy." And one friend of mine said, "All right, I'll tell you something fantastic. Ten years ago, I went to the children's room of the library of such-and-such a city, and asked for *The Hobbit*; and the librarian told me, 'Oh, we keep that only in the adult collection; we don't feel that escapism is good for children.'"

My friend and I had a good laugh and shudder over that, and we agreed that things have changed a great deal in these past ten years. That kind of moralistic censorship of works of fantasy is very uncommon now, in the children's libraries. But the fact that the children's libraries have become oases in the desert doesn't mean that there isn't still a desert. The point of view from which that librarian spoke still exists. She was merely reflecting, in perfect good faith, something that goes very deep in the American character: a moral disapproval of fantasy, a disapproval so intense, and often so aggressive, that I cannot help but see it as arising, fundamentally, from fear.

So: Why are Americans afraid of dragons?

Before I try to answer my question, let me say that it isn't only Americans who are afraid of dragons. I suspect that almost all very highly technological peoples are more or less antifantasy. There are several national literatures which, like ours, have had no tradition of adult fantasy for the past several hundred years: the French, for instance. But then you have the Germans, who have a good deal; and the English, who have it, and love it, and do it better than anyone else. So this fear of dragons is not merely a Western, or a technological, phenomenon. But I do not want to get into these vast historical questions; I will speak of modern Americans, the only people I know well enough to talk about.

In wondering why Americans are afraid of dragons, I began to realize that a great many Americans are not only antifantasy, but altogether antifiction. We tend, as a people, to look upon all works of the imagination either as suspect, or as contemptible.

"My wife reads novels. I haven't got the time."

"I used to read that science fiction stuff when I was a teenager, but of course I don't now."

"Fairy stories are for kids. I live in the real world."

Who speaks so? Who is it that dismisses *War and Peace, The Time Machine*, and *A Midsummer Night's Dream* with this perfect self-assurance? It is, I fear, the man in the street—the hardworking, over-thirty American male—the men who run this country.

Such a rejection of the entire art of fiction is related to several American characteristics: our Puritanism, our work ethic, our profit-mindedness, and even our sexual mores.

To read *War and Peace* or *The Lord of the Rings* plainly is not "work"—you do it for pleasure. And if it cannot be justified as "educational" or as "self-improvement," then, in the Puritan value system, it can only be self-indulgence or escapism. For pleasure is not a value, to the Puritan; on the contrary, it is a sin.

Equally, in the businessman's value system, if an act does not bring in an immediate, tangible profit, it has no justification at all. Thus the only person who has an excuse to read Tolstoy or Tolkien is the English teacher, because he gets paid for it. But our businessman might allow himself to read a best-seller now and then: not because it is a good book, but because it is a best-seller—it is a success, it has made money. To the strangely mystical mind of the money-changer, this justifies its existence; and by reading it he may participate, a little, in the power and mana of its success. If this is not magic, by the way, I don't know what is.

The last element, the sexual one, is more complex. I hope I will not be understood as being sexist if I say that, within our culture, I believe that this antifiction attitude is basically a male one. The American boy and man is very commonly forced to define his maleness by rejecting certain traits, certain human gifts and potentialities, which our culture defines as "womanish" or "childish." And one of these traits or potentialities is, in cold sober fact, the absolutely essential human faculty of imagination.

Having got this far, I went quickly to the dictionary.

The *Shorter Oxford Dictionary* says: "Imagination. 1. The action of imagining, or forming a mental concept of what is not actually present to the senses; 2. The mental consideration of actions or events not yet in existence."

Very well; I certainly can let "absolutely essential human faculty" stand. But I must narrow the definition to fit our present subject. By "imagination," then, I personally mean the free play of the mind, both intellectual and sensory. By "play" I mean recreation, re-creation, the recombination of what is known into what is new. By "free" I mean that the action is done without an immediate object of profit— spontaneously. That does not mean, however, that there may not be a purpose behind the free play of the mind, a goal; and the goal may be a very serious object indeed. Children's imaginative play is clearly a practicing at the acts and emotions of adulthood; a child who did not play would not become mature. As for the free play of an adult mind, its result may be *War and Peace*, or the theory of relativity.

To be free, after all, is not to be undisciplined. I should say that the discipline of the imagination may in fact be the essential method or technique of both art and science. It is our Puritanism, insisting that discipline means repression or punishment, which confuses the subject. To discipline something, in the proper sense of the word, does not mean to repress it, but to train it—to encourage it to grow, and act, and be fruitful, whether it is a peach tree or a human mind.

I think that a great many American men have been taught just the opposite. They have learned to repress their imagination, to reject it as something childish or effeminate, unprofitable, and probably sinful.

They have learned to fear it. But they have never learned to discipline it at all.

Now, I doubt that the imagination can be suppressed. If you truly eradicated it in a child, he would grow up to be an eggplant. Like all our evil propensities, the imagination will out. But if it is rejected and despised, it will grow into wild and weedy shapes; it will be deformed. At its best, it will be mere ego-centered daydreaming;

at its worst, it will be wishful thinking, which is a very dangerous occupation when it is taken seriously. Where literature is concerned, in the old, truly Puritan days, the only permitted reading was the Bible. Nowadays, with our secular Puritanism, the man who refuses to read novels because it's unmanly to do so, or because they aren't true, will most likely end up watching bloody detective thrillers on the television, or reading hack Westerns or sports stories, or going in for pornography, from *Playboy* on down. It is his starved imagination, craving nourishment, that forces him to do so. But he can rationalize such entertainment by saying that it is realistic—after all, sex exists, and there are criminals, and there are baseball players, and there used to be cowboys—and also by saying that it is virile, by which he means that it doesn't interest most women.

That all these genres are sterile, hopelessly sterile, is a reassurance to him, rather than a defect. If they were genuinely realistic, which is to say genuinely imagined and imaginative, he would be afraid of them. Fake realism is the escapist literature of our time. And probably the ultimate escapist reading is that masterpiece of total unreality, the daily stock market report.

Now what about our man's wife? She probably wasn't required to squelch her private imagination in order to play her expected role in life, but she hasn't been trained to discipline it, either. She is allowed to read novels, and even fantasies. But, lacking training and encouragement, her fancy is likely to glom on to very sickly fodder, such things as soap operas, and "true romances," and nursy novels, and historico-sentimental novels, and all the rest of the baloney ground out to replace genuine imaginative works by the artistic sweatshops of a society that is profoundly distrustful of the uses of the imagination.

What, then, are the uses of the imagination?

You see, I think we have a terrible thing here: a hardworking, upright, responsible citizen, a full-grown, educated person, who is afraid of dragons, and afraid of hobbits, and scared to death of fairies. It's funny, but it's also terrible. Something has gone very wrong. I don't know what to do about it but to try and give an honest answer to that person's question, even though he often asks it in an aggressive and contemptuous tone of voice. "What's the good of it all?" he says. "Dragons and hobbits and little green men—what's the *use* of it?"

The truest answer, unfortunately, he won't even listen to. He won't hear it. The truest answer is, "The use of it is to give you pleasure and delight."

"I haven't got the time," he snaps, swallowing a Maalox pill for his ulcer and rushing off to the golf course.

So we try the next-to-truest answer. It probably won't go down much better, but it must be said: "The use of imaginative fiction is to deepen your understanding of your world, and your fellow men, and your own feelings, and your destiny."

To which I fear he will retort, "Look, I got a raise last year, and I'm giving my family the best of everything, we've got two cars and a color TV. I understand enough of the world!"

And he is right, unanswerably right, if that is what he wants, and all he wants.

The kind of thing you learn from reading about the problems of a hobbit who is trying to drop a magic ring into an imaginary volcano has very little to do with your social status, or material success, or income. Indeed, if there is any relationship, it is a negative one. There is an inverse correlation between fantasy and money. That is a law, known to economists as Le Guin's Law. If you want a striking example of Le Guin's Law, just give a lift to one of those people along the roads who own nothing but a backpack, a guitar, a fine head of hair, a smile, and a thumb. Time and again, you will find that these waifs have read *The Lord of the Rings*—some of them can practically recite it. But now take Aristotle Onassis, or J. Paul Getty: could you believe that those men ever had anything to do, at any age, under any circumstances, with a hobbit?

But, to carry my example a little further, and out of the realm of economics, did you ever notice how very gloomy Mr. Onassis and Mr. Getty and all those billionaires look in their photographs? They have this strange, pinched look, as if they were hungry. As if they were hungry for something, as if they had lost something and were trying to think where it could be, or perhaps what it could be, what it was they've lost.

Could it be their childhood?

So I arrive at my personal defense of the uses of imagination, especially in fiction, and most especially in fairy tale, legend, fantasy, science fiction, and the rest of the lunatic fringe. I believe that maturity is not an outgrowing, but a growing up: that an adult is not a dead child, but a child who survived. I believe that all the best faculties of a mature human being exist in the child, and that if these faculties are encouraged in youth they will act well and wisely in the adult, but if they are repressed and denied in the child they will stunt and cripple the adult personality. And finally, I believe that one of the most deeply human, and humane, of these faculties is the power of imagination: so that it is our pleasant duty, as librarians, or teachers, or parents, or writers, or simply as grownups, to encourage that faculty of imagination in our children, to encourage it to grow freely, to flourish like the green bay tree, by giving it the best, absolutely the best and purest, nourishment that it can absorb. And never, under any circumstances, to squelch it, or sneer at it, or imply that it is childish, or unmanly, or untrue.

For fantasy is true, of course. It isn't factual, but it is true. Children know that. Adults know it too, and that is precisely why many of them are afraid of fantasy. They know that its truth challenges, even threatens, all that is false, all that is phony, unnecessary, and trivial in the life they have let themselves be forced into living. They are afraid of dragons, because they are afraid of freedom.

So I believe that we should trust our children. Normal children do not confuse reality and fantasy—they confuse them much less often than we adults do (as a certain great fantasist pointed out in a story called "The Emperor's New Clothes"). Children know perfectly well that unicorns aren't real, but they also know that books about unicorns, if they are good books, are true books. All too often, that's more than Mummy and Daddy know; for, in denying their childhood, the adults have denied half their knowledge, and are left with the sad, sterile little fact: "Unicorns aren't real." And that fact is one that never got anybody anywhere (except in the story "The Unicorn in the Garden," by another great fantasist, in which it is shown that a devotion to the unreality of unicorns may get you straight into the loony bin). It is by such statements as, "Once upon a time there was a dragon," or "In a hole in the ground there lived a hobbit"—it is by such beautiful non-facts that we fantastic human beings may arrive, in our peculiar fashion, at the truth.

Discussion Questions for Chapter Four

For Timothy Snyder

1. Look up the definition of the word *tyranny*. Write it out. Is tyranny at work in our "free society"? If so, where? If not, how and why can you be sure? Explain your stance.
2. Is the Internet "one great, bloody accident" as Snyder describes it? Be specific in your agreement or disagreement with his assessment. How do you safeguard the truth for yourself and for others on the Internet, in particular in your use of social media—Facebook, Twitter, Instagram, and Snapchat?
3. Is journalism a protected profession? If so, why? Identify a *print* journalist who respects this privilege and one who violates it. Be specific.
4. What is the primary argument that Snyder is presenting? What methods of organization does he use in his support of it? Point out specific examples.

For Mark Twain

1. Can you think of a task or occupation—in the same way Twain views the river as an experienced riverboat captain— that loses its allure once it is mastered? Is this loss a necessity to completing the job correctly? Can this work conversely: beauty emerging from the mastery of a task or job?
2. What pattern of organization does Twain use: continuous or alternating? Explain what would be gained or lost by employing the other method.
3. Write out three of Twain's most detail-driven sentences. Then rewrite each of the three, twice creating a new end focus.

For Nicola Davis

1. Many deem knuckle-cracking an annoyance and not a medical phenomenon. Make a list of physical tics and behaviorisms that with further study may provide greater insight into the

workings of the human body and mind. What do you think could be some of the causes and effects of these actions?

2. Around what key event does Davis organize her article? What are the causes of this key event? What are the effects? Consider the transitions that she uses to move her reader through her article.

3. Pretend you are the anthropologist in Horace Miner's essay "Body Ritual among the Nacirema," or perhaps a more contemporary anthropologist, and satirize the act of cracking one's knuckles.

For Paul Kelley

1. Kelley relies on a causal chain to discuss the relationship between the loss of sleep and behavior. Identify the key event of this chain and the effects of it that he presents in his piece.

2. Describe your sleep routine. Do you consider it healthy for you and those around you? Explain.

3. Lack of sleep is not the only societal "counterproductive" behavior. Name another one. Briefly describe its causes and effects on the one who acts this way and on the individuals with whom this person interacts.

4. Kelley mentions lack of sleep and its relation to shift work. Shift work disorder affects many workers. Identify a specific occupation where this problem persists. What is being done (or should be done) to help these workers?

For Lucinda Everett

1. Identify a children's film that taught you a lesson or helped you cope with a difficult emotion or experience. How did the film comfort you? What did it teach you about yourself and your experience?

2. Identify an individual(s) or a group that dismisses children's and young adult literature and films as being unimportant. Discuss why you think these individuals hold such a view.

3. In what paragraph does Everett put forward her thesis? Write it out. What organization strategies does she use to arrange her support of it?

4. Everett speaks to film helping children cope with life-changing experiences—death, abuse, racism, and others. What is an important coping strategy that you rely on? Describe it. How has it helped you in your life?

For Ursula K. Le Guin

1. "Why Are Americans Afraid of Dragons?" was first presented in 1973 as a talk Le Guin gave to the Pacific Northwest Library Association. Does the piece still hold truth? Are Americans today still afraid of dragons? If so, why? If not, how have Americans squelched their fear of dragons? What proof do you have of this?

2. According to Le Guin, the purpose of fantasy is to "deepen your understanding of your world, and your fellow men, and your own feelings, and your destiny." Do you agree with that assertion? Do you think this is the purpose of all literature or just of fantasy? Explain.

3. Le Guin utilizes more than one mode of writing. Identify specific types of development (description, definition, cause and effect, classification, narration, etc.). Why is it effective for her to use multiple types? How does her organization frame her development?

4. Some of Le Guin's paragraphs are quite short in length. Is her choice of length due to the work originally being a speech? Or is there another reason? Which paragraphs work well transitioning from one idea to the next? What words does she use to move from idea to idea—both within the paragraphs and between them?

5. Both Le Guin and Everett have something to say about how children react to difficult or traumatic events or how they perceive fantasy and reality. Compare and contrast their views. Do the two writers agree? Where do they disagree?

Chapter 5

Mechanics

Mechanics are the nuts and bolts of writing and of preparing your manuscript for submission. You must pay special attention to your instructor's requirements for submitting your essays because those requirements will make the writing (and the reading) process easier. In particular, you will have to keep in mind seven areas: **format of paper, documentation, vocabulary, spelling, punctuation, grammar**, and **sentence construction**.

The *format* of the paper includes how you put your name, course, assignment title, and other pertinent information on your manuscript. It also includes settings for margins, paragraph alignment, headers, page numbers, and other details that pertain to the appearance of your text on the page. Many instructors in the humanities will ask you to follow the Modern Language Association (MLA) guidelines that are explained in most student handbooks. However, many instructors may want you to follow their own method of formatting your assignments. Make sure you understand your instructor's requirements before you sit down to write.

The process of *documentation* applies when your instructor has asked you to write a research paper or a literature essay. In either case, you must follow the rules of documentation set out in a style guide such as the *MLA Handbook* or the *Publication Manual of the American Psychological Association*. These rules will also be set out in most student handbooks. The process of documentation has two main parts: a parenthetical citation that appears in the body paragraphs, and a works cited (or references) list. Please make sure that you understand the documentation rules that your instructor requires as you are writing your essay.

113

Using the correct *vocabulary* in your writing is also important. Generally, your instructor will be looking for two things: the proper use of **key terms**, and appropriate **diction**. A key term is the name of a specific concept in a certain field of study. For example, in a literature class (or elsewhere in this book!), you may learn about concepts such as plot, character, and setting. If you are writing an essay in which you must use one of these concepts, the instructor will determine if you have defined that term correctly and applied it accurately to the material you are covering. Diction, on the other hand, pertains to your choice of words in your writing. In an academic setting, your instructor will probably prefer that you use more formal words. It's okay, among friends, to say something like *I got four flats on my ride*, but in your essays, it's probably better if you write *I have four flat tires on my car*.

Checking the *spelling* of unfamiliar words, of important vocabulary words, and of words that you frequently misspell should be one of your final tasks when writing your paper. If you work on a computer, your word processor's spell checker is a handy tool—but it is not perfect. You may misspell a word that the spell checker may not recognize as an error. For example, if you type *an* when you meant to type *and*, the spell checker will not see your misspelling as an error because *an* is a word. An extra pass through your assignment—or the eyes of a classmate or friend—may help you catch many spelling mistakes. Another handy tool, if you are drafting on a computer, is a text-to-speech reader. Mac users have a text-to-speech reader built into their System Preferences menu under the Accessibility icon (click on Speech); Windows 10 users can use Narrator. With this tool, highlight each paragraph in your text and listen closely as you read along. You may be surprised by how many errors you hear that your eyes do not see. You might even hear some of the other errors described below, an added benefit. A classmate or a friend can help you here as well if he or she is willing to read your work aloud.

Errors of *punctuation, grammar,* and *sentence construction* tend to be the most frustrating for students. You may sense that you have made such an error, but you are not sure what that error might be or how to fix it—until you have the assignment handed back with your instructor's marks. Knowing what your instructor is looking for may help you see which errors you commit. Instructors tend to see errors of punctuation, grammar, and sentence construction as belonging to two groups: **frequency errors** and **status errors**.

Frequency errors are those which your instructor sees most often when grading student assignments. Many of these are as simple as a missing comma, but some are as serious as sentence fragments. Following is a list taken from a study conducted by Robert J. Connors and Andrea A. Lunsford in 1988 (qtd. in Noguchi 58–59) showing the twenty most frequent punctuation, grammar, and sentence construction errors:

1	No comma after introductory element (presentence modifier, sentence)
2	Vague pronoun reference
3	No comma in compound sentence (independent clause, independent clause)
4	Wrong word
5	No comma in nonrestrictive element
6	Wrong or missing inflected endings (noun/verb)
7	Wrong or missing preposition
8	Comma splice
9	Possessive apostrophe error
10	Tense shift (main verb, auxiliary verb)
11	Unnecessary shift in person (first, second, third person)
12	Sentence fragment (sentence or independent clause)
13	Wrong tense or verb form (main verb, auxiliary verb)
14	Subject-verb agreement
15	Lack of comma in series
16	Pronoun agreement error
17	Unnecessary comma with restrictive element
18	Run-on or fused sentence
19	Dangling or misplaced modifier
20	Its/It's error

Focusing your attention on the errors that appear at the top of this frequency list may help you to cut down on the number of errors you commit in your own writing. You may also want to look most closely for comma errors, since they appear six times (counting the comma splice). You may wish, therefore, to consult a handbook to learn more about all of these errors.

Status errors are those which stigmatize the writer—that is, mark the writer's social status or educational background—and which elicit the strongest response in a reader. Following is a list taken from a study conducted by Maxine Hairston in 1981 (qtd. in Noguchi 59–60) showing the most serious status-marking punctuation, grammar, and sentence construction errors:

Status Marking
Nonstandard verb forms in past or past participle: *we knowed* instead of *we knew*
Lack of subject-verb agreement: *we was* instead of *we were; he don't think* instead of *he doesn't think*
Double negatives: *I don't want no trouble*
Objective pronoun as subject: *Him and me found the dog*
Very Serious
Sentence fragments (sentence or independent clause)
Run-on sentences
Noncapitalization of proper nouns
Would of instead of *would have*
Lack of subject-verb agreement, nonstatus marking
Insertion of comma between verb and complement: *She is, an engineer*
Nonparallelism: *We enjoy hiking, swimming, and to go to the movies*
Faulty adverb forms: *He treats his men bad*
Use of transitive verb *set* for intransitive *sit: I set down in the chair*

Again, focusing your attention on the errors that appear on this list may help you to cut down on the errors you commit in your own writing, but you will also be reducing the number of errors that your instructor will see as being the most serious. Comparing this list with the previous one may also give you an idea of which errors you may wish to focus your attention on. As with the previous list, you should consult a handbook to learn more about these errors.

Before you submit any essay to an instructor, you should line-edit your manuscript to make sure that your sentences are grammatically and mechanically clean. The process can be laborious, but it will add polish that a careful reader will appreciate. Below follow three suggestions to make the line-editing process smooth and helpful.

1. *Look first at the subjects and the verbs of your sentences.* Seventy-five percent of all errors can be corrected by following this step. For example, look at the sentences below:

   <u>Sarah</u> **pours** the water into the simmering pot and **begins** to boil.

   Different <u>syrups</u> **were lined** up on the counter next to the espresso machine, such as vanilla, amaretto, and coconut.

   The subjects of the sentences have been underlined, and the verbs have been boldfaced. By reading aloud just the subject and the verbs of the first sentence, we can detect the main fault with it—Sarah can't possibly be boiling herself. This sort of mixed construction must be fixed by recasting the whole sentence. One revision might be

   <u>Sarah</u> **pours** the water into the simmering pot and the <u>water</u> **begins** to boil.

   Adding another subject (*water*) creates a sentence that logically connects the actions of the verbs to their actors.

   The problem in the second sentence lies in the unnecessary use of the passive voice. Passive voice constructions tell the reader that the subject of the sentence is receiving rather than doing the action of the verb. However, in this sentence, the syrups are indeed performing the action—they are lining the counter. To revise the sentence, we might write

> Different <u>syrups</u> **lined** the counter next to the espresso machine, such as vanilla, amaretto, and coconut.

If you are having trouble finding subjects and verbs in a passage, follow these two steps: one, rewrite the passage, changing plural words into singular words and singular words into plural words, and underline the words changed; and two, take the rewritten passage and shift words showing present time into the past and words showing past time into the present. Boldface the words changed.

The words you underlined should be nouns, pronouns, or verbs (or helping verbs in front of the main verbs); the words you boldfaced should be verbs. You may also have added or eliminated determiners or changed adverbs of time such as *yesterday* or *today*. However, verbs showing command and verbals may remain unchanged. Here is an example of the exercise:

Originals

> Sarah pours the water into the simmering pot and begins to boil.

> Different syrups were lined up on the counter next to the espresso machine, such as vanilla, amaretto, and coconut.

Step One

> <u>Sarahs</u> <u>pour</u> the <u>waters</u> into the simmering <u>pots</u> and <u>begin</u> to boil.

> Different <u>syrup</u> <u>was</u> lined up on the <u>counters</u> next to the espresso <u>machines</u>, such as <u>vanillas</u>, <u>amarettos</u>, and <u>coconuts</u>.

Step Two

> Sarahs **poured** the waters into the simmering pots and **began** to boil.

> Different syrup **is** lined up on the counters next to the espresso machines, such as vanillas, amarettos, and coconuts.

All words underlined and boldfaced are nouns, main verbs, or helping verbs. The plural -s ending was added, very awkwardly, to change *Sarah* to *Sarahs*. The subject nouns here are *Sarah* and *syrups*; we know this because when those words changed their spellings, the verbs *pour, begin*, and *is* changed to agree with them. Furthermore, because of the changes from past time to present, we know that the main verbs are *pour, begin*, and *lined* (*is* is a helping verb for *lined*). When you use these steps on your own writing, you should be able to pick out the subject(s) and the verb(s) more easily.

2. *Make sure the modifiers go where they should go.* Modifiers include adjectives, adverbs, prepositional phrases (on, of, to, etc.), participial (-ing and -ed words) and infinitive (to go, to eat, etc.) phrases, and relative clauses (who, which, that, etc.). In most cases, modifiers describe nouns and verbs, though they can modify other modifiers. Generally, modifiers should be placed next to the words they modify, either directly in front of or directly behind. The sentences we used in our previous examples have unnecessary modifiers or modifiers placed in the wrong positions:

> Sarah **pours** the water into the simmering pot and the water **begins** to boil.

> Different syrups **lined** the counter next to the espresso machine, such as vanilla, amaretto, and coconut.

In the first sentence, the participle *simmering*, describing the word *pot*, is not used accurately. Pots do not simmer; the contents of a pot simmer. Hence, we can delete the modifier:

> Sarah **pours** the water into the pot and the water **begins** to boil.

In the second sentence, the list beginning with the phrase *such as* has been placed next to *machine* as if the machine could come in different flavors. The list should logically be placed next to the word *syrups*:

> Different <u>syrups</u>, such as vanilla, amaretto, and coconut **lined** the counter next to the espresso machine.

3. *Make sure your punctuation goes where it should.* Addressing the first two suggestions will help you to find and correct many common punctuation errors. In the sentences we created with step two, punctuation is missing or unnecessary:

> <u>Sarah</u> **pours** the water into the pot and the <u>water</u> **begins** to boil.

> Different <u>syrups</u>, such as vanilla, amaretto, and coconut **lined** the counter next to the espresso machine.

The first sentence now has two subject/verb pairs joined by the word *and*. Though some handbooks may say that you do not need to add punctuation to this sentence because of its brevity, you should be aware that careful readers will notice you have omitted a comma; a comma and the word *and* (a coordinating conjunction) should join subject/verb pairs.

> <u>Sarah</u> **pours** the water into the pot, and the <u>water</u> **begins** to boil.

In the second sentence, the modifying phrase *such as vanilla, amaretto, and coconut* has been placed next to the word it describes, *syrups*, but it now comes between the subject *syrups* and the verb *lined*. Whenever a modifying word, phrase, or clause comes between the major elements of a sentence (subject, verb, object, etc.), then the phrase must be set off with two commas or no commas.

> Different <u>syrups</u> such as vanilla, amaretto, and coconut **lined** the counter next to the espresso machine.

Removing the comma in front of the word *such* makes the most sense. Yet even this version of the sentence is not quite accurate. Looking at the sentence again in light of the first suggestion above brings out another fault: Syrup can't really line a counter unless it has been spilled there. We can improve the sentence even more by writing

<u>Bottles</u> of different syrups such as vanilla, amaretto, and coconut **lined** the counter next to the espresso machine.

Because we have neatly placed the syrups within their containers, this version of the sentence can stand, for now, without need of more revision.

★

We hope that this brief look into the process of essay writing will help you through your drafting stages. As stated at the outset, the first draft of an essay is not the final draft. You should get into the habit of writing multiple drafts of each assignment so that you will give yourself the chance to form and organize your ideas and to proofread for errors. To close this chapter, we have provided three readings that should further illustrate the importance of good mechanics. The first, from Timothy Snyder's *On Tyranny*, explains how certain vocabulary can affect political discourse. The second, from Lynne Truss's *Eats, Shoots & Leaves*, provides an amusing look at what happens when punctuation goes badly wrong. And the third, from Roxane Gay's "To Scratch, Claw, or Grope Clumsily or Frantically," shows how good spelling becomes a life or death skill in the world of competitive Scrabble.

We have also included exercises you may use to practice your punctuation and sentence construction skills. The first set needs simple punctuation changes, but the second set will require that you follow the three-step line-editing process outlined above. (Possible answers come at the end of this chapter as well—don't peek!)

Works Cited

Noguchi, Rei R. *Grammar and the Teaching of Writing: Limits and Possibilities*. NCTE, 1991.

Excerpt from *On Tyranny*
by Timothy Snyder
Chapter 17, "Listen for Dangerous Words"

Be alert to the use of the words *extremism* and *terrorism*. Be alive to the fatal notions of *emergency* and *exception*. Be angry about the treacherous use of patriotic vocabulary.

The most intelligent of the Nazis, the legal theorist Carl Schmitt, explained in clear language the essence of fascist governance. The way to destroy all rules, he explained, was to focus on the idea of the *exception*. A Nazi leader outmaneuvers his opponents by manufacturing a general conviction that the present moment is exceptional, and then transforming that state of exception into a permanent emergency. Citizens then trade real freedom for fake safety.

When politicians today invoke *terrorism* they are speaking, of course, of an actual danger. But when they try to train us to surrender freedom in the name of safety, we should be on our guard. There is no necessary tradeoff between the two. Sometimes we do indeed gain one by losing the other, and sometimes not. People who assure you that you can *only* gain security at the price of liberty usually want to deny you both.

You can certainly concede freedom without becoming more secure. The feeling of submission to authority might be comforting, but it is not the same thing as actual safety. Likewise, gaining a bit of freedom may be unnerving, but this momentary unease is not dangerous. It is easy to imagine situations where we sacrifice both freedom and safety at the same time: when we enter an abusive relationship or vote for a fascist. Similarly, it is none too difficult to imagine choices that increase both freedom and safety, like leaving an abusive relationship or emigrating from a fascist state. It is the government's job to increase both freedom and security.

Extremism certainly sounds bad, and governments often try to make it sound worse by using the word *terrorism* in the same sentence. But the word has little meaning. There is no doctrine called *extremism*. When tyrants speak of *extremists*, they just mean people who are not in the mainstream—as the tyrants themselves are defining that mainstream at that particular moment. Dissidents of the twentieth century, whether they were resisting fascism or communism, were called *extremists*. Modern authoritarian regimes, such as Russia, use laws on *extremism* to punish those who criticize their policies. In this way the notion of *extremism* comes to mean virtually everything except what is, in fact, extreme: tyranny.

Excerpts from *Eats, Shoots & Leaves*
by Lynne Truss
From "Introduction—The Seventh Sense"

Punctuation has been defined many ways. Some grammarians use the analogy of stitching: punctuation as the basting that holds the fabric of language in shape. Another writer tells us that punctuation marks are the traffic signals of language: they tell us to slow down, notice this, take a detour, and stop. I have even seen a rather fanciful reference to the full stop and comma as "the invisible servants in fairy tales—the ones who bring glasses of water and pillows, not storms of weather or love." But best of all, I think, is the simple advice given by the style book of a national newspaper: that punctuation is "a courtesy designed to help readers to understand a story without stumbling."

Isn't the analogy with good manners perfect? Truly good manners are invisible: they ease the way for others, without drawing attention to themselves. It is no accident that the word "punctilious" ("attention to formality or etiquette") comes from the same original root word as punctuation. As we shall see, the practice of "pointing" our writing has always been offered in a spirit of helpfulness, to underline meaning and prevent awkward misunderstandings between writer and reader. In 1644 a schoolmaster from Southwark, Richard Hodges, wrote in his *The English Primrose* that "great care ought to be had in writing, for the due observing of points: for, the neglect thereof will pervert the sense," and he quoted as an example, "My Son, if sinners intise [entice] thee consent thou, not refraining thy foot from their way." Imagine the difference to the sense, he says, if you place the comma after the word "not": "My Son, if sinners intise thee consent thou not, refraining thy foot from their way." This was the 1644 equivalent of Ronnie Barker in *Porridge*, reading the sign-off from a fellow lag's letter from home, "Now I must go and get on my lover," and then pretending to notice a comma, so hastily changing it to, "Now I must go and get on, my lover."

To be fair, many people who couldn't punctuate their way out of a paper bag are still interested in the way punctuation can alter the sense of a string of words. It is the basis of all "I'm sorry, I'll read that again" jokes. Instead of "What would you with the king?" you can have someone say in Marlowe's *Edward II*, "What? Would you? *With the king?*" The consequences of mispunctuation (and re-punctuation) have appealed to both great and little minds, and in the age of the fancy-that email a popular example is the comparison of two sentences:

A woman, without her man, is nothing.
A woman: without her, man is nothing.

Which, I don't know, really makes you *think*, doesn't it? Here is a popular "Dear Jack" letter that works in much the same fundamentally pointless way:

Dear Jack,

I want a man who knows what love is all about. You are generous, kind, thoughtful. People who are not like you admit to being useless and inferior. You have ruined me for other men. I yearn for you. I have no feelings whatsoever when we're apart. I can be forever happy—will you let me be yours?

Jill

Dear Jack,

I want a man who knows what love is. All about you are generous, kind, thoughtful people, who are not like you. Admit to being useless and inferior. You have ruined me. For other men I yearn! For you I have no feelings whatsoever. When we're apart I can be forever happy. Will you let me be?
Yours,

Jill

But just to show there is nothing very original about all this, five hundred years before email a similarly tiresome puzzle was going round:

Every Lady in this Land
Hath 20 Nails on *each* Hand;
Five & twenty on Hands *and Feet;*
And this is true, without deceit.

(Every lady in this land has twenty nails. On each hand, five; and twenty on hands and feet.)

So all this is quite amusing, but it is noticeable that no one emails the far more interesting example of the fateful mispunctuated telegram that precipitated the Jameson Raid on the Transvaal in 1896—I suppose that's a reflection of modern education for you. Do you know of the Jameson Raid, described as a "fiasco"? Marvellous punctuation story. Throw another log on that fire. The Transvaal was a Boer republic at the time, and it was believed that the British and other settlers around Johannesburg (who were denied civil rights) would rise up if Jameson invaded. But unfortunately, when the settlers sent their telegraphic invitation to Jameson, it included a tragic ambiguity:

It is under these circumstances that we feel constrained to call upon you to come to our aid should a disturbance arise here the circumstances are so extreme that we cannot but believe that you and the men under you will not fail to come to the rescue of people who are so situated.

As Eric Partridge points out in his *Usage and Abusage*, if you place a full stop after the word "aid" in this passage, the message is unequivocal. It says, "Come at once!" If you put it after "here," however, it says something more like, "We might need you at some later date depending on what happens here, but in the meantime—don't call us, Jameson, old boy; we'll call you." Of course, the message turned up at *The Times* with a full stop after "aid" (no one knows who put it there) and poor old Jameson just sprang to the saddle, without anybody wanting or expecting him to.

All of which substantiates Partridge's own metaphor for punctuation, which is that it's "the line along which the train (composition, style, writing) must travel if it isn't to run away with its driver." In other words, punctuation keeps sense on the rails. [. . .]

★

What happened to punctuation? Why is it so disregarded when it is self-evidently so useful in preventing enormous mix-ups? A headline in today's paper says, "DEAD SONS PHOTOS MAY BE RELEASED"—the story relating to dead sons in the plural, but you would never know. The obvious culprit is the recent history of education practice. We can blame the pedagogues. Until 1960, punctuation was routinely taught in British schools. A child sitting a Country Schools exam in 1937 would be asked to punctuate the following puzzler: "Charles the First walked and talked half an hour after his head was cut off" (answer: "Charles the First walked and talked. Half an hour after, his head was cut off"). Today, thank goodness, the National Curriculum ensures that when children are eight, they are drilled in the use of the comma, even if their understanding of grammar is at such an early age a bit hazy. [. . .] [W]e visited a school in Cheshire where quite small children were being taught that you use commas in the following situations:

1. in a list
2. before dialogue
3. to mark out additional information

Which was very impressive. Identifying "additional information" at the age of eight is quite an achievement, and I know for a fact that I couldn't have done it. But if things are looking faintly more optimistic under the National Curriculum, there remains the awful truth that, for over a quarter of a century, punctuation and English grammar were simply not taught in the majority of schools, with the effect that A-level examiners annually bewailed the condition of examinees' written English, while nothing was done. Candidates couldn't even *spell* the words "grammar" and "sentence," let alone use them in any well-informed way. [. . .]

But to get back to those dark-side-of-the-moon years in British education when teachers upheld the view that grammar and spelling got in the way of self-expression, it is arguable that the timing of their grammatical apathy could not have been worse. In the 1970s, no educationist would have predicted the explosion in universal written communication caused by the personal computer, the internet and the key-pad of the mobile phone. But now, look what's happened: everyone's a writer! Everyone is posting film reviews on Amazon that go like this:

> I watched this film [*About a Boy*] a few days ago expecting the usual hugh Grant bumbling . . . character Ive come to loathe/expect over the years. I was thoroughly suprised. This film was great, one of the best films I have seen in a long time. The film focuses around one man who starts going to a single parents meeting, to meet women, one problem He doesnt have a child.

Isn't this sad? People who have been taught nothing about their own language are (contrary to educational expectations) spending all their leisure hours attempting to string sentences together for the edification of others. And there is no editing on the internet! Meanwhile, in the world of text messages, ignorance of grammar and punctuation obviously doesn't affect a person's ability to communicate messages such as "C U later." But if you try anything longer, it always seems to turn out much like the writing of the infant Pip in *Great Expectations*:

> MI DEER JO I OPE U R KRWITE WELL I OPE I SHAL SON B HABELL 4 2 TEEDGE U JO AN THEN WE SHORL B SO GLODD AN WEN I M PRENGTD 2 U JO WOT LARX AN BLEVE ME INF XN PIP. [. . .]

Taking our previous analogies for punctuation, what happens when it isn't used? Well, if punctuation is the stitching of language, language comes apart, obviously, and all the buttons fall off. If punctuation provides the traffic signals, words bang into each other and everyone ends up in Minehead. If one can bear for a moment to think of punctuation marks as those invisibly beneficent fairies (I'm sorry), our poor deprived language goes parched and pillowless to bed. And if you take the courtesy analogy, a sentence no longer holds the door open for you to walk in, but drops it in your face as you approach.

The reason it's worth standing up for punctuation is not that it's an arbitrary system of notation known only to an over-sensitive elite who have attacks of the vapours when they see it misapplied. The reason to stand up for punctuation is that without it there is no reliable way of communicating meaning. Punctuation herds words together, keeps others apart. Punctuation directs you how to read, in the way musical notation directs a musician how to play. [. . .]

Words strung together without punctuation recall those murky murals Rolf Harris used to paint, where you kept tilting your head and wondering what it was. Then Rolf would dip a small brush into a pot of white and—to the deathless, teasing line, "Can you guess what it is yet?"—add a line here, a dot there, a curly bit, and suddenly all was clear. Good heavens, it looked like just a splodge of colours and all along it was a kangaroo in football boots having a sandwich! Similarly, take a bit of unpunctuated prose, add the dots and flourishes in the right place, stand back, and what have you got?

My dear Joe,

I hope you are quite well. I hope I shall soon be able to teach you, Joe—and then we shall be so glad. And when I am apprenticed to you, Joe: *what larks!* Believe me, in affection,

Pip

To Scratch, Claw, or Grope Clumsily or Frantically[1]

by Roxane Gay

My third tournament started with a brutal game where I lost by more than 200 points. I was the fifth seed, ranked like tennis with words, and feeling confident—too confident, really. "We Are the Champions" may have been on an infinite loop in my head. And yet. It was also early on a Saturday morning. I am not a morning person. Before the tournament started, people milled around the hotel meeting room, chatting idly about the heat, what we had done since the last time many of us had seen one another (the previous tournament in Illinois), and some of the more amazing plays we had made recently.

Scrabble[2] players love to talk, at length, with some repetition, about their vocabulary triumphs.

There were twenty-one of us with various levels of ability, but really, if you're playing this game at the competitive level, you generally have some skill and can be a contender. The more experienced players, the Dragos to my Rocky, studied word lists and appeared intensely focused on something the rest of us couldn't see. Many wore fanny packs without irony—serious fanny packs bulging with mystery. As I waited for the tournament to begin, I studied the table of game-related accessories—books, a travel set, a towel, a deluxe board, and some milled French soaps clearly taken from someone's closet—all for drawings to be held later in the day.[3]

---

1 This is the definition of the word "scrabble" according to *Merriam-Webster's Collegiate Dictionary*.

2 In all seriousness, Scrabble was invented by a man named Alfred Mosher Butts.

3 Scrabble tournaments are a lot like soccer tournaments for four-year-olds in that, oftentimes, everyone goes home with a little something.

At nine o'clock, sharp, the tournament director,[4] Tom, began making announcements, one of which was that his wife had died just days earlier. The tournament was going to go on, he said. It was an awkward, touching moment because grief is so personal and this man was clearly grieving. The room was silent. It was difficult to know what to do. He announced that the first pairings would be posted in a few minutes, so we waited quietly until the pairings were posted around the room. We all hovered around the sheet of paper, quickly writing down the names of our first two opponents. I sat across from my first challenger. She was seeded nineteenth. My confidence swelled vulgarly. She stared at me, smug, almost imperious. I felt an uncomfortable chill. We determined she would go first. She drew her seven tiles. I started her time and fixed her with a hard stare as she began shuffling the seven plastic squares back and forth across her rack. I began drawing my tiles. Beneath the table, my legs were shaking.

This is competitive Scrabble.[5]

You have to understand. I was lonely in a new town where I knew no one. I wanted to be back home, with my boyfriend, in our apartment, complaining about how *SportsCenter* seems to air perpetually or

---

4   Officially rated tournaments are run by NASPA-approved tournament directors. NASPA is the North American Scrabble Players Association. Tournament directors are generally encyclopedic in their knowledge of Scrabble and can easily clarify any confusion about the rules or negotiate disputes that arise during a tournament. Disputes, they arise.

5   This is how serious competitive Scrabble is: there is a national championship, held annually during the summer. The first national tournament was held in 1978. There are also world competitions (the first world championship was held in 1991), a cottage industry of Scrabble-related merchandise, game timers, boards, tiles, etc., plus books, documentaries, and academic articles on the nuances of competitive Scrabble. There are Scrabble-related apps for your iDevices (I use Zarf, CheckWord, the official Scrabble game, Lexulous, and Words With Friends). There are Scrabble games on Facebook (I play the official Hasbro game and Lexulous). Elsewhere online, there's the Internet Scrabble Club (ISC), where I also play. There is a website, cross-tables.com, dedicated to tracking all the official tournaments in the country with scores and rankings. I am ranked 1,336th in the country. I'm guessing that's out of 1,400 players, given my lowliness.

listening to him nag me about my imaginary Internet friends. My apartment was empty, no furniture, because I left my sad graduate-student furniture behind. After work, I'd sit on my lone chair, a step above sad, purchased at Sofa Mart, wondering how my life had come to this.

When my new colleague invited me to her home to play with her Scrabble club,[6] I was so desperate I would have agreed to just about anything—cleaning her bathrooms, watching the grass grow in her backyard, something smarmy and vaguely illegal involving suburban prostitution, whatever.

I didn't quite know what a Scrabble club was, but I assumed it was a group of people enjoying friendly games of Scrabble on a Saturday afternoon. I told my mother I was going to play Scrabble and she laughed, called me a geek, her accent wrapping around the word strangely. I was roundly mocked by my brothers, who were always the popular kids while I was the shunned nerd, a fact they gleefully reminded me of as they made a series of increasingly absurd Scrabble-related jokes, like, "You sure are going through a *DRY SPELL*." The man I left behind said, "Come home. You're freaking me out." I ignored them all.

My colleague Daiva and her husband, Marty, live in a large home in a wooded neighborhood on the very edge of our very small town. Everything is modern and unique and interesting to look at—slick leather chairs, pottery, African art. In their finished basement, there is enough space for ten to twenty people, sometimes more, to get together once a month to play Scrabble all day.

Marty[7] is a nationally ranked player, top fifteen. He knows every word ever invented as well as each word's meaning. If you give him

---

6   There are more than two hundred Scrabble clubs in the United States. The club in my town meets monthly, while the club in Champaign, Illinois, meets weekly. In bigger cities, some clubs will even meet twice a week.

7   He is my Scrabble sensei. I almost beat him once, where "almost" is "not so much." Early in the match I played TRIPLEX for around 90 points. Then I played another bingo. I was way ahead and deluded myself into thinking I was on easy street. The sweetness of my imagined victory was nearly unbearable. Marty would go on to play ENTOZOAN across two Triple Word Score spaces for 203 points. He was Sub-Zero in *Mortal Kombat* tearing out my Scrabble spine with his bare hands—FATALITY. We have not played since. I have been properly humbled.

a seven-letter combination, he'll tell you all the possible anagrams. I would not be surprised to learn he thinks in anagrams. There are thirty-nine possible Scrabble words in "anagram."[8]

When you are new to the club, Marty carefully explains the rules of competitive Scrabble, and rules, there are many. You have to keep score. When you have completed your turn, you have to press a button on a game timer. You have to monitor time because there are penalties if you exceed twenty-five total minutes for your plays. There's a proper etiquette for drawing tiles (tile bag held above your eyes, head turned away).[9] There's a procedure if you draw too many tiles. There's a protocol for challenging if you believe your opponent has played a phony, a word that isn't in the Official Tournament and Club Word List.[10]

As Marty told me all these rules that first day, I laughed and rolled my eyes like an asshole and struggled to take any of it seriously. Until that day, my Scrabble playing had mostly involved drinking, friends, crazy made-up words, haphazard score keeping, and never ever any time constraints. It was an innocent time.

People slowly filed in with large round cases. One woman's case was wheeled, like a suitcase. They set their cases on tables and pulled out custom turntable scrabble boards, timers, tile bags, and racks. They

---

8   I love anagrams. When I was a kid, my mom would write big words on lined paper and ask me to find all the possible words. Now, finding words is kind of my superpower.

9   In the seventh round of the 2011 World Scrabble Championships, Edward Martin, while playing Chollapat Itthi-Aree, realized a tile was missing. The tournament director came up with a reasonable solution, but Itthi-Aree demanded Martin prove he wasn't hiding the missing tile on his person. Play resumed, and Martin eventually won by a single point. My friend/sensei Marty was totally sitting right next to these guys when this went down. He said, "It was a distraction."

10   There are multiple official word lists. In North America, most Scrabble players use the Official Tournament and Club Word List (OWL). Outside of North America, players use the *Collins English Dictionary*. At some tournaments here in the United States, you will find smaller Collins divisions for those Scrabble players who want to test their skills using the Collins dictionary. The challenge is remembering which words are acceptable for Collins and then remembering which words are acceptable for OWL when returning to traditional play.

got out their scoring sheets and personal tokens. The games started, and the room hushed. I realized this was no time to crack jokes. I realized Scrabble is very serious business.

I have a Scrabble nemesis. His name is Henry.[11] He has the most gorgeous blue-gray eyes I have ever seen. The beauty of his perfect eyes only makes me hate him more. He has been known to wear a fanny pack and often scowls. Nemeses aren't born. They are made.

Shortly after I started playing with my local Scrabble club, Marty told me about a charity tournament he holds in Danville, said it would be a great experience for me to play. I had nothing to lose so I agreed. I had no idea what to expect as I walked into the main building of the community college in Danville. After I registered, I stood awkwardly, wondering what to do, until my club friends took mercy on me and showed me the lay of tournament land.

Serious Scrabble people study words and remember matches from eight years ago where they played a word for 173 points. They remember when they didn't challenge a phony and lost the match. They remember everything. Some serious Scrabble players are poor losers. I am a good loser. I love Scrabble so much I don't care if I lose. I also have to be a good loser because I lose a lot, so practicality plays a role. Unlike most serious Scrabble players, I don't have the patience to study all the possible three- and four-letter words, for example, but still, I am extremely competitive.[12] It's an awkward combination.

I began the tournament thinking, *I am going to win this tournament.* I approach most things in life with a dangerous level of confidence to balance my generally low self-esteem. This helps me as a writer. Each time I submit a story to fancy magazines like, say, *The New Yorker* or *The Paris Review*, I think, *This story is totally going to get published.*

My heart gets broken more than it should.

---

11   Henry is not his name.

12   I have always enjoyed board games. I love rolling dice and moving small plastic or metal pieces around game boards. I collect Monopoly sets from around the world. I will play any game so long as there is a possibility I can win. I take games seriously. Sometimes I take them too seriously and conflate winning the Game of Life with winning at life.

After getting all my paperwork and such, I looked around at the other word nerds. I felt like people were checking me out. I was prepared to reenact the beginning of "Beat It" when everyone is silently stalking one another, trying to size up the competition. There were thirty-two players, four groups (based on ranking) with eight players in each. We would play seven rounds to determine the one Scrabble player to rule them all. The tournament director read off the name of each person in each group along with his or her seed. He read my name last, and I understood my place. I was the lowest-ranked (worst) player in the room.[13] I was the last kid who would be picked for dodge ball.

I sat down for my first round with the top seed in my division, and she was pretty cocky. I was too, or I was trying to project cockiness and calm. My hands were shaking under the table I was so nervous. My primary ambition was to not humiliate myself, make any missteps where Scrabble etiquette is concerned,[14] or shame the members of my Scrabble club, several of whom were in attendance.

---

13   Scrabble people are really quite friendly and gracious, but to be clear, they are also intense and serious as hell. I have an imagination. In my head, as we prepared to word rumble, I felt as if we were about to throw down like in the music video for Michael Jackson's "Bad." A lot of my life can be described in terms of Michael Jackson's music. I'd explain the significance of "Man in the Mirror," but then you'd think I was crazy.

14   Players can be very . . . *particular* about how you comport yourself during a Scrabble game. Some players want complete silence during matches, so they won't appreciate your idle chatter. Some players think you're cheating if you play with your phone. Don't take a call should your phone ring, that's for sure. I once got a dirty look for tapping on my phone without muting it. Apparently, the gentle beeps were simply too much for that player. The longer you play, the more you finely hone these particularities. I, for example, have developed several Scrabble-related pet peeves and preferences. I have strong opinions on the type of scoring sheets I use and the kind of pens I use to keep score (Uni-ball .5mm roller ball). I now have a very low tolerance for players who draw their tiles in annoying ways. I am particularly aggravated by players who do a lot of mixing the tiles up before each draw. IT DOES NOT CHANGE THE OUTCOME. I also do not look kindly upon players who tap the tiles on the board as they tally their points. Why are they doing that? What really sets me over the edge, though, is when players recount my word scores after I've announced my score at the end of a turn as if I am incapable of simple math. Certainly, math is not my strong suit, but in general, I have addition under control. When this unnecessary score verification occurs, I sometimes have to sit on my hands to keep from punching a player in the face.

My opponent looked up and said, "I was in the next highest division yesterday." The gauntlet was thrown. She said it with a kind, warm smile, but she was trying to intimidate me. I could tell by the way her upper lip curled. Well played. I wondered if I could purchase adult diapers at the nearest gas station.

The tournament started, and I managed to spell my words and use the timer correctly. I got into a rhythm. I placed a bingo.[15] I was feeling good. My skin flushed warmly with early success. I started thinking I had a chance. Then Number-One Seed proceeded to wipe the board with my ass; the final score was 366–277. I smiled and shook her hand, but a small piece of my soul was destroyed. I thought, *Je suis désoleé*.

When I composed myself, I took stock of what happened. I played decently and had two bingos overall. There was simply nothing I could do. I kept drawing terribly (JVK) and getting outplayed, and she was so damn confident the entire time. Worse yet, Number-One Seed played me better than she played the game.[16] At the beginning of the match, she asked if I was a student.[17] I said, "No, I teach writing," and she said, "Oh, I'm in trouble," pretending to be the weaker prey. Here's the thing. I play poker. I know a bluff when I see one. Once she got going, she kept smirking, letting me know her foot was leaving an ugly mark on my neck.

I was determined to win my second match because I am that competitive and I have pride and winning feels way better than losing. My opponent was really quiet and taciturn. It was not fun playing her. I slaughtered her 403–229 and I wanted to scream I was so happy. I was very tempted to jump on the table and shout, "IN YOUR FACE." For the sake of sportsmanship, I remained quiet and polite and thanked her for the game. She coldly walked away without so much as a by-your-leave. Later, as I drove home, I did gloat. I gloated a lot.

---

15   A bingo is when you play all seven letters on your rack. This is one of the most coveted Scrabble plays. I am a bingo player. I have no time to learn all the three-letter words and random obscure words, so I spend most of my time going for bingos because, in addition to the points you earn from the board, you also earn a fifty-point bonus. There are twenty-three possible Scrabble words in "bingo."

16   Don't get it twisted. Competitive Scrabble is both word chess and word poker. You need a game face, and you need to wear that game face hard.

17   I choose to believe she asked this because I look so fresh and youthful.

The third match was with a woman I play regularly. She's really nice and we get along well. She always beats me, and that day would be no exception—score: 390–327. My ambitious, delusional goal of winning the tournament was faltering. There were four matches left after the break, so before resuming play, we had lunch and I ate a vegetable sandwich. I told Daiva, the woman who had introduced me to the craziness of competitive Scrabble, "I'm going to win this tournament." She gave me the saddest look, as if to say, *There, there, crazy little Scrabble baby.*

There's something to be said for the delusion of confidence. I won my next four matches (389–312; 424–244; 352–312; 396–366). I was a demon. I had my word mojo. I was seeing bingos everywhere and making smart, tight plays, blocking triple play lanes and tracking perfectly.[18] With each win, I felt increasingly invincible. I wanted to beat my chest. I was also trying to distract myself.

In the middle of the night, hours before the tournament began, I received a frantic call from my mother, the kind of call, as your parents get older, you hope to never receive. My normally healthy father had to be rushed to the hospital—chest pains and shortness of breath. My first instinct was to say, "I am coming home," but fortunately, my youngest brother lives nearby and was able to be there. Throughout the tournament, I was getting updates on my father's condition, trying to reassure my mother that everything would be fine.[19] I was trying not to lose my shit[20] completely. There are 227 possible Scrabble words in "completely."

---

18   Much like in poker where you try to make an educated guess as to the cards your opponent is holding, great Scrabble players will track the letters played throughout a game. By the end of the game, you should know exactly what your opponent has on his rack. It is also important to track because it allows you to make smarter strategic decisions. It's good to know if high-value letters (J, X, Q, K, V, etc.) are in play because if there are few letters left and you're holding on to a U or an I and you know the Q is still in the bag, you want to be smart about where you play those vowels so your opponent cannot build a word with his Q unless he has the necessary vowels in his own rack.

19   Everything turned out fine.

20   "Shit" is a valid Scrabble word.

In my last match of the day, it became clear the winner of our match would win the entire tournament for our division. This is how my nemesis was born.

Henry with the beautiful, piercing blue-gray eyes was sly like a fox. At the start of the match, he kept playing two-letter words, so I did the same. We were stalking each other around a cage. You know the naked fight scene in *Eastern Promises*? It was like that, only we weren't criminals, naked, or in a Turkish bath, and I was the only one with a number of visible tattoos. He wore a T-shirt that read, "World's Best Scrabble Player." It was the T-shirt that made me extra motivated to win. The level of competition was very strong, and as the game unfolded, my excitement grew.

As the second seed, Henry the Nemesis was confident he would defeat me. I could smell the confidence on him. He reeked of it. I played three bingos during the course of the match. He tried to play TREKING[21] for 81 points, but I knew that was not a word. "Trekking" takes two Ks. I challenged. He rolled his eyes like he couldn't believe I had the nerve to challenge his bad spelling. My hands shook as I typed his word into the computer. I won the challenge. By the end of the match, he was irate and I was giddy. When I won, he realized he wasn't going to win the tournament and had fallen to third place. Because I was seeded so low, his ranking was going to take a hit. He refused to shake my hand and stalked off angrily. I thought he was going to throw the table over. Male anger makes me intensely uncomfortable, so I tried to sit very still and hoped the uncomfortable moment would pass quickly. Henry's bad sportsmanship did not temper my mood for long. I won my first tournament despite being the lowest-seeded[22] player in the field and took home a small cash prize. The size of my ego for the following week was difficult to measure. It would not last, though. What Scrabble giveth, another player, at another tournament, will taketh away.

---

21   There are no bingos with the letters T, R, E, K, I, N, and G. If Henry studied, he would know that.

22   I ended up with an amazing ranking, high enough to almost place me a division up. In the next tournament I played, I would be seeded much higher and I would pay for that, dearly.

When you succeed early at an endeavor, you convince yourself you will easily replicate that success. Ask child actors.[23] Three months later, I played in another tournament, the Arden Cup, a twenty-match, two-and-a-half-day affair where I won eight games and lost twelve. I learned a lot. I especially learned that it is insane to believe you will walk into a competitive tournament, among a much larger field, with a fragile and inflated ranking, and somehow win that tournament.

Henry the Nemesis was in attendance, as was a host of equally intriguing and intense players who would get under my skin nearly as much as Henry does. My least favorite player was Donnie,[24] who tried to mansplain Scrabble because he didn't recognize me[25] and took me for a neophyte. As we sat down to start our match, he said, "Now, you just play this the same way you play Scrabble at home." I made it my life's purpose, right then, to destroy him. Another opponent asked if we should play at his board or mine. When I told him I didn't have my own set, he gave me a pitying look.[26] I quickly realized I was swimming with Scrabble sharks. I was the blood in the water.

There was one redemptive moment despite the humiliation of that tournament, one where I lost so many times the matches blended into a depressing blur, where I lost mostly to mansplainers who defined words[27] even though I did not ask for definitions, regaled me with tales of their sordid Scrabble histories, and otherwise drove me

---

23   The child actors from *Diff'rent Strokes*, among others, know a little something about this. I was thinking I would pull a Mary-Kate and Ashley. Such was not the case.

24   Also not his name.

25   The Scrabble community is fairly small, and once you start attending tournaments regularly, you will see the same people over and over.

26   I have my own tournament board now as well as a timer (with pink buttons), tiles (pink), and long tile racks (sadly not available in pink). I also have a carrying case with a shoulder strap so I can rock my Scrabble board slung across my shoulders like a boss.

27   Qoph is a Hebrew letter. My opponent not only shared the word's meaning, he also explained the origins (something about a sewing needle; frankly, I had tuned him out at that point) and pronunciation. After the exciting word lesson, he started telling me all the possible Q words one can spell without a U. I wondered, *Is there a Q in "motherfucker"?*

crazy. I beat Henry the Nemesis again. We played twice during the tournament—he won a game and I won a game. At the end of our second game, the one I won, he stood and pointed at me. He said, "You've won two out of three times. Two. Out. Of. Three." I looked down, bit my lower lip to keep from smiling my face off.

"I wasn't keeping track," I said.[28]

I excused myself and ran to the restroom, where in the privacy of my stall, I whispered, "I beat you, I beat you, I beat you." There was fist pumping.

And so. My third tournament started brutally and the brutality was unrelenting. I ended up winning six matches (one was a bye) and losing six and took fifteenth place. My friends told me that was a good outcome. I'm pretty sure they were just being nice given the increased fragility of my Scrabble ego.

I did not get to play my nemesis, but he was there and he performed well. I took that personally.

A new nemesis was also made early during that tournament. In my first match of the day, I was tired. I had slept for only three hours after a late night in the city with friends. I am not a morning person. I did not have time to find the nearest Starbucks. I could not find any dollar bills to buy a Diet Pepsi. I could not find my Visine. I was hungover—gin, which doesn't settle well with me the day after. My stomach kept turning uncomfortably. I was drowsy. If I closed my eyes, I would simply fall into an uncomfortable sleep. I was a mess.

I was the fifth seed in a field of twenty-one, so I was stupidly pleased with myself to still be seeded so high after the previous tournament. My opponent was unseeded and had no ranking so I mistakenly assumed she was a novice player.[29] From the outset I was certain I would win the match handily even though I was hungover and barely able to cope with the dryness of my eyeballs.

---

28   That was a pretty little lie.
29   I willfully ignored the memory of the outcome of my first tournament, where I won as the lowest-seeded player, without a ranking.

Toward the end of the match, I played BROASTED and BO for a Triple Word Score. My opponent challenged, and she won. When you challenge multiple words, though, the computer only tells you if the word combination is good or bad. If the combination is bad, it will not tell you if one or all the words in the combination are bad. I thought, because I was mentally incapacitated, that BO must not be a valid word. I may not know my three-letter words, but I do know my two-letter words. I was confused. I was not at my best.

A couple moves later, I played BROASTED and BA in the same location. My opponent's eyes widened. She stared at me like I was the stupidest person alive. In that moment, I hated every last cell in her body.

"You're going to do *that* again?" she asked, but it wasn't quite a question.

It was her tone that totally set me off. I had just laid down the tiles, thereby making it crystal clear I was going to make the same, ridiculous, amateurish mistake twice. What did she fail to understand?

In my defense, I was so convinced BROASTED[30] was a word, because it actually *is* a word, that I remained unwavering in my commitment to play the word. Had I succeeded, I would have earned 87 points. As we walked to the challenge computer, I could feel her laughing at me. I wanted to cry, but my eyes were still so terribly dry, and also there is no crying at a Scrabble tournament unless you're in the bathroom and you have carefully checked all the stalls to make sure you are alone.

The next time I see New Nemesis, I must explain, "I am not the idiot you think I am, or at least I am not an idiot for the reasons you think."

The match was a massacre. The final score: 500–263. That match set the tone for the tournament. Time and again, lower-ranked players

---

30   "Broasting" is a proper noun, and proper nouns are not valid Scrabble words. Broasting is a trademarked method of cooking chicken.

taught me painful lessons. Time and again, I was humbled. At the end of the tournament, after the prizes were handed out and we applauded each of the winners and the players who had played the highest-scoring words, we losers stood in small clumps of failure bemoaning how terribly we had played while those who played well tried not to gloat. Their modesty was good-naturedly false. We packed up our boards, and the excitement of the tournament slowly seeped out of our muscles. We shook hands and bid one another good-bye until the next club meeting or tournament. We were no longer adversaries.

Discussion Questions for Chapter Five

1. As discussed by Snyder, fear is often the mechanism by which politicians coerce individuals to trade freedom for safety. Discuss other examples of specific language used by a politician or a political party that demonstrate this same technique.

2. Truss relates how grammar and punctuation were not widely taught in Great Britain after 1960, leading to problems today in popular forms of communication such as Web sites and text messages. What problems have you seen in these communication media? Also, looking over some of the terms used in this chapter (noun, subject, participle, comma, etc.), reflect on your own education in these skills when you were an elementary or high school student.

3. Compare and contrast how Snyder and Truss use vocabulary and punctuation in their own essays. Which writer do you feel uses a wider vocabulary? A vocabulary closer to everyday speech? Which writer tends to use more punctuation? Does one writer or the other follow the "rules" more closely?

4. In her essay, Gay expresses her love of Scrabble and of words. List and define your five favorite words (look up each in a dictionary) and identify their parts of speech. Why do you enjoy these words? Their sounds? Their meanings? The associations they have for you?

5. When facing her nemesis Henry during a Scrabble match, Gay challenges him when he tries to play TREKING. Why is this not the spelling of the word? What is the rule that makes TREKKING the proper spelling?

Exercises—Set One

Add the correct punctuation to the following sentences.

Example

Original: John is going to the store but Cindy is going to the mall
Revision: John is going to the store, but Cindy is going to the mall.

1. On Tuesday John is going to break the world record for eating donuts.
2. Wow Did that really just happen
3. When I come back he said lets go out to a movie.
4. You my friend just made a big big mistake.
5. Davy Smith we shouldnt consider anyone else should be our next leader.
6. After school lets out Charlie who is a game junkie is going to sit all night at his Xbox.
7. Computers TVs and cameras are all on sale today at Leftys Electronics
8. Candy is drinking a latté Sylvia is drinking a chai tea
9. She said Ill see you tomorrow
10. Here are the things youll need for the trip a polar jacket which will keep you warm mittens which will save your fingers from frostbite and earmuffs which will keep your ears from freezing off.

Exercises—Set Two

Using the three-step line-editing process, fix the punctuation and sentence-construction errors in the following sentences.

Example

Original: Laughing and giggling the elevator took us to the seventh floor.

Revision: Laughing and giggling, we took the elevator to the seventh floor.

1. Various creatures could be seen out of the corner of the eye scurrying away.
2. Tomatoes, corn, cucumbers, and the sweet scent of watermelon permeate the air.
3. Large teardrops dampened the edge of the glasses as they ran down her face and fell to her lap in a small puddle.
4. The volume of each radio raised to highest level, canceled each other, creating an incoherent babbling of words and sounds.

Answers to Set One

1. On Tuesday, John is going to break the world record for eating donuts.
2. Wow! Did that really just happen?
3. "When I come back," he said, "let's go out to a movie."
4. You, my friend, just made a big, big mistake.
5. Davy Smith—we shouldn't consider anyone else—should be our next leader.
6. After school lets out, Charlie, who is a game junkie, is going to sit all night at his Xbox.
7. Computers, TVs, and cameras are all on sale today at Lefty's Electronics.
8. Candy is drinking a latté; Sylvia is drinking a chai tea.
9. She said, "I'll see you tomorrow."
10. Here are the things you'll need for the trip: a polar jacket, which will keep you warm; mittens, which will save your fingers from frostbite; and earmuffs, which will keep your ears from freezing off.

Answers to Set Two

1. Out of the corner of his eye, he saw various creatures scurrying away.
2. The sweet scent of tomatoes, corn, cucumbers, and watermelon permeates the air.
3. Large teardrops ran down her face, dampened the edge of her glasses, and fell into a small puddle in her lap.
4. The volume of each radio, raised to the highest level, created a babble of words and sounds.

Chapter 6
The Research Essay

Research is part of scholarship, but it is not limited to college assignments, as many of us will find ourselves digging for truths and best practices throughout our lives. While in college, students will research topics and implement their findings into their writing. In this text, we give the research essay its own chapter because nearly every student must write one in multiple classes, including those outside of English. Whatever is learned in a composition class regarding research can be applied to other fields.

Competent research skills should promote honesty. When students enter college, they become part of a community that must follow certain academic standards. These standards, typically listed on the learning institution's Web site, should be read and understood by all members. For example, the Academic Integrity Policy at the College of Southern Nevada informs students that they must "accept the expectation to always take the ethical path, uphold the standards for integrity and honesty in their individual academic studies, and encourage others to do the same." One very important way to "uphold the standards" is to conduct research that is both meaningful and transparent, identifying credible sources and citing those sources according to the assigned documentation standards. When this occurs, students avoid plagiarism and can be proud of their efforts.

The discussion below, contributed by Pamela Kandaris Cha, instructor of English and Communications at Utah State University Eastern-Price, is a map for creating a research essay. Keep in mind that a research essay begins the way any essay begins—by understanding the assignment, or by asking questions of your instructor to eliminate confusion. Let's start.

★

The research essay strikes fear and terror in the hearts of all college students. Do not let this happen. If approached correctly, the research paper can become a meaningful assignment. The key not just to a successful paper, but to an enjoyable and educational experience, is in the approach.

All classes are unique, so the nature of the paper will vary depending on the class and the assignment. However, all papers have some necessary elements. First, remember that when research is used, it must be documented. Second, a good research paper uses the research to support the writer's position. The paper is not driven by research but by analysis. The writer must be present in the paper, using her voice and not the voice of the research.

Investment

When beginning the research paper, remember this: The writer must be invested in the subject. Whether writing a term-long persuasive paper or a shorter essay intended to inform, the writer must pick a topic that he finds important and interesting. As in any relationship that requires commitment, if the writer chooses a companion (topic) based on familiarity rather than interest, he will learn to resent the involvement. After all, he has devoted time and effort to this endeavor. By the end of the relationship, there should be a feeling of satisfaction—of time well spent—even if the writer and his companion never meet again. Consequently, the writer should pick a topic that she can live with over the time of the assignment. An example of an essay that represents a writer's healthy relation with a topic is Nina Jensen's "An Abundance of Love." In her essay, Jensen outlines her interest in the foster care system, a system with which she and her family had firsthand involvement. But because of her willingness to investigate beyond her own experience, Jensen generated a well-developed paper. Her success began with her topic selection.

Contributed by Pamela Kandaris Cha. © Kendall Hunt Publishing Company

Selection

How does the writer go about picking a topic? Research papers in an English class are not just a collection of facts, but also literary pieces. This means the topic will include all three elements of persuasion: *logos* (factual appeal), *pathos* (emotional appeal), and *ethos* (moral appeal). As we look at the Jensen paper, we see examples of *logos* in the facts and figures of the foster care system; of *pathos* in the story of Michael Oher; and of *ethos* in the theme that every child deserves a loving home. Further, the idea must not be so broad as to overwhelm the writer with too much information or too narrow to limit the writer's ability to write a comprehensive research paper. Thus, rather than just presenting the issue from her experience, Jensen examined it on a broader spectrum. The result is a well-researched topic that contains the necessary elements of a successful essay.

Inquiry

Once the writer chooses a topic, she may be required to develop a research proposal. Often, the proposal helps the instructor to verify that the student is on the path to a successful outcome. Even if such a task is not mandatory, the creation of a proposal can help her generate a better essay. The most effective way to form the proposal is to answer the following questions:

- What is the question the writer wants to explore?
- Does the writer know what information has already been discussed or researched on this topic?
- What is the best search strategy, and what challenges can be foreseen at this point?

Although these questions may seem overwhelming, finding the answers to them allows the writer to fully understand the topic, and in turn, commit to researching and writing the paper. With the answers, the writer will have not only the basis for a proposal, but also an outline of research strategies with which she can form an organized template to begin the essay's drafting process.

Sorting

Templates are helpful for research, drafting, and revision. A common organizational template for the research essay looks like this:

- Introduction. The introduction contains the essay's thesis even if the thesis is a working thesis, one that will change while the research process occurs. The writer may also choose a strategy by which to engage his reader—present a personal experience, establish a mood, pose a problem, describe a relevant person or place.

- Background Information/History of the Issue. This section of the essay explores the evolution of the issue to its present condition—the condition on which the essay will primarily focus in the majority of the essay's body paragraphs.

- Opposing Viewpoint (optional depending on the essay assignment). This section is necessary if the essay is presenting an argument—arguing for or against a particular law, code, or policy. For example, if Nina Jensen had focused her essay on the effectiveness of her state's foster care laws, this section would have allowed her to define the dissenting opinion.

- Body of Proofs. This is the most important section of any research essay. The body is created through the effective development and support of multiple paragraphs. The body of proofs validates the thesis. If the essay's thesis is broad, the body will require more points of proof. This section may also include a rebuttal of the opposing viewpoint.

- Conclusion. This section brings closure to the essay. Depending on the requirements of the assignment, the conclusion may restate the thesis in fresh language, present a call to action, or speculate on how the issue may develop in the future.

By following the template, the writer knows what kind of research he will need to complete each of the sections and has a ready-made organizational plan for presenting that research.

Working Fit Thesis

Regardless of whether the writer's process or assignment requires the use of a template, the writer cannot avoid developing a working thesis. As discussed earlier in this book, the thesis is the essay's brain. Humans cannot function without a brain, and essays cannot function without a thesis. The research essay demands a fit thesis that frames the writer's issue. Further, the thesis must give the reader an idea of what direction the paper is going to take. When creating the thesis, therefore, the writer should know the scope of the issue he has chosen and the effects he hopes to produce with his research. In her essay, Nina Jensen, after using the strategy of posing a problem in her introduction, lets her readers know that "every child deserves a family." Her research validates this thesis and attempts to persuade the reader of the value of the foster-to-adopt program.

Sources

If the thesis statement is what the writer wants to prove, the research is the map. It is the development and support of the paper. To begin the research process, all writers must become critical thinkers. The writer must have the ability to look at the information he is gathering with a rational eye. Facts must be examined and crosschecked against other sources. Sources must be unbiased and substantive. A variety of sources ensures that the paper is credible. Keep in mind that the writer's opinion is only as valid as the research she is using to support it. Ideally the student will use a combination of primary and secondary sources. Primary sources such as autobiographies, letters, diaries, and personal interviews provide information that comes directly from the source. Secondary sources such as biographies, printed or broadcast interviews, articles, and books have an intermediary between the source and the information. A student's first search is usually on the Internet. Be careful when searching the Internet without any parameters. The safest starting point for research is to use your school's library database, which has thousands of vetted and reliable sources.

Jensen uses a variety of sources in her paper: primary sources such as autobiographies and her own experience with an autistic child; and secondary sources such as articles, fact sheets, and literary sources (books and movies). Using a combination of literary and substantive sources enables her to broaden her perspective and expand it beyond her personal experience. By reviewing different sources, she is able to support her stance about foster care and adoption. Her research allows her to create an analytical and literary-driven paper rather than a simple position paper based on her own opinions.

As the writer is gathering her information, she must keep track of where that information is coming from. The writer should note the author, title, publisher, date of publication, page numbers, and URL or digital object identifier (DOI) on all of the sources. The writer should also briefly summarize, in her own words, the information from the source. These steps will make outlining, writing the paper, and perhaps most importantly, documenting the sources on a bibliography page much easier. A bibliography (or works cited) page is necessary because the writer must acknowledge the original sources of the evidence used in the paper. Quotations, diagrams, illustrations, paraphrases, and any other borrowed material must be cited. Citations not only respect the original source but also provide a place for the reader to find additional information on the topic. Always ask your instructor about the assigned bibliographic source requirement. The most common bibliographical style for an English or humanities paper is the Modern Language Association (MLA) format. Resources that aid the writers in proper formatting rules include EasyBib <easybib.com> and the Purdue University Online Writing Lab <owl.english.purdue.edu>. Failure to adhere to the assigned standard typically results in a failing assignment grade and often is considered plagiarism.

Most writers do not intentionally plagiarize but forget to keep track of the information they have gathered so it gets used without the necessary citations. You will need to cite your sources twice: once at the end of the paper on the works cited page, and again in the body of the paper immediately after you use the source. When presenting the source in the paper, be sure to use signal phrases—or narrow-down language—to let the reader know that the information about to be presented is from an outside source. Finish your quotation with a parenthetical citation.

Jensen does this throughout her paper. Notably in her first paragraph she lets the reader know there is a documented source by signaling the *Fox 13 News* report, citing the figures, and then including the reporter's name in the parenthetical citation. This citation allows the reader to go to the works cited page, find the original source, and, if the reader desires, read the source in its entirety. Some readers, especially instructors who question the writer's use of the source material, will seek the original source to determine if the writer has used the material correctly.

Organizing the Paper

The template provided above is a good, all-purpose organizational plan that will help you get started with your drafting and that may provide the final shape of your paper. However, you may have to choose a different plan based on the subject matter and the direction of the persuasive arguments used. Generally, material can be organized by the development patterns discussed elsewhere in this book: chronological, spatial, cause-effect, topical, or comparative advantage. Another good choice, especially for a persuasive research paper, is Monroe's Motivated Sequence. Initially, Monroe brings in readers by getting their attention with an interesting introduction. It then continues by presenting the need. It moves from the need to the solution step. It then adds a visualization step that paints a picture of the world with the implemented solution. Finally, there is an action step to tell readers what they specifically need to do. Think of modern-day infomercials to understand the effectiveness of the approach. To use Monroe's effectively, the writer must evaluate the research she has found, determine the arguments she is most moved by, and use the most persuasive sequence available. To learn more about Monroe's Motivated Sequence, students can consult the following resources:

<mindtools.com/pages/article/MonroeMotivatedSequence.
    htm>
<changingminds.org/techniques/general/overall/monroe_
    sequence.htm>

Whatever plan the writer chooses, she should create an outline to visualize how the pieces of the paper will fit together. A scratch outline with bullet points will help get the process started, but later, the writer should move to a formal outline. A formal outline uses a system of Roman numerals, capital letters, and Arabic numbers to organize and rank the material. Each subdivision has one thought, and giving equal thoughts equal rank keeps the paper mechanically and linguistically parallel. Additionally, if the writer identifies the locations of the research information in the outline, she lessens the chance of plagiarism. The writer will find that once the outline is completed, the paper is ready to be written. The road map is in place and the writing begins.

The Drafting. Let It Begin.

The introduction of the paper should captivate the reader. Along with the strategies mentioned in the template, stories, statistics, quotations, rhetorical questions, and surprising statements are all good ways to begin. As noted above, Jensen's posing of a problem makes an exccllent introduction. However, you may find that the strategy you start with may not be suitable for the content of the essay. You will not know the essay that you want to introduce until *after* you have written it. As with all essays, revise the introduction and the conclusion after the body paragraphs are completed.

The body itself organizes and presents the writer's thoughts and arguments in a persuasive manner. Many students will compartmentalize the drafting of the body paragraphs based upon the importance of the paragraph's controlling ideas. For example, if the majority of the research speaks to three points, then those ideas should be written and rewritten multiple times. Give them the proper time to unfold on the page. Do not rush them. And always make sure that you understand the research that you have chosen to support your claims. Look at your outline and identify the areas that will require the most time, and start with those paragraphs. Then fill in the other areas as needed. There is no single way to construct the body paragraphs of a research essay.

When deciding the order of your body paragraphs, keep in mind the best-for-last principle. If, say, your topic is banning school uniforms, and you have three arguments in support of your stance, then ask yourself which of the three best makes your case. That argument should be saved for last because your reader will recall it more readily and it will make a stronger impression. Jensen follows this principle by discussing the positive effects of encouragement at the end of her essay. By showing how encouragement allowed Michael Oher, a famous football player, to reach his goals, Jensen implies that other adopted children will benefit in the same way.

An additional priority is to review the arguments for fallacies. Fallacies can be found in defective evidence, defective proofs, or defective designs. It is vital to convince, stimulate, or actuate the reader with arguments that use facts, values, and policies (where applicable) and meet the standards of *logos*, *pathos*, and *ethos*. Jensen does this effectively throughout her paper. She points out the need for foster care. She then discusses the needs of the child she and her husband have chosen to adopt, takes the stance that such a child deserves a family, support, and love, brings in the well-known case of Michael Oher, and broadens her argument to include all children. She avoids a problem with fallacies by drawing not only from Michael Oher's autobiography, but also Leigh Anne Tuohy's autobiography (both primary sources) and the movie *The Blind Side* (a secondary source). By exploring factual information together with all points of view, she is finding evidence that supports her positions and meets the standards of *logos*, *pathos*, and *ethos*.

The conclusion should remind the reader of the paper's main ideas, without dully repeating them. Conclusions do not need to be lengthy. As noted above, the writer can summarize key points and propose a course of action if it is appropriate to the paper. Jensen's challenges, phrased as questions such as "Are you willing to . . .", are a very effective conclusion. New ideas should never be introduced in the conclusion. The writer needs to be sure of the essay's position, meaning the content stands by the arguments presented. The essay ends with punctuated confidence.

When writers reach this point, they have successfully completed the research paper. They have found a topic that is relevant for a chosen audience. They have chosen an organization plan based upon the most effective way to arrange the research and achieve the essay's purpose. They have written a conclusion that gives the reader a last, favorable impression. We hope that when you successfully navigate the research paper, you have discovered that the experience was favorable as well.

Nina Jensen

Professor Cha

English 2010

3 August 2017

An Abundance of Love

Many of us watch the news on a regular basis. If you do, you know about the "Wednesday's Child" segments on KSL. Each Wednesday, a child in foster care is introduced and the child's story is told. What do you do when you see these? Do you think about what that child has gone through? Do you wonder if someone else is going to adopt him or her? Do you wonder where he or she is living right now? Do you think that you could make a difference in this child's life? Are you willing to make the effort to help someone who really needs it? Are you willing to go through the process of adopting through the foster care system? Utah Foster Care states that there are about 2,700 children in the foster care system in Utah at any given time (*Statewide*). A recent *Fox 13 News* report stated that in May of this year, there were 2,900 kids in foster care, but there were foster homes for only 2,400 (Lawrence). That means five hundred children were not in a home; they were in a shelter until a place was found for them.

When my husband and I met and married, we started our family in the traditional way. We talked about how many kids we wanted and how we would raise them. The discussion of fostering children came up occasionally, but we weren't really serious about it. We knew there were kids needing a family, but we were busy with what we had and we figured someone else would help those in need. Most of us think that we don't need to do something because someone else already is. But that statement isn't true. In her reporting, Danica Lawrence says there is more need for foster parents than ever. Most couples look forward to having children of their own, but that isn't always possible. There are also many reasons for choosing to adopt through the foster

care system. In the book *When Adoptions Go Wrong*, experts assert that

> [a]doptive parents are intentional parents, i.e., they choose to become parents. In
>
> most cases, they have fertility problems that have kept them from parenthood,
>
> but there are other reasons as well to choose to adopt one or more children.
>
> Today, single adults with no partner, homosexuals with or without partners,
>
> couples who want more children but not more pregnancies, and people who
>
> simply want to save a child from a life with no family all turn to adoption. (6)

Twenty-three years and five kids later, our perspective has changed. In May of

this year, my husband, Eric, was browsing online and came across an article about the

foster-to-adopt program in Utah. At the beginning of the article there was a picture of a

young man looking for a family. Eric found the "Wednesday's Child" segment for this

young man and decided that "this boy needs us and we need him." He showed me

what he'd found, and after thinking about it for a few days, I was in complete

agreement. We contacted Utah Foster Care and started training classes that are required

to become a licensed foster-care family. We turned in an application, submitted

fingerprints for a background check, found four references, and started making

significant changes to our home. We are now waiting for a home inspection by the state.

However, during all of this, we learned that there's more to this young man's story. He

has autism, among other things that we don't know about yet, and has a Division of

Services for People with Disabilities (DSPD) certification. Because of this, we have to be

licensed by a different state agency so he can keep that DSPD certification and have

those services throughout his life, especially after he's adopted. We've completed

another application, asked for another reference letter from our references, turned in another background check, and reorganized our home so that he can have his own bedroom; we will have the training classes completed by August 15, 2017.

So why are we doing this? The process is confusing and frustrating; we keep learning that there's something more that we need to do! We are doing this for him. We haven't met him yet, but we already love him. We are doing this because we believe we can give him the love and family that he needs and that he deserves. We will do whatever it takes to bring him home. Every child deserves a family. Every child deserves love. Every child deserves a safe home. Every child deserves to be supported in his or her struggles. Every child deserves to be supported in his or her interests. Every child deserves a chance to have a good life.

The children in foster care have lost so much, but the most important thing they've lost is family. Whatever the reason was for them to be removed from their home, they've lost family. Sometimes it's just one parent that they've lost, but sometimes it's both. Sometimes they've been separated from siblings. As he explains in his book *I Beat the Odds*, Michael Oher lost a mom and eleven siblings (11). In the case of the young man we're trying to bring home, he was removed from both parents and he now has a baby sibling. In addition, there are many who have aged out of the foster care system who still want a family. In Leigh Anne Tuohy's book, *In a Heartbeat*, the Tuohy family shares a story about a twenty-seven-year-old woman who had aged out. She told them, "I still want to be adopted. People think just because I'm twenty-seven years old that I don't want to be adopted anymore. That's just not the case. I want a family. I want somebody to send me a birthday card. I want to know that someone, when they wake up in the morning, cares whether I'm alive or dead" (262). If you look on *The Adoption Exchange* Web site, you will find quite a few who have aged out, yet they are still on the adoption page. They are still looking for a family. Every person, regardless of age, deserves to be part of a family.

When a child is placed in foster care, they've also lost love. They've possibly lost it even before they entered the system. In his book, Michael Oher talks about how his mother loved her children, but that didn't stop her from locking her kids out of the house when she would disappear to go buy drugs. She would be gone for days and the kids would find food and shelter with other families (11). When the kids were removed from her home, they were split up and placed in different foster homes. Michael and his brother, Carlos, were placed in a home together (40). In talking about his foster mom, he said, "She was a stranger to me and I sure didn't think that she loved me. After all, who could love a bunch of kids they don't even know who get dumped on their doorstep? That was what I believed at the time, anyway, and I think a lot of kids in my situation feel the same way" (44). When a child is placed in foster care, it's harder for them to believe that they are loved. They've already lost so much. Why should they believe they can be loved? In *Martian Child*, the main character is a widower thinking about adopting a child. He and his wife had talked about adopting because she had been adopted as a child. He is matched with a child who claims to be from Mars. In an argument with his sister about adopting this boy, he says, "I want to do something meaningful, ya know? And I get all the arguments against it. I even get the one that says I don't know if I want to bring another kid into this world. But how do you argue with the logic of loving one that's already here?" It's so important that children feel loved. It is the foundation of self-confidence and self-belief. Foster parents can help their child believe that they are loved, that they are wanted, and that they are a part of a new family. It's up to us to continually show love and exercise patience until they truly know that they are loved. It can take a long time. Every child deserves to love and to be loved.

When a child is placed in foster care, they lose a home. Sometimes there is abuse, sometimes there is neglect, and sometimes there is drug use. Whatever the reason, their home is no longer safe. In our application to foster-to-adopt, we have to show that our home is safe and that we are safe. We have to pass a background check. We will also have to pass a home inspection by the state. They will make sure that we have smoke and carbon monoxide detectors, that all hazardous items are locked up, and that any and all medications are locked up. Further, we need to have the right size of fire extinguisher, and have proof that each of us and even our pets are current on our immunizations. In the movie *The Blind Side*, the Tuohy family sees a young man who got into a private school based on his athletic ability, not his GPA, and they start to wonder about him. They see him cleaning up bleachers after a volleyball game; they see him walking in the wintertime in shorts and without a coat. They see him carrying all his things in a plastic grocery bag and they also learn that he doesn't have a home. At first, it was just giving him a place to spend the night, but it quickly became apparent that Leigh Anne Tuohy was not going to just let him wander away. She insisted that he stay with them. She clothed Michael, fed him, and gave him his own room. In his book, *I Beat the Odds*, Oher talks about the Tuohy family and their effect on his life. He says, "The more time I spent with that family, the more I felt like I had found a home" (137). Every child deserves a safe home.

We know that when we foster to adopt, we are going to need to help our new child. We know he's been diagnosed with autism and that he struggles with staying in school for the full day. We also know that he has an Individual Education Plan (IEP) to help him get through school. What are we going to be able to do to really help? We are going to be able to help him because we have had the experience of helping one of our own children deal with a similar problem. Our fourth child shows a lot of the symptoms of autism. He stopped talking around eighteen months old, he didn't (and still doesn't) handle loud noises well, we couldn't leave the house without his notebook and pencil for years, he needed a paraeducator to make it through the day at school, and he's had an IEP since he was three years old. He's thirteen now and he still has an IEP, and I'm going to make sure he keeps his IEP until he's completed high school and is in college. He just finished his first year of junior high and, in spite of his struggles, did very well. The front office and all of his teachers got to know me because I was there when there were problems. Whether it was schoolwork, behavior in class, or others bullying him, I was there. Because of this experience, I know I can help another child in the same way. There might be different answers to be found, but I know how to go to the school and the teachers and get my child whatever help is needed. The Tuohy family recalls how they did the same thing for Michael Oher. They write about preparing for his senior year and realizing that Michael's GPA wasn't going to be high enough to get into college on a football scholarship. Sean Tuohy suggested delaying college by finishing his senior year and then enrolling in another school to improve his GPA. Michael decided that he didn't want to wait for another year to go to college. He said, "That would be a setback. I'm ready to go to college and get to work—I'm going for it" (Tuohy et al. 185). The family found him a tutor. Leigh Anne contacted each of Michael's teachers and asked them what he could do to pull his grades up. She said, "We were going to see that Michael had everything he needed to succeed" (187). They did everything they could to help him overcome his educational struggles. We are going to do everything we can to help our foster child succeed and overcome the difficulties he's had. Every child deserves to be supported in his or her struggles.

The child we are trying to bring home loves anything and everything to do with technology. His case worker let us know that he's taught her things about her phone that she doesn't know and he loves to do it. Each of our children has talents and interests and we are doing what we can to encourage them in those interests. We can give our foster child the same encouragement and even learn from him, too. I am not very technology educated myself and would love to have him teach me. We can help him prepare for the future by focusing on what he is good at and finding a way to make it a part of his life. Michael Oher had his own goals for his future. He puts it in his own words in his book when he says, "My sights were set on the future from the time I was seven, and then even more as I became a teenager. I always seemed to have my eyes on what was ahead" (12). Michael knew that his sports abilities would get him out of the life his mother had, and the Tuohys totally supported him in that goal. He loved basketball, but his size made it difficult to play without fouls being called on him constantly (148). When he started playing football, his size became an asset. He may have been big, but he was also very fast. He knew that sports would get him out of the projects permanently. His interest in sports became his strength and also became his career. Every child deserves to be supported in his or her interests.

As our children have grown, we've tried our hardest to make sure they've each had what they needed in order to take care of themselves and to make good choices. Foster kids aren't able to think of the future for the most part because their lives are so unstable. They are used to taking care of what they need immediately, which is usually food to eat and a place to sleep. Bringing a foster child into our home and wanting to adopt him will give him a chance to not have to worry about those things because food will always be available and his bed will always be in his room. Over time, our new son will know that we totally support him and want his life to be good. We will do whatever he needs in order to help him have a secure home and future. We want him to feel as Michael Oher did when he said, "To be a part of a community at Briarcrest [his school], as well as starting to feel like part of a supportive family, made all the difference in the world for me, because I'd never been around people who were cheering me on" (137-38). Every child deserves a chance to have a good life. Every child deserves to have someone that cheers them on!

While we took the pre-service training classes offered by Utah Foster Care, we saw a diverse group of people wanting to do the same thing we want to do. We were all there because we each want to help children have a home. Some wanted young children under the age of five, some wanted elementary-aged children, some wanted teenagers, like us, and some wanted to focus on those about to age out. Some already had kids, like us. Some weren't able to have children on their own. Some had been through the foster system themselves. We were all there because we wanted to make a difference in a child's life. Are you at a point in your life that you would consider doing this, too? Are you willing to open your life and home to inspection? Are you willing to make the necessary changes in your home to make it safe? Are you willing to accept that the child you bring into your home will have struggles and challenges you might not have any experience with? If you can answer yes to any of these questions, you might be ready to become a foster parent, too. In our situation, we already have a family, so why are we adopting, you ask? We are adopting this young man because we know he needs us and we also need him. We are adopting him because we know we can help him. Our kids are very aware of our efforts and look forward to having a new brother. They often ask us, "When is he going to be here?" We are making these changes and going through the application and training process to make a difference in this child's life. When he's adopted, we are seriously considering bringing in another foster child. Each of us has the ability to help. I hope that more people have the determination to do so, because he is not the only one in need. Whatever your circumstances, you could be a foster parent, too. You may have kids already or you may not. If there is room in your heart, there is room in your home for a child in need. Every child deserves and needs a family, home, love, and support. Let's make sure each child gets one.

Works Cited

The Blind Side. Directed by John Lee Hancock, performance by Sandra Bullock, Warner
    Brothers Pictures, 2009.

Lawrence, Danica. "Need for Foster Parents in Utah Grows As More Children Than
    Ever Need Care." *FOX 13 Salt Lake City*, Tribune Broadcasting, 13 May 2017,
    fox13now.com/2017/05/12/resources-stretched-thin-as-more-children-entering-
    foster-care-in-utah-than-ever-before/.

Martian Child. Directed by Menno Meyjes, performance by John Cusack, New Line
    Cinema, 2007.

Oher, Michael, with Don Yaeger. *I Beat the Odds: From Homelessness to the Blind Side and
    Beyond*. Penguin Group, 2011.

Schwartz, Lita Linzer. *When Adoptions Go Wrong: Psychological and Legal Issues of
    Adoption Disruption*. Haworth Press, 2006.

Statewide Facts: Children in Foster Care. Utah Foster Care, Sept. 2016,
    utahfostercare.org/wp-contnets/uploads/2013/04/ufc-factsheet-general.pdf.

Tuohy, Leigh Anne, et al. *In a Heartbeat: Sharing the Power of Cheerful Giving*. Henry Holt
    and Company, 2010.

Avenido 1

Lorraine Avenido

Professor Eliopulos

English 101-2003

1 December 2014

Simply a Fad or Simply Offensive?

For many decades, society's fascination with pop culture has found its way into the fashion industry. With varying degrees of success, designers integrate cultural symbols onto clothing in an attempt to create something unique, the next style that the world will want to wear. However, some of these products have sparked controversy because of the designer's ignorance about the culture being represented on the product. Although some see designs inspired by cultures on clothing as trendy (and trending) fashion statements, in actuality these statements are often perceived as offensive and culturally inappropriate.

Cultural appropriation often appeals to society's greed. More specifically, according to James Lull, "Cultural appropriation is how people take something that is given to them by a culture and use it for their own purposes" (104), purposes that often generate monetary gain or fame. Whether it's a design pattern or a song, the art form is reintegrated and as a result its original meaning is altered (104). One historic example of how cultural appropriation has been applied was during the age of punk rock. James Lull explains that during this age, the youth started rejecting mainstream, progressive rock bands such as Rush, Genesis, and King Crimson with their poetic lyrics and replaced them with more simple, angry songs (105). As a result, safety pins that would have been normally used for clothing were now utilized as body piercings that symbolized the movement of a social and musical revolution (105). A common example of cultural appropriation manifests in clothing fads such as feather clips or kimono cardigans inspired by a certain culture. However, the ever-changing market makes it difficult to draw the line between appropriating a cultural design to celebrate diversity or creating offense.

Culture appropriation can encourage diversity, especially in the U.S. where embracing differences is welcomed as a means to eliminate boundaries and heighten awareness. The United States is the melting pot of the world. It is the place where movements can expand awareness of different sects of religion and new forms of music or create new designs artistically (Lull 105). Eugene Volokh points out that artists, designers, and musicians should be able to work in any field they want regardless of their skin color or ancestry. Telling someone to work in a particular field or integrate a certain aspect because of their race or ethnic origin creates a wall within society (Volokh). In his article, Volokh further explains that the line is drawn when something such as blackface is meant to be a mockery of and objection to a race. However, if the costuming is a means to dress the part, such as a non-European ballet dancer dancing in traditional European costumes, then the tradition is honored and not mocked (Volokh). This is how cultures learn from one another.

The counterpart, or rather the more difficult aspect of cultural appropriation, is trying not to intentionally abuse and offend a certain group, especially if that group has been oppressed historically. During the 2013 Victoria's Secret fashion show, Karlie Kloss walked out on the runway wearing turquoise jewelry and a Native American headdress paired with lingerie (Li). Many viewers took offense at the presentation of the traditional clothing. The headdress, or war bonnet, is intended to commemorate men who have performed great deeds in battle (Li). To see this same clothing on a model with the sole intention of marketing sexy lingerie insults the Native American community. Ruth Hopkins, a columnist for *Indian Country*, viewed the selection as "[m]aking a mockery of Native identity" (qtd. in Li). Hopkins said, "I am repaid with the mean-spirited, disrespectful trivialization of my blood ancestry and the proud Native identity I work hard to instill in my children" (qtd. in Li). Someone wanting to share their culture with their children with high reverence faces difficultly when those honored traditions are mishandled and misused, especially in such public ways. This level of appropriation can spread quickly through social media's trending nature.

Several years ago, Urban Outfitters released a clothing line they referred to as the "Navajo hipster" brand that ranged from graphic patterned clothing to accessories. What deemed this line offensive was the use of the name "Navajo," a Native American tribe. From a legal standpoint, the clothing brand violated the Indian Arts and Crafts Act which states, "It is illegal to sell arts and crafts in a way that falsely suggests they were produced by Native Americans" ("Navajo"). In defense, Ed Looram, the company spokesman, countered that the term "Navajo" has been cycling through fashion, fine arts, and design throughout the past few years and is trending ("Navajo"). An easy fix to this would have been for Urban Outfitters to simply research and rename the brand as a "graphic print." But adding further insult to the Native Americans was Outfitters' expansion of the "Navajo hipster" line to include a "Navajo hipster panty" and a "Navajo print fabric wrapped flask." These items are considered derogatory and scandalous in many tribes, and alcohol consumption is banned on many reservations ("Navajo"). The Urban Outfitters example shows the extent of damage that can be done through "branding." Their actions exploited an entire group of people and encouraged ignorance among a public willing to buy those products.

A majority of consumers will buy clothing on impulse and especially around a holiday. During Halloween, few consumers think about a costume selection being deemed "culturally appropriate." Classic costumes such as a "Sexy Geisha" or "Indian" being sold annually may seem harmless to the consumer, but are viewed as offensive by members of the culture linked to the costume. These costumes are mass produced every year; yet some of them come with exaggerated characteristics and create a caricature of a certain race all for the sake of sales. The seemingly innocent costume perpetuates stereotyping or stigmatizing of a certain group (Lazo). The consumer may only wear the costume for a single day as a "harmless joke" or "small gesture of appreciation" but the damage to the culture can be long lasting (Lazo). Consumers should take the time to question if a costume is actually offensive and do a bit of research before making the purchase. Wearing a costume on Halloween is not embracing diversity.

Culture appropriation in clothing can be used to bring people together, but it must be done so in an informed manner. More importantly, it is essential that the everyday consumer get a clue. If it offends more than it trends, then maybe it is a good idea to place the item back on the rack.

Works Cited

Lazo, Kat. "Is Your Halloween Costume Racist?" *Everyday Feminism*, Everyday

Feminism, 29 Oct. 2013, everydayfeminism.com/2013/10/is-your-halloween-

costume-racist/.

Li, Shan. "Victoria's Secret Apologizes for Use of Native American Headdress." *Los*

Angeles Times, Los Angeles Times,

articles.latimes.com/2012/nov/13/business/la-fi-victorias-secret-native-

american-20121113.

Lull, James. "Cultural Appropriation." *The Media*, edited by Robin Andersen and

Jonathan Gray, vol. 1., Macmillan Reference USA, 2014, pp. 103-108. *Gale Virtual*

Reference Library,

link.galegroup.comezproxy.library.csn.edu/apps/doc/CX3402900180/GVRL?u

=las55353sid=GVRLxid=39ea2afa. Accessed 14 Nov. 2014.

"Navajo Nation Sues Urban Outfitters for Trademark Infringement." *The Guardian*,

Guardian News and Media, 1 Mar. 2012,

www.theguardian.com/world/2012/mar/01/navajo-nation-sues-urban-

outfitters.

Volokh, Eugene. "What Would *Salon* Think of an Article Called, 'Why I Can't Stand

Asian Musicians Who Play Beethoven'?" *Washington Post*, The Washington Post,

6 Mar. 2014, www.washingtonpost.com/news/volokh-

conspiracy/wp/2014/03/06/what-would-salon-think-of-an-article-called-why-i-

cant-stand-asian-musicians-who-play-

beethoven/?noredirect=on&utm_term=.c72177df017d.

Chapter 7
The Literature Essay

One task you may perform in your English class is a literature essay. For this task, you will read (or view) a work such as a play, poem, novel, movie, or short story; then you will write an essay in which you discuss how that work was put together. Ideally, this task will give you a better appreciation of the work. Practically, the task will prepare you for times in your career when you might provide an analysis of a report, or a proposal, or the costs and benefits of adopting a certain course of action. Below you will find the points a literature essay may cover and directions for how to write it.

The Basic Tools of Storytelling

If you are experiencing a work that is telling a story, such as a play, novel, movie, or short story, then you will need to look for the six following elements: **setting**, **character**, **plot**, **point of view**, **symbolism**, and **theme**.

Setting

The *setting* is the time and place during which a story occurs. Few authors will tell you this information directly. You will have to look closely at how places and people are described to pick up the clues you will need. For example, if a group of people is sitting in a cave around a fire, wearing animal skins, and using tools of stone and bone, then the story might be set in prehistoric times. If a group of people is escaping in a spaceship from hostile aliens firing at them with laser cannons, then the story might be set in the future or in an alternate universe.

173

Setting is important because it limits how characters can act and thus creates expectations in the reader. If in the opening pages of a story a man is riding a horse and wearing a ten-gallon hat, a gingham shirt, leather chaps, and a gun belt circled by bullets, then the reader will expect the story to be a Western, or at the least a story set in the American West. The reader will also expect this man to act and think the way people acted and thought during that time.

In a fantastical setting like that of *The Lord of the Rings* or *Star Wars*, looking at the details will be even more important. As viewers, we will not know the rules for how these worlds work until we see how the characters interact with their settings.

Character

A *character* is any agent that exhibits a distinct personality and affects the outcome of the story. A character can be human, animal, machine, or some other imaginative form. Again, as readers (and viewers), we must pay attention to how characters are described so that we can determine how they fit into the story, how they may act, and how we should respond to them (Is this person likeable? Should I be sympathetic?).

The most important character in a story is the *hero* or *protagonist*. This is the character that the story seems to be about, the one who has the most effect on the outcome. Other characters can be ranked as *major* or *minor* based on how much influence they have. The protagonist's love interests, family, allies, or rivals (the main rival being the story's *antagonist*) are usually major characters. Other characters met in passing during the course of the story are usually minor characters.

Two aspects of the major characters to consider are their *motivations* and *goals*. A motivation is the cause of a character's action; a goal is a character's desired outcome. Sometimes these two are the same, but sometimes they are not. If all we know about a character is that she hopes to run her own bakery someday, then her motivation and goal are the same. But if we know that the character wants to run the bakery because her mother once owned one, then motivation and goal are different. Something in her past provides a reason for something she wants in the future.

It is important to know the characters' motivations and goals because they often shape the action and the outcome of a story. For instance, if two rival characters hope to find a buried treasure, we immediately sense a conflict between them. We must weigh the reasons each has for finding the treasure, and examine the actions they take, to determine whom we should root for, and we should have a sense of what would happen if our chosen character should fail. The moment when our character is closest to achieving or losing his goal is typically the moment of highest tension in the story. Our enjoyment of the story may well hinge on his success or failure and on the circumstances surrounding this outcome.

Plot

The basics of *plot* have already been laid out for you in chapter 4 (in the discussion of the best-for-last organizational strategy). But because of the plot's importance in storytelling and analysis, we have provided more information here.

Plot and story are not the same. A story is a series of events that involves a set number of characters. A plot is the structure behind those events. The author chooses which event opens a story, which event closes it, and which events make up its contents. The author also chooses the order in which the events occur: sometimes in chronological order, but sometimes not. A *loop plot*, for example, will pose a mystery or problem in the opening and then lead us into the past to solve the puzzle for us. Such a plot shapes movies like *Titanic* or *Inception*. *Flashbacks*, like loops, return us to the past, but only for a moment or for a scene before the plot resumes its normal flow of time. A story with *subplots*—storylines featuring characters other than the protagonist—may have many events occurring at the same time as the events in the main plot.

To analyze a story's plot, you must look at the events of the story. An *event* is an action that changes the course of a character's life. If a woman chooses to leave her betrothed at the altar, for example, or if she learns her husband has been unfaithful, or if her bakery suddenly goes bankrupt, then we have an action important to her life—and, in turn, to the direction of the story. These examples, by the way, illustrate three of the most important actions to look for: *decision, discovery*, and *reversal*. Sometimes, however, an action is simply a random happening that the universe may interpose at a crucial moment. If, for example, two characters need to climb to the top of a mountain and it suddenly begins to snow, the universe has stepped in to throw an obstacle in their path. Here, too, we have an action becoming an event.

Plots usually are shaped by three types of conflict: *internal, personal,* and *extrapersonal*. Internal conflicts typically happen inside a character's mind, body, or heart. A woman may be torn, for example, between her feelings for her lover and her obligations toward her sickly parents. Or she may be battling a drinking problem caused by low self-esteem. Or she may feel that her life in general is lacking direction. Personal conflicts happen between two (or more) characters, like the two treasure seekers above. The two characters may be at odds over an heirloom, or a parking space, or a beautiful woman. Or perhaps one character causes an injury to a second, and the second seeks redress. Or perhaps the characters are engaged in a power struggle in their relationship. Extrapersonal conflict usually sees the characters arrayed against a large impersonal force such as nature, or big government, or a heartless corporation, or the universe itself. Extrapersonal conflicts between countries or corporations or other forces may also serve as part of the setting against which the characters operate.

As you can see in these conflicts, plot is heavily influenced by character. In a good story, neither exists without the other. The number of characters in a story often governs the type of conflict within it. If the story has one major character, for example, then the plot usually forms around a struggle the character has with the universe around him, or with his inner demons, or with a lack she perceives within her life. With two major characters, the plot revolves around the contest between them or an injury one causes the other. With three major characters, the plot springs from the triangles they form: A and B both love C; A loves B, but B loves C; A and B gang up on C. A two-character plot can also include the conflicts that arise in a one-character plot, and a three-character plot can include the conflicts that arise in a one- or two-character plot. In stories with more than three characters, we usually see extensions or modifications of these basic conflicts.

A plot begins with an event that knocks the hero's life, or the universe around him, out of its usual path. This event may be called the *inducer* (in the Aristotelian plot, the initial conflict). Any action that precedes the inducer is the *exposition*, often describing the setting and the hero's circumstances. The story may form a loop, or use flashbacks, to show us the events that led to the inducer or to take us back to the inducer itself. Aside from it being near the start, there is no set moment when the inducer occurs. In *Titanic*, the inducer—the moment when the older Rose Calvert sees the news story about the ship on television—happens after Brock Lovett and his team discover the safe in the wreckage; they are still in the present time of the story. In contrast, in *Inception*, the inducer—the moment when businessman Saito offers Dom Cobb the job of planting the inception into rival Robert Fischer—takes place well after the story has entered the loop.

Another kind of inducer arises when at the story's outset the universe of the hero is already off track and the hero has not yet been affected. Alternately, the hero may be in a state of paralysis created by his universe's disorder, unable to act. (In many legends, the hero has yet to be born.) The inducer occurs either when the disorder touches the hero's life or when the hero breaks out of his paralysis (as at his birth). Again, the story may take the form of a loop, or use flashbacks, to show the events that led to the inducer or to take us back to the moment when the inducer occurred. The inducer in *Inception* is actually of this kind: Saito's job offer will allow Cobb to break out of the legal paralysis that has prevented him from returning to America and seeing his children.

The hero has three responses to the inducer. First, the hero can react immediately. Second, the hero can delay reaction, the delay occurring for a number of reasons. For example, the inducer may occur at some time or place away from the hero and the hero may not learn of it until later. Or the hero may be prevented from immediate action. Or the hero is not ready to act. And third, the hero may resist reaction or deny the inducer has occurred; in this case, a second event will occur that forces the hero to react. Rose reacts immediately, calling Lovett to ask him if he has found the Heart of the Ocean, the necklace he is seeking. Dom also reacts immediately, accepting Saito's offer and moving forward to assemble his team.

A plot ends when one of three events occurs. First, the hero restores order to his life or to the universe. Second, the hero assimilates to the new conditions brought by the inducer. Or third, the hero is overcome by the new conditions brought on by the inducer. This event is a permanent change that no further action by the characters or the universe can affect (though in a sequel . . .). Rose makes peace with her life and a final avowal of her love for Jack Dawson by dropping the necklace into the deep. Dom, too, finds a measure of peace by successfully completing his job and returning to his children—though the final image of the spinning top creates a final tease of doubt.

Point of View

Point of view is the perspective through which the story is told. Of course, the author is ultimately the person who wrote the story. However, another persona, the *narrator*, may actually give the story its voice. Thus, you may see the I-pronoun used, but you must never assume that it is the author behind the I.

We label the narrator by his or her distance from the story and by the pronouns used to identify him or her. A *first-person narrator* is one who frequently appears as a character in the story and refers to him- or herself with the I-pronouns. The first-person narrator can be *central* or *peripheral*. If central, the narrator is also the story's protagonist. If peripheral, the narrator is either one character chronicling another character's story (as Nick Carraway does in *The Great Gatsby*) or else someone telling the story to a waiting audience (as Nelly Dean does in *Wuthering Heights*). In the latter case, the action of the story is often already complete, and the narrator is telling it in retrospect.

A *second-person narrator* stands somewhat outside the story and addresses all of the characters as *you*. The effect of this narration is to create a story that reads like an extended one-sided dialogue or else a series of challenges to the characters.

A *third-person narrator* stands completely outside the story and addresses all characters as *he* or *she*. The third-person narrator is further categorized by the control she has over the characters and their environment. An *omniscient* narrator can enter the thoughts of any of the characters, offer judgment on them and their actions, move the story backwards and forwards through time, or transport the setting to any place in the universe. A *limited omniscient* narrator allows the reader access to the thoughts of only one character (who thus becomes our point-of-view character) and narrows our perceptions of the universe to those of that character. This narrator offers no judgments except those of the character herself. Time and place change only if the character changes position. An *objective* narrator stays completely out of the thoughts of the characters and simply records the surface details of their appearances and actions. In this mode, the narrator is like a camera that follows the characters around.

Symbolism

Symbolism is the use of symbols, and *symbols* in turn are objects or actions that have a meaning beyond themselves. For example, on a first date, a man gives a woman a bird he has folded out of paper. The bird is just that to an outside observer—a bird. However, for the man it might symbolize the effort he is willing to make to please the woman. For the woman, the bird might represent that first date and the beginning of their relationship. If, later in the story, the woman encases the bird in glass, or throws it into a fire, then her action becomes symbolic: an acknowledgment or a rejection of the man's efforts, or her feelings about the relationship itself.

Symbols grow out of the meanings that the characters, the narrator, and we as readers attach to those objects and actions. They may create a web that stretches under the surface of the story. When that web is discovered, it may help our understanding of the characters' motivations and goals, of the shape of the plot, and of the theme of the story.

Theme

A *theme* is a broad conclusion that the work as a whole draws about the characters and their actions. Typically, a theme involves an idea such as love, time, fate, or some other cultural or universal concept.

Thus, if in a story a man and a woman grow to love each other but must endure separations, temptations, struggles, and other obstacles before they can unite happily at the end, a theme of the story might be that love is worth the difficulties one might face.

Because of its scope, a theme depends upon the other elements described above. Setting, character, plot, and the rest will all have something to contribute to the building of a theme, so you will have to pay close attention to them. Rarely will a modern storyteller simply lay out a theme in the introduction or in the conclusion the way a fable might, or the way we present a controlling idea when writing expository essays.

Since stories are individual creations with their own settings, characters, plots, and so on, they will each have a unique vision in their themes even if they tackle the same ideas. The movies *Titanic* and *Inception* both treat the idea of love—they even feature the same lead actor—but the theme they each develop is quite different. In the first, when Rose takes Jack's last name after her rescue and, much later, sends the necklace to his grave, the theme is that love (not precious jewelry) is worth keeping. In the second, when Dom finds his life increasingly troubled by his memories of his dead wife, Mal—at the end, she tries to prevent his return from the realm of dreams to the real world—the theme is that when love becomes obsessive and dangerous, it must be let go.

It is also possible that a well-crafted story has more than one theme. If two or more ideas are in play in the characters' actions, then the story will say something about each. *Titanic* has something to say about human arrogance: The moment when humanity thinks itself invulnerable is the moment when the universe will put an iceberg in its path. *Inception* warns us that perhaps the suggestive power of dreams should not be manipulated toward selfish ends.

Theme may also be shaped by another element: **irony**. We frequently use *verbal irony* when we say things we do not really mean: "Oh, sure, I like sushi," we may say to a friend even though we really do not like sushi at all. Theme, however, usually springs from more complex forms of irony. *Dramatic irony* may arise when we, the audience, know things that the characters or the narrator does not. Such irony shapes Edgar Allan Poe's story "The Cask of Amontillado": We know that Montresor is leading Fortunato to his death though the character does not realize it until too late. *Situational irony* is at work when appearance and reality, expectation and fulfillment are at odds. A key moment in Julian Mortimer Smith's story "Headshot" comes when Marine Corporal Peters must gain the approval of a quorum of parents and peaceniks in order to assassinate a dangerous terrorist. Finally, *cosmic irony* comes into play when it seems like the universe itself is working against the characters. This form of irony gives us the catastrophic ending of Kate Chopin's "The Story of an Hour," when Louise Mallard's expectation of a life of freedom, occasioned by the news of her husband's death, is dashed when the universe returns her husband to her safe and sound.

The Basic Tools of Poetry

When you experience a poem, you will need to use all of the elements described above. However, you will also have four others to consider.

Narrative or Lyric

All poems can be broadly categorized as *narrative* or *lyric*. A narrative poem is one that tells a story. It can be long or short, but it will have a clearly defined plot following the model described above. To understand the narrative poem, then, you must closely follow the events of the plot. Certain types of poems, like the epic or the ballad, will almost always be narratives. Thus, poems such as Homer's *Iliad* and *Odyssey* (both epics) and Samuel Coleridge's "The Rime of the Ancient Mariner" (a ballad) fall into this category.

A lyric poem is one that surrounds a central image or series of images. An *image* is a picture, though in poetry (and in storytelling) images must be created using words rather than paint or clay or film. Typically, the lyric poem is short, no more than a page or two, though some can run longer. The image at the heart of the poem will likely have a symbolic meaning that will be central to its theme; identifying the image, then, is paramount to understanding the poem.

Closed Form or Open Form

In form, all poems distinguish themselves from prose by the use of line breaks and stanzas. A *line break* is the poet's conscious ending of a line before the margin of the page. In prose forms such as the short story, novel, or essay, the lines run to the margin, breaking only at the ends of paragraphs. Poems, on the other hand, have internal rules, determined by the poet or by the poem itself, as to when lines end. The result is that a poem looks quite different from a short story or a novel when printed.

A *stanza* is a series of lines set together as a unit. It is the rough equivalent of the paragraph in prose writing. Usually, stanzas are separated from one another by an extra blank line, though there are other methods. Stanzas, too, have internal rules governed by the poet or by the type of poem; thus, a poem could be written as a series of two- or three-line stanzas, or it could have stanzas of different lengths, or it could have no stanzas at all, just one continuous stream of lines.

Beyond these similarities, though, all poems can further be categorized as *closed form* or *open form*. A closed-form poem has strict rules for the length of lines and stanzas, the use of rhymes and repetition, and the pattern of stressed and unstressed syllables (called a *foot*). A sonnet, for example, has fourteen lines of ten syllables each, the syllables generally in an unstressed-stressed pattern (an *iambic* foot). It also has two rhyme schemes that affect the organization of the poem. A ballad usually relies on four-line stanzas following an 8-6-8-6 or a 4-4-6, 4-4-6 syllable count and an alternating rhyme scheme. Villanelles, pantoums, and sestinas have a set pattern of repeated lines (or words) and stanza lengths. The poet, however, may create her own closed form by following an original pattern of rhymes, syllables, and stanza lengths.

An open-form poem follows no strict patterns of rhyme, syllable count, repetition, or stanza length. Hence, most open-form poems are called *free verse*. Open-form poems, however, are not simply poems without rules, and they are not prose passages forced into a poetic form with arbitrary line breaks. The poet's use of stanzas and line breaks still follows a conscious design, and we as readers must determine the nature of that design. Further, the poet uses other resources of language to distinguish his work as a poem. Some of those resources are described below.

Concrete versus Abstract

As you learned earlier, description is the most basic mode of essay writing. However, all writers, no matter what they are writing, must use details to make an effective impression upon the reader. Essays use details to support a thesis or tell a narrative. Fiction uses details to bring settings, characters, and symbols to life. But poetry, in particular lyric poetry, is largely defined by the skill with which writers create and use details that appeal to the senses.

Sensory details must be *concrete* rather than *abstract*. We have touched upon this difference, and the importance of concreteness, before, but this concept bears repeating. A concrete detail such as *red 1966 Mustang convertible* makes a far bigger impression than does the abstract *vehicle*. Not only will a reader be able to visualize the car, but all readers will be able to visualize the same car, a necessary step in creating images. Poems that repeat vague terms like *love, sorrow, death,* or *joy,* will never make the experience of these concepts personal to the reader.

Some poets, like Christine Boyka Kluge in her "Inventing New Bodies," will try to overwhelm the reader with sensory details not to cause confusion but to break open the shell of our consciousness and lift us to a greater level of physical, moral, or spiritual awareness. Done correctly, a poem will forevermore change how we view the world around us. Hence, Kluge, by taking such great pains to describe the snails' music, the garden in which they live, and their unexpectedly vivid anger toward humans, has changed our apprehension of their simple existence from mere curiosity to high transcendence.

Compression

All writers may use *figures of speech* to make their language musical, meaningful, or memorable. Speechwriters use these figures so that listeners will retain the key themes of the speech. Fiction writers use figures to subtly underscore dramatic moments in a story. But again, however, poets go a step further. Poetry might be described as the art of using concentrated figures to squeeze the greatest amount of meaning into the fewest number of words. This art is also known as *compression*.

The fundamental figures are widely known: *simile, metaphor, metonymy*, and *synecdoche*. These can be classified as figures of comparison. There are also figures of opposition such as *litotes, paradox*, and *antithesis*. Others, such as *parallelism, anaphora*, and *epistrophe*, create pleasing forms of repetition. *Ellipsis* drops unneeded words so that sentences are more compact. *Function shift* lets poets turn nouns into verbs, or verbs into adjectives, and so on, to create colorful descriptions that arrest the eyes. The *rule of three* can create harmonies of sound, sense, and structure that reinforce the connection between a poem's form and its content.

Essay Model

When writing a literature essay, start by stating the name of the author (if known) and the title of the work. In the same sentence and into the next, set forth the work's *premise*—that is, a very brief summary of what happens or what major ideas are in play. You can usually assume that the reader of your essay is familiar with the work you are analyzing, so your premise should have just enough detail to show that you have read and understood the work. The next two sentences should present the element you will be analyzing in your paper (setting, plot, theme, compression, etc.) and your thesis. Much like the argument paper, a literature essay requires that you take a stand. Your thesis must clearly state how your chosen element appears in your work, how it affects that work, or what greater meaning it may hold.

The body of the literature essay then supports the stance you take in your thesis. The structure of the body paragraphs should follow the five-step model set forth in chapter 4: topic sentence, narrow down, quotation, explanation, and conclusion. Each body paragraph should start with a topic sentence that, piece by piece, restates your stance. The rest of the paragraph then develops and explains your stance. The main source of support is the work itself. You must be able to show where in the work your chosen element appears and why you believe it functions as it does. For example, if you are analyzing the plot of a story, you must be able to name the events you believe are the inducer, the hero's reaction, and the climax (or alternately, the initial conflict, gradual rise in tension, and climax) and explain how those events fulfill the definitions supplied above.

To point out where your element appears in the work, you must use and cite quotations, much like you did in your research essay. Quotations can be direct (word for word from the text and enclosed in quotation marks) or indirect (a paraphrase written in your own words and not enclosed). To cite your sources, you must use Modern Language Association (MLA) format, again as you did for your research essay. Typically, for works of prose (novel, short story), you will cite by author's last name and the page number on which the quoted passage appears in your printed source. Poems are cited by author's last name and line number. Plays, if they are divided into act, scene, and line numbers (as Shakespeare's are), should be cited by those numbers; if not, then by page number.

However, the literature essay is not simply an exercise in stringing quotes together. Never assume your reader sees the same meanings in the passages that you do. You will have to take the time to introduce your quotations to your reader (much like you would handle introductions at a party) and then, perhaps most importantly, take the time to explain how and why the passages support your stance.

The final paragraph of your essay should clearly signal that you have finished your analysis. As with the other essay types, you can simply restate your thesis and summarize your main points. However, depending on your instructor's guidelines, you also have the option of judging the effectiveness of your chosen element, relating your essay topic to a broader concept, or deciding whether the work as a whole deserves its reputation (i.e., Was it worth saying?). You may also, if allowed, raise and refute an alternative interpretation of your element.

Based on the model described above, an introduction and body paragraph of a literature essay might look like this:

> While reading William Shakespeare's play *The Tragedy of Othello*, we are saddened by the deaths of Othello and Desdemona, and we are appalled by Iago's treachery. Often,

an audience will ask itself, Why did Iago do it? This question, though simple, is important to our understanding of the play because Iago's actions move the play forward. Iago is motivated by his jealousy of Othello and by his ambition to rise through the ranks of the Venetian army.

The first of Iago's motivations is jealousy for Othello. He first expresses this jealousy when he relates a rumor concerning his wife, Emilia, and Othello: "It is thought abroad that 'twixt my sheets / H'as done my office" (1.3.360-1). The "office" he refers to is the duty of a husband to maintain sexual relations with his wife, so he is stating his belief that Othello has slept with Emilia. This belief, denied later by Emilia herself, is nevertheless a major reason why Iago seeks revenge against Othello.

Here is another example:

In the short story "The Story of an Hour," Kate Chopin describes how Louise Mallard longs to experience the world beyond her house. When an acquaintance brings news of her husband's death, she sees a chance to escape her limitations. Chopin uses the window of Louise's room to symbolize the freedom that beckons her forward to a new life. Little does Louise realize, however, that her excitement for her prospects will ultimately turn against her, with fatal results.

The attention given to Louise's sensory awareness of the world outside her window emphasizes her strong desire to break free of her repressed life. For example, when she sits in the chair facing the window, her body is "haunted" by a "physical exhaustion" that reaches "into her soul" (197). These are signs of the fatigue that her current life with her husband has brought her. Immediately contrasted with this exhaustion, however, is the description of the first impressions that reach her through the window, the trees "all aquiver with the new spring life," the "delicious breath of rain," and the "twittering" of "countless sparrows" (197). In this short passage it is clear that her senses are awake and that these impressions have already begun to renew her energies. Soon, her body will physically respond to these new stimuli.

Here is a breakdown of the steps used in the sample essay on Shakespeare:

Introductory Paragraph

Author-Title + Premise: While reading William Shakespeare's play *The Tragedy of Othello*, we are saddened by the deaths of Othello and Desdemona, and we are appalled by Iago's treachery.

Introduction of Literary Element: Often, an audience will ask itself, Why did Iago do it? This question, though simple, is important to our understanding of the play because Iago's actions move the play forward.

Thesis: Iago is motivated by his jealousy of Othello and by his ambition to rise through the ranks of the Venetian army.

Body Paragraph

Topic Sentence: The first of Iago's motivations is jealousy for Othello.

Narrow Down: He first expresses this jealousy when he relates a rumor concerning his wife, Emilia, and Othello:

Quotation: "It is thought abroad that 'twixt my sheets / H'as done my office" (1.3.360-1).

Explanation of Key Term: The "office" he refers to is the duty of a husband to maintain sexual relations with his wife, so he is stating his belief that Othello has slept with Emilia.

Conclusion: This belief, denied later by Emilia herself, is nevertheless a major reason why Iago seeks revenge against Othello.

Here is a breakdown of the steps used in the sample essay on Chopin:

Introductory Paragraph

Author–Title + Premise: In the short story "The Story of an Hour," Kate Chopin describes how Louise Mallard longs to experience the world beyond her house. When an acquaintance brings news of her husband's death, she sees a chance to escape her limitations.

Introduction of Literary Element: Chopin uses the window of Louise's room to symbolize the freedom that beckons her forward to a new life.

Thesis: Little does Louise realize, however, that her excitement for her prospects will ultimately turn against her, with fatal results.

Body Paragraph

Topic Sentence: The attention given to Louise's sensory awareness of the world outside her window emphasizes her strong desire to break free of her repressed life.

Narrow Down: For example, when she sits in the chair facing the window,

Quotation: her body is "haunted" by a "physical exhaustion" that reaches "into her soul" (197).

Explanation of Key Term: These are signs of the fatigue that her current life with her husband has brought her.

Narrow down: Immediately contrasted with this exhaustion, however, is the description of the first impressions that reach her through the window,

Quotation: the trees "all aquiver with the new spring life," the "delicious breath of rain," and the "twittering" of "countless sparrows" (197).

Explanation of Key Term: In this short passage it is clear that her senses are awake and that these impressions have already begun to renew her energies.

<u>Conclusion</u>: Soon, her body will physically respond to these new stimuli.

The body paragraph in the Chopin essay is more complex, repeating steps two, three, and four to examine the relevant details surrounding Louise Mallard's window. Note, however, that all quotations used are carefully introduced, cited, and explained so that the author has clearly located and documented his sources.

Summary

The literature essay examines the elements which make up plays, poems, novels, movies, and short stories. As noted earlier in this book, the essay works like a division essay, breaking an object (in this case a story or a poem) into its parts, but it usually focuses on the use of just one or two of the parts. The essay is also like an argument paper, in which you take a stance by presenting your interpretation of how the element is used. The essay is also like the research essay in that you must use and cite quotations in support of your stance. Much of what you learned about the narrative essay—initial conflict, rise in tension, climax, and so on—applies to literary works as well. If you enjoy learning how things work and have ever taken apart a toy or a gadget to see what it looks like inside, then the literature essay should appeal to your sense of discovery.

Below, you will find a collection of short stories and poems, including the complete version of Chopin's "The Story of an Hour," that build upon the elements described above. At the end, you will also find a student paper written about *Harry Potter and the Sorcerer's Stone* so that you can see how the entire literature essay is put together.

The Cask of Amontillado
by Edgar Allan Poe

The thousand injuries of Fortunato I had borne as I best could, but when he ventured upon insult, I vowed revenge. You, who so well know the nature of my soul, will not suppose, however, that I gave utterance to a threat. *At length* I would be avenged; this was a point definitely settled—but the very definitiveness with which it was resolved precluded the idea of risk. I must not only punish, but punish with impunity. A wrong is unredressed when retribution overtakes its redresser. It is equally unredressed when the avenger fails to make himself felt as such to him who has done the wrong.

It must be understood that neither by word nor deed had I given Fortunato cause to doubt my good will. I continued, as was my wont, to smile in his face, and he did not perceive that my smile *now* was at the thought of his immolation.

He had a weak point—this Fortunato—although in other regards he was a man to be respected and even feared. He prided himself on his connoisseurship in wine. Few Italians have the true virtuoso spirit. For the most part their enthusiasm is adopted to suit the time and opportunity to practice imposture upon the British and Austrian *millionaires.* In painting and gemmary Fortunato, like his countrymen, was a quack, but in the matter of old wines he was sincere. In this respect I did not differ from him materially: I was skillful in the Italian vintages myself, and bought largely whenever I could.

It was about dusk, one evening during the supreme madness of the carnival season, that I encountered my friend. He accosted me with excessive warmth, for he had been drinking much. The man wore motley. He had on a tight-fitting parti-striped dress, and his head was surmounted by the conical cap and bells. I was so pleased to see him, that I thought I should never have done wringing his hand.

I said to him—"My dear Fortunato, you are luckily met. How remarkably well you are looking to-day! But I have received a pipe of what passes for Amontillado, and I have my doubts."

"The Cask of Amontillado" by Edgar Allan Poe, 1846.

"How?" said he. "Amontillado? A pipe? Impossible! And in the middle of the carnival?"

"I have my doubts," I replied; "and I was silly enough to pay the full Amontillado price without consulting you in the matter. You were not to be found, and I was fearful of losing a bargain."

"Amontillado!"

"I have my doubts."

"Amontillado!"

"And I must satisfy them."

"Amontillado!"

"As you are engaged, I am on my way to Luchesi. If anyone has a critical turn, it is he. He will tell me—"

"Luchesi cannot tell Amontillado from Sherry."

"And yet some fools will have it that his taste is a match for your own."

"Come, let us go."

"Whither?"

"To your vaults."

"My friend, no; I will not impose upon your good nature. I perceive you have an engagement. Luchesi—"

"I have no engagement; come."

"My friend, no. It is not the engagement, but the severe cold with which I perceive you are afflicted. The vaults are insufferably damp. They are encrusted with niter."

"Let us go, nevertheless. The cold is merely nothing. Amontillado! You have been imposed upon; and as for Luchesi, he cannot distinguish Sherry from Amontillado."

Thus speaking, Fortunato possessed himself of my arm. Putting on a mask of black silk, and drawing a *roquelaure* closely about my person, I suffered him to hurry me to my palazzo.

There were no attendants at home; they had absconded to make merry in honor of the time. I had told them that I should not return until the morning, and had given them explicit orders not to stir from the house. These orders were sufficient, I well knew, to insure their immediate disappearance, one and all, as soon as my back was turned.

I took from their sources two flambeaux, and giving one to Fortunato, bowed him through several suites of rooms to the archway that led into the vaults. I passed down a long and winding staircase, requesting him to be cautious as he followed. We came at length to the foot of the descent, and stood together on the damp ground of the catacombs of the Montresors.

The gait of my friend was unsteady, and the bells upon his cap jingled as he strode.

"The pipe," said he.

"It is farther on," said I; "but observe the white web-work which gleams from these cavern walls."

He turned towards me, and looked into my eyes with two filmy orbs that distilled the rheum of intoxication.

"Niter?" he asked, at length.

"Niter," I replied. "How long have you had that cough?"

"Ugh! ugh! ugh!—ugh! ugh! ugh!—ugh! ugh! ugh!—ugh! ugh! ugh!—ugh! ugh! ugh!"

My poor friend found it impossible to reply for many moments.

"It is nothing," he said, at last.

"Come," I said, with decision, "we will go back; your health is precious. You are rich, respected, admired, beloved; you are happy, as once I was. You are a man to be missed. For me it is no matter. We will go back; you will be ill, and I cannot be responsible. Besides, there is Luchesi—"

"Enough," he said; "the cough is a mere nothing; it will not kill me. I shall not die of a cough."

"True—true," I replied; "and, indeed, I had no intention of alarming you unnecessarily—but you should use all proper caution. A draught of this Medoc will defend us from the damps."

Here I knocked off the neck of a bottle which I drew from a long row of its fellows that lay upon the mould.

"Drink," I said, presenting him the wine.

He raised it to his lips with a leer. He paused and nodded to me familiarly, while his bells jingled.

"I drink," he said, "to the buried that repose around us."

"And I to your long life."

He again took my arm, and we proceeded.

"These vaults," he said, "are extensive."

"The Montresors," I replied, "were a great and numerous family."

"I forget your arms."

"A huge human foot *d'or*, in a field azure; the foot crushes a serpent rampant whose fangs are imbedded in the heel."

"And the motto?"

"*Nemo me impune lacessit.*"

"Good!" he said.

The wine sparkled in his eyes and the bells jingled. My own fancy grew warm with the Medoc. We had passed through walls of piled bones, with casks and puncheons intermingling, into the inmost recesses of the catacombs. I paused again, and this time I made bold to seize Fortunato by an arm above the elbow.

"The niter!" I said; "see, it increases. It hangs like moss upon the vaults. We are below the river's bed. The drops of moisture trickle among the bones. Come, we will go back ere it is too late. Your cough—"

"It is nothing," he said; "let us go on. But first, another draught of the Medoc."

I broke and reached him a flagon of De Grave. He emptied it at a breath. His eyes flashed with a fierce light. He laughed and threw the bottle upwards with a gesticulation I did not understand.

I looked at him in surprise. He repeated the movement—a grotesque one.

"You do not comprehend?" he said.

"Not I," I replied.

"Then you are not of the brotherhood."

"How?"

"You are not of the masons."

"Yes, yes," I said, "yes, yes."

"You? Impossible! A mason?"

"A mason," I replied.

"A sign," he said.

"It is this," I answered, producing a trowel from beneath the folds of my *roquelaure*.

"You jest," he exclaimed, recoiling a few paces. "But let us proceed to the Amontillado."

"Be it so," I said, replacing the tool beneath the cloak, and again offering him my arm. He leaned upon it heavily. We continued our route in search of the Amontillado. We passed through a range of low arches, descended, passed on, and descending again, arrived at a deep crypt, in which the foulness of the air caused our flambeaux rather to glow than flame.

At the most remote end of the crypt there appeared another less spacious. Its walls had been lined with human remains, piled to the vault overhead, in the fashion of the great catacombs of Paris. Three sides of this interior crypt were still ornamented in this manner. From the fourth the bones had been thrown down, and lay promiscuously upon the earth, forming at one point a mound of some size. Within the wall thus exposed by the displacing of the bones, we perceived a still interior recess, in depth about four feet, in width three, in height six or seven. It seemed to have been constructed for no especial use within itself, but formed merely the interval between two of the colossal supports of the roof of the catacombs, and was backed by one of their circumscribing walls of solid granite.

It was in vain that Fortunato, uplifting his dull torch, endeavored to pry into the depths of the recess. Its termination the feeble light did not enable us to see.

"Proceed," I said; "herein is the Amontillado. As for Luchesi—"

"He is an ignoramus," interrupted my friend, as he stepped unsteadily forward, while I followed immediately at his heels. In an instant he had reached the extremity of the niche, and finding his progress arrested by the rock, stood stupidly bewildered. A moment more and I had fettered him to the granite. In its surface were two iron staples, distant from each other about two feet, horizontally. From one of these depended a short chain, from the other a padlock. Throwing the links about his waist, it was but the work of a few seconds to secure it. He was too much astounded to resist. Withdrawing the key I stepped back from the recess.

"Pass your hand," I said, "over the wall; you cannot help feeling the niter. Indeed it is *very* damp. Once more let me *implore* you to return. No? Then I must positively leave you. But I must first render you all the little attentions in my power."

"The Amontillado!" ejaculated my friend, not yet recovered from his astonishment.

"True," I replied; "the Amontillado."

As I said these words I busied myself among the pile of bones of which I have before spoken. Throwing them aside, I soon uncovered a quantity of building stone and mortar. With these materials and with the aid of my trowel, I began vigorously to wall up the entrance of the niche.

I had scarcely laid the first tier of masonry when I discovered that the intoxication of Fortunato had in a great measure worn off. The earliest indication I had of this was a low moaning cry from the depth of the recess. It was *not* the cry of a drunken man. There was then a long and obstinate silence. I laid the second tier, and the third, and the fourth; and then I heard the furious vibrations of the chain. The noise lasted for several minutes, during which, that I might hearken to it with the more satisfaction, I ceased my labors and sat down upon the bones. When at last the clanking subsided, I resumed the trowel, and finished without interruption the fifth, the sixth, and the seventh tier. The wall was now nearly upon a level with my breast. I again paused, and holding the flambeaux over the masonwork, threw a few feeble rays upon the figure within.

A succession of loud and shrill screams, bursting suddenly from the throat of the chained form, seemed to thrust me violently back. For a brief moment I hesitated—I trembled. Unsheathing my rapier, I began to grope with it about the recess; but the thought of an instant reassured me. I placed my hand upon the solid fabric of the catacombs, and felt satisfied. I reapproached the wall. I replied to the yells of him who clamored. I re-echoed—I aided—I surpassed them in volume and in strength. I did this, and the clamorer grew still.

It was now midnight, and my task was drawing to a close. I had completed the eighth, ninth, and tenth tier. I had finished a portion of the last and the eleventh; there remained but a single stone to be fitted and plastered in. I struggled with its weight; I placed it partially in its destined position. But now there came from out the niche a low laugh that erected the hairs upon my head. It was succeeded by a sad voice which I had difficulty in recognizing as that of the noble Fortunato. The voice said—

"Ha! ha! ha!—he! he! he!—a very good joke indeed—an excellent jest. We will have many a rich laugh about it at the palazzo—he! he! he!—over our wine—he! he! he!"

"The Amontillado!" I said.

"He! he! he!—he! he! he!—yes, the Amontillado. But is it not getting late? Will not they be awaiting us at the palazzo, the Lady Fortunato and the rest? Let us be gone."

"Yes," I said, "let us be gone."

"*For the love of God, Montresor!*"

"Yes," I said, "for the love of God!"

But to these words I hearkened in vain for a reply. I grew impatient. I called aloud:

"Fortunato!"

No answer. I called again—

"Fortunato!"

No answer still. I thrust a torch through the remaining aperture and let it fall within. There came forth in return only a jingling of the bells. My heart grew sick—on account of the dampness of the catacombs. I hastened to make an end of my labor. I forced the last stone into its position; I plastered it up. Against the new masonry I re-erected the old rampart of bones. For the half of a century no mortal has disturbed them. *In pace requiescat!*

The Story of an Hour
by Kate Chopin

Knowing that Mrs. Mallard was afflicted with a heart trouble, great care was taken to break to her as gently as possible the news of her husband's death.

It was her sister Josephine who told her, in broken sentences; veiled hints that revealed in half concealing. Her husband's friend Richards was there, too, near her. It was he who had been in the newspaper office when intelligence of the railroad disaster was received, with Brently Mallard's name leading the list of "killed." He had only taken the time to assure himself of its truth by a second telegram, and had hastened to forestall any less careful, less tender friend in bearing the sad message.

She did not hear the story as many women have heard the same, with a paralyzed inability to accept its significance. She wept at once, with sudden, wild abandonment, in her sister's arms. When the storm of grief had spent itself she went away to her room alone. She would have no one follow her.

There stood, facing the open window, a comfortable, roomy arm-chair. Into this she sank, pressed down by a physical exhaustion that haunted her body and seemed to reach into her soul.

She could see in the open square before her house the tops of trees that were all aquiver with the new spring life. The delicious breath of rain was in the air. In the street below a peddler was crying his wares. The notes of a distant song which some one was singing reached her faintly, and countless sparrows were twittering in the eaves.

There were patches of blue sky showing here and there through the clouds that had met and piled one above the other in the west facing her window.

She sat with her head thrown back upon the cushion of the chair, quite motionless, except when a sob came up into her throat and shook her, as a child who has cried itself to sleep continues to sob in its dreams.

"The Story of an Hour" by Kate Chopin, 1894.

She was young, with a fair, calm face, whose lines bespoke repression and even a certain strength. But now there was a dull stare in her eyes, whose gaze was fixed away off yonder on one of those patches of blue sky. It was not a glance of reflection, but rather indicated a suspension of intelligent thought.

There was something coming to her and she was waiting for it, fearfully. What was it? She did not know; it was too subtle and elusive to name. But she felt it, creeping out of the sky, reaching toward her through the sounds, the scents, the color that filled the air.

Now her bosom rose and fell tumultuously. She was beginning to recognize this thing that was approaching to possess her, and she was striving to beat it back with her will—as powerless as her two white slender hands would have been.

When she abandoned herself a little whispered word escaped her slightly parted lips. She said it over and over under her breath: "free, free, free!" The vacant stare and the look of terror that had followed it went from her eyes. They stayed keen and bright. Her pulses beat fast, and the coursing blood warmed and relaxed every inch of her body.

She did not stop to ask if it were or were not a monstrous joy that held her. A clear and exalted perception enabled her to dismiss the suggestion as trivial.

She knew that she would weep again when she saw the kind, tender hands folded in death; the face that had never looked save with love upon her, fixed and gray and dead. But she saw beyond that bitter moment a long procession of years to come that would belong to her absolutely. And she opened and spread her arms out to them in welcome.

There would be no one to live for her during those coming years; she would live for herself. There would be no powerful will bending hers in that blind persistence with which men and women believe they have a right to impose a private will upon a fellow-creature. A kind intention or a cruel intention made the act seem no less a crime as she looked upon it in that brief moment of illumination.

And yet she had loved him—sometimes. Often she had not. What did it matter! What could love, the unsolved mystery, count for in the face of this possession of self-assertion which she suddenly recognized as the strongest impulse of her being!

"Free! Body and soul free!" she kept whispering.

Josephine was kneeling before the closed door with her lips to the keyhole, imploring for admission. "Louise, open the door! I beg; open the door—you will make yourself ill. What are you doing, Louise? For heaven's sake open the door."

"Go away. I am not making myself ill." No; she was drinking in a very elixir of life through that open window.

Her fancy was running riot along those days ahead of her. Spring days, and summer days, and all sorts of days that would be her own. She breathed a quick prayer that life might be long. It was only yesterday she had thought with a shudder that life might be long.

She arose at length and opened the door to her sister's importunities. There was a feverish triumph in her eyes, and she carried herself unwittingly like a goddess of Victory. She clasped her sister's waist, and together they descended the stairs. Richards stood waiting for them at the bottom.

Some one was opening the front door with a latchkey. It was Brently Mallard who entered, a little travel-stained, composedly carrying his grip-sack and umbrella. He had been far from the scene of the accident, and did not even know there had been one. He stood amazed at Josephine's piercing cry; at Richards' quick motion to screen him from the view of his wife.

But Richards was too late.

When the doctors came they said she had died of heart disease—of joy that kills.

Headshot
by Julian Mortimer Smith

@JMitcherCNN: Corporal, first of all, let me thank you for agreeing to this interview. By now all of America has seen the footage of your amazing headshot last week. Could you tell us the story, in your own words?

@CplPetersUSMC: Well sure, Jim. As you know, things went kinda crazy after I made that kill. I'm pushing 12k followers now. At the time the most I'd ever had online at once was . . . maybe a couple dozen? Fact is, there were only two people with me when it happened—@PatriotRiot2000 and @FrendliGhost. This was the night of the assault on Peshawar, remember? So half the nation was following the boys from First Airborne. No one wanted to miss a jump like that. I appreciate all the fans who've been with me since the beginning, but I want to give credit where it's due. It was just me, Riot, and Ghost that night.

@JMitcherCNN: Interesting. So you didn't even have quorum for engagement?

@CplPetersUSMC: No, sir. Not at first. But that night I wasn't even worrying about quorum. It was just a routine patrol and we weren't expecting any trouble. I was just chatting with Ghost and Riot. Both of those dudes have always had my back with nav and sit-reps and shit like that. But they were also just there when I needed someone to talk to, you know? That's even more important sometimes. When you're in the middle of a war zone, it's nice to hear the voice of some suburban kid from Detroit in your headset.

@JMitcherCNN: So how many other soldiers were taking part in this patrol?

@CplPetersUSMC: It was a six-man squad, but the tactical-scale guys had split us up to cover more ground. Ghost and Riot both thought that was dumb, but they'd been outvoted in the war room. When the numbers are small, bad ideas can get through more easily. That's the whole point of quorum. I admit, we were doing a bit of trash talking. They told me there were a lot of tac-scale folks online who had never even really followed a soldier. They just spend all their time zoomed-out, looking at satellite feeds, moving us around like chess pieces. I'm not saying that's wrong, but it can be dangerous. No one who's spent time with a soldier on patrol would have made that kind of call.

@JMitcherCNN: So it was just you, alone in an alley. No backup.

@CplPetersUSMC: That's right. So then Riot notices this big black car parked in the alley. It was dark as hell in there. All the streetlights were out, so I didn't notice it. But Riot, he's a real tech-head. He has my feed running in infrared, thermal, and laser-gated, each in a separate window. He don't miss much. And he's from Detroit, so he knows his cars. Anyway it was a Lincoln. Most of the cars here are these shitty Soviet models from the '70s. Ain't that the ultimate irony? You can tell the guys on the Most Wanted list 'cause they all drive American cars.

@JMitcherCNN: So you knew someone important was nearby.

@CplPetersUSMC: Well, we suspected. Ghost is looking at the satellite heat maps, pulling up floor plans, checking the locations of windows. I knew I couldn't just storm in there by myself, but Ghost and Riot didn't trust the guys in the war room so they wanted to wait before calling in the cavalry. Those tac-scale yahoos would probably just send the squad in, guns blazing, just for the thrill of it. So Ghost guides me into this bombed-out office building across the street. I hoof it up five stories 'til I'm level with the building opposite. Sure enough, a light is on and I can see into the room. There are six or seven bearded dudes there with AKs slung over their shoulders. It looks like they're arguing and for a while I think they're going to shoot each other and save me the bother, but then another guy comes in. You can tell just by looking at him that he's some sort of head honcho—the owner of the car. I didn't recognize him myself. I ain't no racist, but with those beards they all look kinda the same. Riot, on the other hand, boots up some face recognition software and IDs him, lickety-split, as Jaques al-Adil.

@JMitcherCNN: The Jack of Clubs.

@CplPetersUSMC: Exactly. This guy's a face card. One of the top ten most wanted terrorists in the world, and I'm sitting in a window across the street from him, lined up for a perfect headshot.

@JMitcherCNN: But . . .

@CplPetersUSMC: But, as I mentioned, I didn't have quorum, so I couldn't take the shot. Legally. So, Ghost and Riot jump on their social networks and try to get the word out. Any patriotic American would upvote a shot like that, but we just didn't have enough bodies in the room. Of course all their friends are watching the assault in Peshawar, and not checking their messages. So you know what they do? Ghost goes and wakes up his parents, and Riot fetches his little sister and her boyfriend. Now, Riot's parents are real traditionalists who have never followed a soldier in their lives. Riot's always complaining about them, going on about how they're not upholding their responsibilities as citizens. They're old-timers, see? Got no interest in direct democracy.

@JMitcherCNN: Were they registered to vote?

@CplPetersUSMC: No! That's the thing. I think they were pre-screened through their driver's licenses or whatnot, but they certainly weren't registered for this theater. So I can hear Riot walking them through registration, trying to convince them how important this is, and they're trying to calm him down, and typing their email addresses wrong and having to start again, just like any other old folks. Have to laugh at it all, now.

@JMitcherCNN: I'm guessing it wasn't so funny at the time.

@CplPetersUSMC: It wasn't. But get this: the situation at Ghost's place is even worse. His sister is a hippie. A real peacenik, you know? She doesn't want anything to do with war. So I can hear him talking philosophy to her, trying to convince her to do the right thing for freedom and democracy just this once. And meanwhile I'm waiting with my rifle cocked and Jaques al-Adil's head in the middle of my sights. I've got to admit, Jim, I was sorely tempted to pull the trigger and just live with the consequences. But I thought to myself, if I shoot now I'm no better than he is. I'm here as a representative of my country. If I shoot without a quorum of consenting citizens, as the Rules of Engagement demand, then I'm no longer defending freedom and democracy, I'm just another terrorist.

@JMitcherCNN: Strong words, Corporal.

@CplPetersUSMC: Well, if I didn't believe them, I never would have enlisted.

@JMitcherCNN: So what happened next?

@CplPetersUSMC: Well then I hear gunfire coming from the next street over. I found out later that it was just Samuels and Gonzales showing off for some kids, but Ghost and Riot were too busy to keep me updated at this point, so it scared the hell out of me at the time. And it scared al-Adil and the rest of the folks around that table. They kill the lights and hit the floor. A minute later, I see the front door of the building open and four figures sprint to the Lincoln. One of them is al-Adil and he gets in the back seat. My HUD was still only showing Ghost and Riot online, but just as the car was pulling away three more followers blipped into existence. I had quorum. Now they just needed to upvote engagement. The car was already turning the corner of the street when the votes came through. Five-out-of-five upvotes. Riot had persuaded his sister's boyfriend to log in and vote. I couldn't even see al-Adil by this point, all I could see was the car, but I had seen him climb into the back right-hand seat, so I aimed for where I thought his head would be.

@JMitcherCNN: And the rest is history.

@CplPetersUSMC: And the rest is history. Although it would never have gone so viral if Samuels hadn't been just around the corner. He was the one who saw all the gore. It's his POV feed that's trending. Over 10M now, I think.

@JMitcherCNN: But seeing yours makes the shot all the more astonishing. I encourage all our followers to watch Corporal Peters's POV of the shot. If it had been a second later . . .

@CplPetersUSMC: Ghost and Riot have both made their screen-feeds public too. Be sure to check them out. Couldn't have done it without them.

@JMitcherCNN: So how do you think your job will change now that you have thousands of fans?

@CplPetersUSMC: Well, I certainly won't have trouble making quorum anymore . . . ROFL. On the one hand, it feels great to have the support of so many patriotic citizens behind me. But it'll be harder to have one-on-one chats with my followers. I'll do what I can to keep that personal connection. I've already set up a private channel for Ghost and Riot, so they'll always be able to talk to me directly, no matter how much chatter is going down. How will it change the job? I guess we'll just have to wait and see.

@JMitcherCNN: Just one more question, Corporal, and then I'll let you go. Sergeant Pearson's recent court-marshal has sparked a grassroots campaign to eliminate quorum altogether. Do you wish you had had more leeway? More freedom to act on your own initiative?

@CplPetersUSMC: Well, that's a great question, Jim. A lot of the older guys in the unit complain a lot about the whole direct democracy thing, but I think I like things the way they are. Maybe if I had missed the shot I would feel differently, but it seems to me that getting your folks out of bed to vote and debating philosophy with your sister before letting a soldier take a shot—that's how it should work. That's democracy.

@JMitcherCNN: Well said, Corporal. And thank you for your service.

The Suitcase
by Meron Hadero

On Saba's last day in Addis Ababa, she had just one unchecked to-do left on her long and varied list, which was to explore the neighborhood on her own, even though she'd promised her relatives that she would always take someone with her when she left the house. But she was twenty, a grownup, and wanted to know that on her first-ever trip to this city of her birth, she'd gained at least some degree of independence and assimilation. So it happened that Saba had no one to turn to when she got to the intersection around Meskel Square and realized she had seen only one functioning traffic light in all of Addis Ababa, population four million people by official counts, though no one there seemed to trust official counts, and everyone assumed it was much more crowded, certainly too crowded for just one traffic light. That single, solitary, lonely little traffic light in this mushrooming metropolis was near the old National Theater, not too far from the UN offices, the presidential palace, the former African Union—a known, respected part of the city located an unfortunate mile (a disobliging 1.6 kilometers) away from where Saba stood before a sea of cars, contemplating a difficult crossing.

Small, nimble vehicles, Fiats and VW Bugs, skimmed the periphery of the traffic, then seemed to be flung off centrifugally, almost gleefully, in some random direction. The center was a tangled cluster of cars slowly crawling along paths that might take an automobile backward, forward, sideward. In the middle of this jam was a sometimes visible traffic cop whose tense job seemed to be avoiding getting hit while keeping one hand slightly in the air. He was battered by curses, car horns, diesel exhaust as he nervously shifted his body weight and tried to avoid these assaults. Saba quickly saw she couldn't rely on him to help her get across. She dipped her foot from the curb onto the street, and a car raced by, so she retreated. A man walked up next to her and said in English, "True story, I know a guy who crossed the street halfway and gave up."

Saba looked at the stranger. "Pardon, what was that?"

"He had been abroad for many years and came back expecting too much," the man said, now speaking as slowly as Saba. "That sad man lives on the median at the ring road. I bring him books sometimes," he said slyly, taking one out of his messenger bag and holding it up. "A little local wisdom: don't start what you can't finish." Saba watched the stranger dangle his toes off the curb, lean forward, backward, forward and back, and then, as if becoming one with the flow of the city, lunge into the traffic and disappear from her sight until he reemerged on the opposite sidewalk. "Miraculous," Saba said to herself as he turned, pointed at her, then held up the book again. Saba tried to follow his lead and set her body to the rhythm of the cars, swaying forward and back, but couldn't find the beat.

As she was running through her options, a line of idling taxis became suddenly visible when a city bus turned the corner. She realized that, as impractical as it seemed, she could hail a cab to get her across the busy street. The trip took ten minutes; the fare cost 15 USD, for she was unable to negotiate a better rate, though at least she'd found a way to the other side. She turned back to see the taxi driver leaning out the window talking to a few people, gesturing at her, laughing, and she knew just how badly she'd fumbled yet another attempt to fit in. All month Saba had failed almost every test she'd faced, and though she'd seized one last chance to see if this trip had changed her, had taught her at least a little of how to live in this culture, she'd only ended up proving her relatives right: she wasn't even equipped to go for a walk on her own. What she thought would be a romantic, monumental reunion with her home country had turned out to be a fiasco; she didn't belong here.

She was late getting back to her uncle Fassil's house, where family and friends of family were waiting for her to say goodbye, to chat and eat and see her one last time, departures being even more momentous than arrivals. Twelve chairs had been moved into the cramped living room. Along with the three couches, they transformed the space into a theater packed with guests, each of whom sat with his or her elbows pulled in toward the torso to make space for all. They came, they said, to offer help, but she sensed it was the kind of help that gave—and took.

It was time to go, and she was relieved when Fassil said—in English, for her benefit—"We are running out of time, so we have already started to fill this one for you." He pointed past the suitcase that Saba had packed before her walk and gestured to a second, stuffed with items and emitting the faint scent of a kitchen after mealtime. At her mother's insistence, Saba had brought one suitcase for her own clothes and personal items and a second that for the trip there was full of gifts from America—new and used clothes, old books, magazines, medicine—to give to family she had never met. For her return, it would be full of gifts to bring to America from those same relatives and family friends.

Saba knew this suitcase wasn't just a suitcase. She'd heard there was no DHL here, no UPS. Someone thought there was FedEx, but that was just for extremely wealthy businessmen. People didn't trust the government post. So Saba's suitcase offered coveted prime real estate on a vessel traveling between here and there. Everyone wanted a piece; everyone fought to stake a claim to their own space. If they couldn't secure a little spot in some luggage belonging to a traveling friend, they'd not send their things at all. The only reasonable alternative would be to have the items sent as freight on a cargo ship, and how reasonable was that? The shipping container would sail from Djibouti on the Red Sea (and with all the talk of Somali pirates, this seemed almost as risky as hurling a box into the ocean and waiting for the fickle tides). After the Red Sea, a cargo ship that made it through the Gulf of Aden would go south on the Indian Ocean, around the Cape of Good Hope, across the Atlantic, through the Panama Canal, to the Pacific, up the American coast to Seattle. An empty suitcase opened up a rare direct link between two worlds, so Saba understood why relatives and friends wanted to fill her bag with carefully wrapped food things, gifts, sundry items, making space, taking space, moving and shifting the bulging contents of the bag.

Fassil placed a scale in front of Saba and set to zeroing it. She leaned over the scale as he nudged the dial to the right. The red needle moved ever so slightly, so incredibly slightly that Saba doubted it worked at all, but then Fassil's hand slipped, the needle flew too far, to the other side of zero. He pushed the dial just a hair to the left now, and the red needle swung back by a full millimeter. He nudged the dial again; now it stuck.

"Fassil, Saba has to go," Lula said, shaking her hands like she was flicking them dry. "Let's get going. Her flight leaves in three hours, and with the traffic at Meskel Square and Bole Road . . ."

Saba leaned toward that wobbly needle as Fassil used his finger-nail to gently coax the dial a breath closer. A tap, nearly there. A gentle pull.

"Looks good, Fassil," Saba said kindly but impatiently.

"It has to be precise," Fassil replied, then turned to the gathered crowd. "Look what you're making the poor girl carry." He pointed to that second suitcase.

Saba tried to lift it, but it was as heavy as an ox. Fassil rushed over and helped her pick it up, and when he felt its weight, he said, "There's no way they'll let her take this." The crowd was unhappy to hear that, and so was Saba. The room hummed with disapproval, punctuated with *tsk*s and clicked tongues. "I can just pay the fee," Saba quickly said, but Lula stood again, put up her hands, and boomed, "You will not pay a fee. It's too much money. You are *our* guest, and *our* guest will pay no fee!"

"It's okay," Saba said. "If we must, we must." But now the resistance came from everyone. Saba looked helplessly at Fassil. "Let me pay. I have to go. What else can I do?" she asked. She looked at the others and wondered if this was one of those times when a "No" was supposed to be followed by a "Please, yes!" "No, no." "Really, I insist." "No, we couldn't." "Really, yes, you must." "Okay." "Okay." Was it that kind of conversation? That call and response? Or was it the other kind, the "No, no!" "Really, I insist!" "No, we just couldn't." "Okay, no, then."

"Of course you can't pay. They will never let you," Fassil said, ending Saba's deliberation. He announced, "I'll weigh the suitcase," and there was a general sigh of approval. "But," Fassil continued, "if it's overweight, which it is, we are going to have to make some tough choices." He turned to Saba. "You are going to have to make some tough choices." She nodded and hoped silently that it would come in at weight, please. If she could be granted one earthly wish in this moment, that was what she would wish for. She watched Fassil heave the suitcase onto the scale and winced as the needle that hovered, almost vibrated, above zero shot to the right. Thirty kilos—ten kilos too heavy.

The crowd began to murmur anxiously, and a few shouted out sounds of frustration. Then one by one, the guests began to speak in turns, as if pleading their cases before a judge.

Konjit was the first up. She was old, at least seventy, a verified elder who settled disputes and brokered weddings and divorces, part of that council of respected persons that held a neighborhood together. As Konjit walked toward Saba, Saba bowed a little.

"Norr," Saba said, a sign of respect.

"Bugzer," Konjit replied, acknowledging that the order of things hadn't been completely turned on its head. Konjit lifted the edge of her shawl, flung it around her shoulder, and walked slowly right up to the suitcase and unzipped it. She took out a package of chickpeas and tossed it on the ground, and though someone grumbled at this, Konjit just smoothed her pressed hair behind her ears as if she were calming herself before an important announcement, an orator about to make a speech, an actress set to perform. Konjit held a hand up to the others who sat on the couches and chairs, and waited for total silence. Then she turned to Saba, put her hands on both her hips, which swayed as she stepped closer to Saba, and said in a low voice that filled the small space, "Please, Sabayaye, I haven't seen my grandchildren since they were two years old. How old are you?"

"Twenty," Saba said apologetically.

"Twenty? Ah, in all the time you've been alive in this world I have not seen them. Imagine! I'm old now. Who can even say how old I am? I'm too old to count and getting older. I want to send this bread so they know people here love them."

Most of the others in the room nodded in agreement, but not Rahel. Rahel shook her head as she stood from the couch and walked right up to Konjit, putting a hand on Konjit's arm. "Who can say how old you are, Konjit? Me, I can say how old you are. Not the number of years of course, but I can say for sure that I am older than you. One month, remember."

Rahel brought up that one-month position of seniority often, and Saba had come to expect it. Within just her first week there, Saba learned that Rahel and Konjit had grown up and grown old fighting often about things like which church had the most blessed holy water, Ledeta (Rahel) or Giorgis (Konjit), or whether it was better to use white teff flour (Konjit) or brown teff flour (Rahel), or where you could get the best deals on textiles, Mercato (Konjit) or Sheromeda (Rahel). Without fail, each argument ended with Rahel staking out a win by virtue of being slightly elder.

Rahel bent down and removed one of the three loaves of bread from the suitcase and tried to hand it back to Konjit, who refused to take it. Saba, wanting to hurry things along, reached out for the loaf, but Rahel placed the bread on the floor by her feet. "You can bake a loaf, Konjit, I give you that, but it takes you three hours to make that bread? Eh? I spent two days—two *days*—making this beautiful doro wat for my nephew. The power kept switching off. I had to go to Bole to freeze it in Sintayu's freezer, and she has all those kids and all those in-laws and hardly any space in her house, let alone her freezer, but still, that's what it took to make this beautiful wat. Then I had to wrap the container so tight that, should any melt in transit, it will stay safe and secure—and with these old old old fingers," she said, putting up her index, middle, and ring fingers. "Can you believe it? These old old fingers," she said, now raising her pinky and thumb. "These fingers a month older than yours, Konjit." She pulled Saba over and put her fanned fingers on Saba's left shoulder, leaning on her. "Just take this beautiful wat for me. It will be no problem, right?"

Before Saba could say that this seemed reasonable, Wurro walked up to Saba, and Saba shifted her attention again. "I may not be the oldest, and my hands don't ache like Rahel's, but please, think about this objectively, Saba," said Wurro, whose utilitarian views led her to make obviously questionable decisions, like employing fifteen workers in her small grocery so that fifteen more paychecks went out each month and fifteen more families would be happy, even if it put her one family on the verge of ruin. Wurro never argued her utilitarian views as forcefully, though, as when they matched her own purposes. She cleared her throat, and Saba waited for what she feared would be another well-argued plea. Wurro began, "If you don't send this bread, Konjit, your family will still eat bread. If you don't send this wat, Rahel, your family will still eat wat." Wurro took Saba's hand and said, "My niece had a difficult pregnancy. You have to take this gunfo because if you don't take it, well, there is no way to get gunfo in America, and who has ever heard of a woman not eating gunfo after labor? If you don't bring it, she won't have it. Milk for the baby, gunfo for the mother. It's natural logic. You can't deny it."

"But American women don't eat gunfo. Do they eat gunfo, Saba?" asked Lula.

"She's never been pregnant in America, right? How would she know?" asked Wurro.

"She's never been pregnant here. Does she even know gunfo?" Konjit asked.

Saba said, "I know gunfo," and was met with whispered words of approval, so she refrained from adding how hard she had to swallow to get a spoonful down of the thick paste made from (she'd heard) corn, wheat, barley, or banana root, she wasn't even sure. Whatever gunfo was, she'd rather not bring it, if it was up to her, but she wasn't actually sure of that either. Was it up to her?

"Saba is a smart girl," Lula said. "She probably read *at least* ten books in the four weeks she was here." Saba felt guilty then, because it was true that she had declined as many invitations as she accepted, choosing sometimes to read alone at home. "She must know Americans have high-tech things for women after their pregnancies. They don't need gunfo," Lula said, rearranging the contents of the suitcase to make room for her own package. "But you know what they do need in America? Have you ever tasted American butter?"

Lula looked at the others as if this would end the discussion. She stood up, opened her arms. "Have you had American butter?" No one spoke. Saba kept quiet, for of course she had eaten American butter, but what good would it do to mention that now? Besides, few had the courage to challenge strong-willed Lula, even with the truth.

"No one here has ever had American butter, so then that settles it." Lula took out another of Konjit's loaves of bread and a bag of roasted grains. "*I* have eaten American butter. *I* have tasted it with my own tongue. *I* can say with certainty that American butter is only the milk part, no spices, no flavor. It just tastes like fat. Please bring this butter to my best friend for her wedding banquet," Lula said with her hands now pressed over her heart and looking pleadingly at Saba. "Ahwe, her wedding! And what a feat to get that man to the altar. His gambling and staying out late and—"

"Aye aye aye," Konjit interrupted, shaking her head and removing Lula's butter and putting a second loaf back into the suitcase. "You want her to bring butter so your friend can marry a bad man? Have you ever heard such nonsense?" Konjit asked Saba. Saba shrugged, and Konjit said, "See, she has never heard such nonsense," and Saba didn't have the heart to correct her and didn't have the heart not to correct her, and she didn't know which would have helped her bring this to the right resolution, so she just made a vague gesture and let them finish.

"He is not a bad man, just a *man* man," Lula said.

"Well, my son is a *good* man raising *good* grandchildren. Lula, my son brought you the stretchy pants you asked for from America when he visited. Wurro, my son brought you a laptop last time he came. Rahel, he brought you cereal with raisins, the kind you always ask for. Fassil, he brought you books, since you have long gone through everything at every library here, I assume. Saba, one day if you live in Ethiopia, he will bring you something too, anything you ask. Name something you miss here."

"Too much talk, Konjit!" Rahel yelled. "The traffic, she has to go!"

Konjit swatted away Rahel's interruption and gestured to Saba.

Saba tried to think of what to say. She didn't want to offend them by making them believe she had lacked for anything. She remembered how hurt Konjit had been when Saba visited after lunchtime, only to find a full meal waiting for her. When Saba refused, Konjit insisted that the dishes were very clean and the food fresh. That wasn't as bad, though, as sitting down to eat "just a little" and passing on the salad, the water, the cheese, the fruit, eating only the lentils and bread, accepting some coffee but not even the milk. "You have all been so kind to me," Saba said, bowing respectfully, pronouncing all her syllables perfectly, precisely, as quickly as she could. "I have not missed a thing. But it's late, and it's true, the traffic is bad . . ."

Konjit dismissed Saba. "She has learned the Ethiopian way. Good girl. Too polite to say you need anything here," Konjit replied, putting an arm on Saba's shoulder. Konjit continued, "Okay, don't tell us, that's okay. But if you visit again to stay a while, and if you find you are homesick for something you grew accustomed to there in America, my son will bring it. He is a good son. I am asking you to take two loaves of bread. Okay, forget about the third, I don't want to ask too much of you, even though I am an old lady who has not seen her grandchildren in, oh, who knows how long. But these two loaves must stay in the suitcase, two loaves for my three grandchildren so they know I am thinking about them. That I have not forgotten them." Saba could see that Konjit was too proud to say what she really meant: she didn't want her grandchildren to forget about her, a fear she must bear, living so far away for so many years with only limited lines of connection.

Konjit's argument hung there in the air until Fikru stood hesitantly and walked over to the suitcase, finding his bags of spices on the floor beside it. He reached into the suitcase and took out three Amharic-English dictionaries and tossed them onto the coffee table. Hanna shouted out, "Aye! Why, Fikru, would you do that?" She ran over and picked up the books, then threw them back in, but Konjit took them out, for they crushed her bread.

Fikru, who kept opening his mouth to speak but found himself overpowered by the more forceful voices, seized his opportunity like a fourth-chair orchestral musician stealing a flourish at the end of a number. He stood next to an overwhelmed Saba and said, "Everyone here has a relative in Seattle, yes? Then why is it that only my son is going to pick Saba up from the airport?" He turned to the others. "You talk about what so-and-so needs or has done, but my son, without asking for anything, has volunteered to get her. He will be carrying this heavy suitcase to his car. Then he will take her to her dorm and bring this heavy suitcase up the stairs, if there are stairs, or down the hall, should there be a hall. What can it hurt to bring a few items for him?" Fikru showed Saba his items. "Just a few bags of spices: corrorima, grain of paradise, berbere. Please, Saba, a humble parcel from my humble son."

Saba turned to her uncle Fassil and discreetly pointed to her watch. "Okay, you all have something to say," Fassil offered, cutting off the remaining guests who gathered around the suitcase, eager to make their appeals. "But the traffic!"

"Yes, the traffic," said Fikru.

"The traffic," Rahel and Konjit said in unison, and Lula nodded.

Fassil turned to Saba. She asked him, "What do you want to do?"

"What do *you* want to do?" Fassil asked her. Though each person in that room had his or her body turned to the suitcase, all eyes were on Saba, who was trying to figure out how to navigate this scene. They looked her over and imagined she looked so . . . what? Different? Just . . . apart with her woven bag, which intermittently glowed with the light from her iPhone or beeped and pinged and vibrated from the sound of her other gadgetry, her American jeans tucked into tall leather boots, a white button-down shirt and gold earrings, while they wore modest clothes and hand-me-downs, some of which she had brought herself.

She had been in the country one whole month and had tried, they must know, to learn the culture, to reacquaint herself with her first home and fit in. And now, here she stood, on the last moments of her last day, still not sure what to do, while they looked at her lovingly and with curiosity too. Saba felt the weight of choosing what should be taken and what should be left behind. She was looking for a way out and a way in, but she realized there really were no shortcuts here.

"You have all been so kind," Saba said. "Rahel, you took me to listen to the Azmaris sing," she said, omitting that she had been too shy to dance such unfamiliar dances no matter how encouraging Rahel had been. A few days later, Rahel came back to take her to one of the fancy new hotels where an American cover band played to a foreign crowd, and Saba pretended to like being there. She imagined Rahel had pretended too.

"Wurro, you took me to the holiday dinner, and we ate that delicious raw meat," Saba said, of course not mentioning that Fassil had to take her to the clinic the next day to get Cipro for her stomach cramps.

"Fikru, you brought me to Mercato to buy a dress," Saba said. But what she most remembered was spending the trip chasing after him through the labyrinthine alleyways; every so often, when Fikru looked back at her, she would wave and smile, and he'd keep going, losing her twice.

She remembered the man with the messenger bag that morning, the one who had crossed the street, and his warning about starting things you can't finish or giving up too soon. Saba walked to the suitcase she had packed herself, filled with her own things, and in one quick gesture opened it, emptied the contents. Her best clothes fell to the floor: her favorite old jeans, most sophisticated dresses, her one polished blazer, a new pair of rain boots, T-shirts collected from concerts and trips and old relationships. She pushed this empty suitcase to the center of the room.

"Dear friends, neighbors, and relatives," she said in forced Amharic, looking at the confused expressions that confronted her, "please, now there is room for it all."

There were gasps, whispers, whistles, an inexplicable loud thud, but no laughter.

"Are you sure?" Fikru asked.

"This is the least I can do," Saba said slowly. "It is the least I can do."

"What about your belongings?" Fassil asked.

"We'll keep them safe for her in case she returns," Konjit said, her voice commanding the space.

"*Until* she returns," Rahel corrected.

"Until you return?" Konjit asked, and Saba said yes.

Fassil got a bag, put Saba's things in, and told her he would store it in his own closet. The two suitcases were packed, weighed (the room applauded when both came in just under the limit), and thrown into the trunk of Fassil's car, which sagged a little in the rear. There were three cars in their little caravan that headed to the airport. The ride was slow. The weight of the overfull cars possibly complicated the trip, as did the rocky side streets and, of course, the congestion at the difficult intersections. They pressed on, and they reached the airport with absolutely no time to spare. Saba said quick, heartfelt goodbyes, thank-yous, made fresh promises, then pulled the two big suitcases onto a luggage cart. Her family and friends of family watched from the waiting area as she moved quickly through the line to get her boarding pass. They looked on as the two suitcases were weighed and thrown on the screening belt, and they saw her pass the main checkpoint. Every time she looked back to the lobby, she could catch glimpses of them on tiptoe, waiting to see if they might connect with her one more time.

Border Lines
by Alberto Ríos

A weight carried by two
Weighs only half as much

The world on a map looks like the drawing of a cow
In a butcher's shop, all those lines showing
Where to cut.

That drawing of the cow is also a jigsaw puzzle,
Showing just as much how very well
All the strange parts fit together.

Which way we look at the drawing
Makes all the difference.
We seem to live in a world of maps:

But in truth we live in a world made
Not of paper and ink but of people.
Those lines are our lives. Together,

Let us turn the map until we see clearly:
The border is what joins us,
Not what separates us.

The Flea
by John Donne

Mark but this flea, and mark in this,
How little that which thou deniest me is;
It suck'd me first, and now sucks thee,
And in this flea our two bloods mingled be.
Thou know'st that this cannot be said
A sin, nor shame, nor loss of maidenhead;
   Yet this enjoys before it woo,
    And pamper'd swells with one blood made of two;
   And this, alas! is more than we would do.

O stay, three lives in one flea spare,
Where we almost, yea, more than married are.
This flea is you and I, and this
Our marriage bed, and marriage temple is.
Though parents grudge, and you, we're met,
And cloister'd in these living walls of jet.
   Though use make you apt to kill me,
    Let not to that self-murder added be,
   And sacrilege, three sins in killing three.

Cruel and sudden, hast thou since
Purpled thy nail in blood of innocence?
Wherein could this flea guilty be,
Except in that drop which it suck'd from thee?
Yet thou triumph'st, and say'st that thou
Find'st not thyself, nor me the weaker now.
   'Tis true; then learn how false fears be;
    Just so much honour, when thou yield'st to me,
   Will waste, as this flea's death took life from thee.

"The Flea" by John Donne, 1633.

Inventing New Bodies
by Christine Boyka Kluge

We become small, we become soft. We turn ourselves inside-out, inventing new bodies. Our skins of oiled silk glide over the beaded grass. For a season, even our ribs disappear. Our hearts expand, ripening like cherries.

Night creatures, we hide from the sun's fierce eye. We fear the feet of heedless humans. We tamp each other into acorn caps, escape beneath fallen branches and moss-haired stones. We sleep for a long time, changing.

In the darkness, only our eyes stay hard. Even dreaming, they never close. They glint like diamond chips at the ends of stalks. Our nights grow infinite, blossoming into secret days. Flowers and leaves are our only lanterns. Veins of roses glow like forked lightning. Maple leaves furl and unfurl, beckoning fingers. We are always hungry. The stars call us to dinner.

Trailing silvery paths across brick walks and patios, we slip into gardens and flowerpots. We paint patterns, leaf to leaf. We fasten our mouths to petals and stems and swallow, knowing nothing but sweetness. We are lost, eating your invisible world.

Come dawn, we disappear. We retreat into tunnels, wrap ourselves in shadows. Swollen with night's offerings, we curl into dreams.

You never hear our slithery music, the sound of molten bronze crawling in rivulets through the lawn. You never look down in search of beauty. Humans rarely do. You only see the holes, the lace made of raspberry and geranium leaves. Angered, you leave us saucers of terrible ale. You sprinkle us with salt like stinging snow. A blind giant, you march across our intricate art, never noticing the glittering graffiti that clings to the soles of your shoes.

"Inventing New Bodies" first appeared in *The Bitter Oleander*, then was published in *Stirring the Mirror*, the author's collection from Bitter Oleander Press. Copyright © by Christine Boyka Kluge. Reprinted by permission.

Black Pearl
by Christine Boyka Kluge

I'm sure she stumbled for miles in high school, that loss cutting into her sole like crushed glass in her shoe, until the drowning dulled and death glowed like a black pearl, pain's accretion of dark luster. She held out the pearl of her father's death like a prize, something we might be tempted to snatch, that kept us in a fascinated circle around her tear-stained face. Teenagers, we were hooked by this mystery and sadness, lured by the story of the tipped boat, the hole in the water he had vanished through.

We all leaned forward when she cried, alarmed by her face, puckered red and ugly as a neglected baby's. But we were drawn to that smoky pearl, grief's sharp-edged grit transformed to strange beauty. We all longed to touch its satin and shiver, but none of us wanted to hold the cold sphere within her own fist.

She looked up at us from our cafeteria table, as if she had dived to the dark bottom of the sea with her father, then alone dared to rise. The pearl of his last breath was cupped in her hands like an iridescent bubble of air, lifting her back to the surface, where light was captured in the water's crazed glass. Beyond that shattered pane, she searched for our soft, blurred faces looking down from their great height, from the safe, sunlit ledge she might never climb back to again.

Tinnitus
by Robert Wrigley

—at the library

The loneliness of a rank of six public
pay phones moves me today almost to tears,
and I wonder, dropping in my quarters,
if you will allow this odd nostalgic

impulse toward anachronism
to go through. That is, if you will answer
this morning's call from an unknown number,
or let it, by the cold mechanism

of that which is called caller ID,
be rerouted to what is known as voice mail.
And then, on hearing your unreal voice, if I will,
nevertheless, tell you that it's me.

But no, I hang up, and from the pay phone
on the far right I call the one one slot left,
and from the third, call the next one left,
and from the fifth, call the sixth and final phone,

creating as I do a carillon
of overlapping, almost identical rings,
disturbing the many students studying
in this building, where no one's home.

As I leave, I dial you on my cell phone,
and you answer, asking if I've just called,
saying the number was strange, that you'd called
back but heard only a busy signal's drone.

Ah, love, let us be true to one another
in almost every way, I also do not say.
I'm at the door now, this cold and snowy day,
thinking of the old high ways one lover

once spoke to another, over wires,
when a call could be a complete surprise.
Still you ask, what is that strange bell noise?
And I answer, just the ringing in my ears.

Daniel Bridges

Professor Moffett

English 223

1 May 2017

From Servant to Warrior

In J. K. Rowling's *Harry Potter and the Sorcerer's Stone*, readers are introduced to Harry and are whisked off on an extravagant adventure with him to find out who is trying to steal the highly coveted Sorcerer's Stone. Before he can do that, however, Harry has to flee the abuse, ridicule, and housework that he has become accustomed to while living with his Aunt Petunia, Uncle Vernon, and Cousin Dudley. Harry Potter, without a doubt, starts this book as a Servant to his aunt and uncle, but he ends up occupying the station of Warrior at Hogwarts.

To have a complete understanding of Harry Potter's rise from Servant to Warrior, certain terms must first be explained. The Servant is a member of the Primal Village, which is "a hypothetical reconstruction of humankind's first tribes and the stories that surround the key members of the tribe" (Moffett). The Servant himself may appear in the role of "the housemaid, the field worker, the slave, the prisoner, the child/apprentice, the helpful animal" (Moffett) or some other. The Servant may also be subject to abuse or ridicule from others in the Village

(Moffett). Among the many storylines surrounding the Servant, one is most relevant to Harry's situation: The Flight from the Cruel Master, which occurs when the hero takes "flight to the home of a better master" (Moffett). In the Flight from the Cruel Master storyline, the Servant may have to return to the Cruel Master either permanently or temporarily. The Warrior, on the other hand, is a prominent member of the Village, belonging to the "second of the three major castes . . . that [form] the basis of society" (Moffett). Given his status as the mediator between the castes, the Warrior's two main roles are to defend the Village from outside threats and to purge it from the inside of any corruption (Moffett). The Warrior's story has many important episodes, two being the *Beot*, or boast, a statement of what he intends to do; and the Exploit, often taking the form of a duel with his foe (Moffett).

At the beginning of his story, Harry falls into the role of the Servant. As some Servants often do, Harry faces physical abuse from his extended family. More than once, readers are told of the many times Dudley has attacked Harry. To be more specific, one passage says that "Dudley's favorite punching bag was Harry, but he couldn't often catch him" (Rowling 20). This statement makes it clear that Dudley hit Harry when he could catch him. Unfortunately, this is clear proof that Harry, having lost his loving parents, now lives with people who guiltlessly tormented him.

Harry also faces a large amount of verbal abuse from his aunt and uncle. The most horrendous verbal abuse Harry faces is the threats he receives. Uncle Vernon tells Harry, before they go out to celebrate Dudley's birthday at the zoo, "I'm warning you now, boy-any funny business, anything at all-and you'll be in that cupboard from now until Christmas" (Rowling 24). Treatment like that is completely unfair to Harry. Unbeknownst to him at the time, Harry is a wizard. This means that he accidentally causes weird things to happen when he is mad, scared, or worried. It is unfair that Harry's uncle threatens to put him in the cupboard for months over things he cannot control.

Adding to the abuse, while with his aunt and uncle at Number 4, Privet Drive, Harry lives in subpar conditions. Until his uncle fears they are being watched, Harry sleeps in the cupboard under the stairs. Things are so bad that Harry is described as being used to spiders because the cupboard is full of them (Rowling 19) and as being small and skinny for his age, which probably has "something to do with living in a dark cupboard" (Rowling 20). Harry is also forced to do household chores that would have been annoying to even the most motivated and resilient child. The value of children having chores is well understood, but it is clear that, to his aunt and uncle, Harry

is the only child deemed fit for chores. Harry is described as
being awoken by his Aunt Petunia screeching at him to get up so
he can "look after the bacon" for his cousin's birthday
breakfast (Rowling 19). They also make Harry do menial tasks
like going to get the mail, when anyone could have done it.
Tasks like this make it clear that Harry is seen as a butler,
not as a member of the family.

Harry's invitation to the Hogwarts School of Witchcraft and
Wizardry is how he takes Flight from his Cruel Masters. The
Dursleys, especially his uncle Vernon, do everything they can to
prevent Harry from receiving the letter, ripping the first one
out of his hands, boarding up the mail slot on their front door,
burning or shredding the stacks that manage to make it through,
and finally fleeing the house. It's when Uncle Vernon takes the
family to the tiny, rain-soaked island that Hagrid himself comes
to deliver the letter to Harry and begin the process of telling
him about his heritage. Unfortunately for Harry, he can't stay
at the school; at the end of his first year, he must return to
the Dursleys and begin another round of maltreatment.

While Harry is at Hogwarts, however, his time to act as the
Warrior begins. Initially, Harry becomes responsible for fixing
corruption. During a flying lesson, Neville Longbottom, thrown
off his broom, loses his Rememberall, and Draco Malfoy takes
possession of it with the intent to hide it from him. Harry

draws matters into his own hands and says, "Give that here,
Malfoy" (Rowling 148). Draco represents everything that is wrong
with the wizarding world: the arrogance of the old Pureblood
families, the entitlement of the rich, and the potential for
evil that grows stronger throughout the series as Lord
Voldemort's influence increases. In this particular case with
Neville, Draco proves himself to be a bully, especially in his
treatment of peers who are not as well off as he is, or not of
his type. It is this sort of corruptive attitude that Harry
battles openly for the first time here, and continuously
throughout the series.

Harry's encounter with Draco during the flying lesson also
represents his first major Exploit in the story. He successfully
faces down Draco, who throws the Rememberall in an attempt to
distract Harry from himself. But like the Warriors of old, Harry
adds to his list of Exploits as the story continues: his (and
Ron's, and Hermione's) subduing of the troll, his successful if
unorthodox catch of the snitch during his first Quidditch match,
his frightful adventure with the dead unicorn in the Forbidden
Forest, and finally, his encounter with Quirrell and Lord
Voldemort before the Mirror of Erised. In this last, we see our
best example of the duel between the Warrior and his foe, Harry
and Quirrell completely isolated from everyone else in Hogwarts.
Harry is clearly outclassed by the older and more experienced

wizard, but he survives because of the protection given him by
his mother's final sacrifice, a protection that Voldemort had
not foreseen. With this final success, Harry both rids Hogwarts
of the corruptive influence of Quirrell, and defends wizardkind
from the imminent threat of Lord Voldemort, whose reign of
terror would have begun again had he obtained the Sorcerer's
Stone.

Before saving the stone with Ron and Hermione, Harry also
follows in the Warrior's tradition of issuing a *Beot* or boast.
When the three friends learn that Dumbledore is not present at
Hogwarts to guard the Stone, Harry tells the others, "I'm going
out of here tonight and I'm going to try and get to the Stone
first" (Rowling 270). This is clearly an announcement of his
intent. When Ron and Hermione express their reservations, Harry
doubles down: "I'm never going over to the Dark Side! I'm going
through that trapdoor tonight and nothing you two say is going
to stop me!" (Rowling 270). It's a daring boast, one that he
almost gives his life to make good.

Although Harry's actions as the Warrior are only temporary,
as he is only a student at Hogwarts and he has to return to his
aunt and uncle every year to become the Servant again, *Harry
Potter and the Sorcerer's Stone* is definitely a story that
connects with many kids. There may have been kids who, like
Harry, have found themselves stuck with an evil and oppressive

family. What power and hope it must have given them to read a
story about a boy who left his prison and became a famous
wizard. They connected to this story and ended up making it the
highest selling book series of all time.

Works Cited

Moffett, Todd. "The Primal Village." English 223: Themes of

Literature. College of Southern Nevada, 29 Feb. 2017, CSN

North Las Vegas Campus H202, North Las Vegas. Lecture.

Rowling, J. K. *Harry Potter and the Sorcerer's Stone.* Scholastic

Books, 1998.

Discussion Questions for Chapter Seven

For Edgar Allan Poe

1. What is the setting for "The Cask of Amontillado"? How is the setting appropriate to the events narrated in this story?
2. What is the inducer in "The Cask of Amontillado"? Does it knock the protagonist's life out of its usual path, or is his universe already off track when the story begins?
3. There is strong evidence of a loop plot underneath "The Cask of Amontillado." What is this evidence? Explain.

For Kate Chopin

1. At what level would you place the conflict faced by Mrs. Mallard: internal, personal, or extrapersonal? Why?
2. Why does Chopin tell the story from a third-person and not a first-person point of view? What are the benefits and the drawbacks of this choice?
3. Chopin uses very little dialogue in the story. Why do you think so little would be used? Do you agree with this decision? If yes, why? If you think the story would benefit from more dialogue, explain why and where dialogue is needed.

For Julian Mortimer Smith

1. "Headshot" is told in an unconventional fashion: without the usual techniques of narration, description, dialogue, and so on. What exactly is the form of this story? What point of view is it told through? How would the story have changed if Corporal Peters had simply narrated the assassination of the Jack of Clubs while he was on patrol?
2. "Headshot" is a story told about an incident that occurred during a war. What is the setting of that war? How are troops engaged in that war? How are the rules of engagement different from those used by the current US military?

3. In "Headshot," what goals does Corporal Peters have? What are his motivations?

For Meron Hadero

1. Even though Saba is visiting Ethiopia, the country of her birth, there are multiple moments in the story when she feels like an outsider. Name five of these moments. How are the moments complicated by her family members' reactions, customs, and treatment of her?

2. During Saba's family's debate about what she should take home with her to Seattle in her second suitcase, Saba appears helpless to mediate the conversation. Have you ever felt like Saba where you have been placed in a situation where your actions were complicated or exploited because of the motives of others? How did you resolve your situation? Be specific.

3. At the opening of the story, Saba meets a stranger who offers her a piece of "wisdom" about crossing the busy intersection in Meskel Square; he tells her in English, "Don't start what you can't finish." How do his words affect the choice she makes at the end of the story? Do you view his words as wise for Saba? Explain.

4. The story contains allusions to ancient mythic conceptions of the journey the soul makes to the land of the dead. What are those conceptions? How do they appear in Hadero's story? How are they relevant to Saba's own journey?

For Alberto Ríos

1. In "Border Lines," what simile opens the poem? How does it set the mood for the rest of the poem?

2. Is Ríos's poem a narrative or a lyric? If the former, what story does it tell? If the latter, what is the central image that shapes the rest of the poem?

3. The first four stanzas of "Border Lines" seem to make assertions: descriptions, observations, or statements. The last stanza,

however, seems to have a different purpose. What is it? And how is that purpose signaled?

For John Donne

1. In "The Flea," whom is the speaker addressing? What is his purpose for speaking to this audience? Why does he not allow the audience to speak directly?
2. The central image of Donne's poem is a flea. What symbolism surrounds this image? How does this symbolism fit with the speaker's purpose?
3. "The Flea" is an example of a closed-form poem. What makes it so? Look specifically at the line and stanza lengths, the syllable patterns, and the rhyme scheme.

For Christine Boyka Kluge

1. In "Inventing New Bodies," whose bodies are being invented? What details in the poem give clues to their identity?
2. "Inventing New Bodies" is strongly lyrical, but there is also a conflict at the heart of it. What kind of conflict: internal, personal, or extrapersonal? What makes up this conflict?
3. "Inventing New Bodies" relies on a number of figures of speech. Which can you find in the poem? Another figure not mentioned above, *personification*, also appears. What is personification, and how is it used in the poem?
4. Kluge's poem "Black Pearl" and Violet E. Baldwin's essay "Drowning," which appears earlier in this book, speak of a similar event, but with decidedly different outcomes. What happens in the poem that is different from what happens in the essay?
5. Who is the speaker in "Black Pearl"? What do we gain from hearing this speaker that we would not if the poem had been told through the perspective of the unfortunate girl?
6. What is the "ledge" mentioned in the last lines of "Black Pearl"? Why can't the unfortunate girl climb to it?

For Robert Wrigley

1. Wrigley's poem "Tinnitus" speaks to differences between old and new forms of technology. To what technologies does he make reference? Why are they important to the poem?
2. Is Wrigley's poem open-form or closed-form? How can you tell?
3. Wrigley's speaker, like that of Donne's "The Flea," is addressing someone outside the poem. To whom is he speaking? What is his purpose for speaking to this person? How is this purpose different from that of the speaker in Donne's poem?

For Daniel Bridges

1. In "From Servant to Warrior," Bridges follows the model for the literature essay given above. Who is the author, and what is the title, of the work to which he is responding? What is the premise of that work? What is Bridges's thesis? Write them out word for word as done in the examples for Shakespeare and Chopin above.
2. In his second paragraph, Bridges defines some key terms he uses later in the essay. What are those terms? Why did he define them here before going on to his analysis?
3. Look closely at Bridges's third paragraph. What is the topic sentence? What is (are) his narrow down(s)? What is (are) his quotation(s)? What is (are) his explanation(s)? What is his conclusion? Write them out word for word as done in the examples for Shakespeare and Chopin above.

Glossary of Important Terms

Abstract—The opposite of *concrete*. The word can be nearly the equivalent of *general*, but for clarity it is useful to distinguish an abstraction from a general word. An abstract word refers to a *quality* of something else—a quality that cannot exist alone, but only in connection with something else. The word *horse* is rather general, but it is concrete. A horse's *strength*, on the other hand, is abstract. It is an entirely different thing from the strength of an oak tree, or the strength of a smell, or the strength of a conviction. In the last case, we have an abstract word modifying another abstract word. Nearly any word ending in *-ism*, *-ness*, *-tion*, *-ment*, or *-ity* is abstract. A helpful way to think of an abstract word is to consider it an adjective (such as *strong*, *polite*, or *courageous*) that has been converted by an act of the intellect into a noun (such as *strength*, *politeness*, or *courage*). In general, beware of using too many abstract words in your writing unless you provide plenty of concrete support.

Anaphora—Anaphora is the repetition of a word or words at the beginning of sequenced word groups: "We are young, we are strong, and we are ready to take over the world."

Anecdote—An anecdote is a brief story or narrative that we incorporate into an essay to support a general statement. For instance, to illustrate the need to know how to fix a flat tire, we might tell the anecdote of a friend who waited many hours in the desert for someone to come along and fix her flat tire.

Antithesis—Antithesis sets ideas of contrasting or opposing value in a parallel structure: "She was kind yet vicious, honorable yet cruel, loving yet deadly." Often the antithesis is signaled by words such as *yet*, *but*, or *though*.

Argumentation—Argumentation is the fourth mode of the essay, along with description, narration, and exposition. In an argumentative essay, the writer seeks to convince readers to accept his position in a debatable issue by using reasons and proofs. Two common forms of argumentative strategies are *induction* and *deduction*. Often argumentative essays require a body of proofs that comes from research of outside sources.

Audience—The term refers to the people or to the person to whom you address your essay. Your audience may influence the selection and arrangement of details in your essay. For instance, say that you are writing an essay on the disintegration of the traditional family unit. Writing to a group of fundamentalist Christians, you might cite many Biblical passages with which they may be familiar. If, on the other hand, you were addressing this essay to a group of sociologists, you might use case studies and facts and statistics that would not be so interesting to the church group.

Body—The body is generally in the middle of the essay, between the introduction and the conclusion. It is here, in the narrative essay, that we develop the action and conflicts leading to the climax. In a description essay, we build up sensory details. In an expository essay, we use one or more of the development patterns studied in this book—for example, comparison and contrast, process, definition—to support the thesis. In an argumentative essay, we use the body to furnish proof supporting the essay's central proposition or claim. The body should also be organized according to one of the several plans set forth in the organization chapter.

Character—A character is an actor in a story that has a distinct personality and influences the outcome of the plot. A *major character* has much influence, and a *minor character* has little or no influence. All characters, major or minor, are products of the writer's imagination.

Cliché—A cliché is a once-clever expression now ineffective because of overuse. Examples of these trite expressions include "chills running up and down my spine," "sharp as a tack," "neat as a pin," "nipped in the bud," "old as the hills," "the grass is always greener on the other side of the fence," and so on. Avoid using them.

Closed Form—Closed-form poetry strictly adheres to a pattern of rhyme, syllable count, word or line repetition, or stanza length.

Coherence—Coherence is one of the qualities that instructors look for in essays. An essay is coherent when, sentence by sentence and paragraph by paragraph, it clearly follows a logical chain of development and organization originating with the issue. When that issue governs the topic sentences of individual paragraphs, and those topic sentences in turn govern each individual sentence within the paragraph, the essay will be unified by a single controlling idea. To write a coherent essay, use transitions and make sure your topic sentences relate to your thesis. See also **Unity**.

Cohesion—Cohesion is a quality that governs the flow of a sequence of sentences. In the sequence, each sentence should open with information learned in a previous sentence and end with information that is new or unknown to the reader. This information, however, must relate to the essay's issue, or the essay will lack coherence. Consider the following passage: "I like doughnuts. The best doughnuts in town are sold at Connie's Bakery. Connie's Bakery stands on the corner of Main Street and First Avenue. First Avenue was torn up in the recent downtown development. The development took a long time." The sentences are cohesive because each opens with information learned in a previous sentence, but they are incoherent because they do not focus on the issue raised in the first (topic) sentence: the speaker's fondness for doughnuts. In contrast, consider this passage: "I like doughnuts. My favorite doughnut is a glazed because I enjoy the taste of the sweet melted sugar surrounding the springy interior. Another doughnut I like is the chocolate cake because the sweetness of the chocolate offsets the slightly heavy texture of the cake." In this passage, the writer has remained focused on the issue.

Conclusion—The final part of an essay, the conclusion may consist of one or more paragraphs in which, in the case of description, the writer may summarize the dominant impression he has been trying to convey through the use of concrete images; in which, in the case of narration, he brings the story to a close; and in which, in the case of exposition, argumentation, or literary analysis, he summarizes or restates the thesis, calls the reader to take action, takes a broader view of the topic, or offers a personal judgment on the topic. However, in writing your concluding paragraph, never introduce a new idea, an idea that has not been developed and supported in the essay's body.

Concrete—The term *concrete* refers to those descriptive words and details that appeal to the five senses: sight, sound, taste, touch, and smell. We could, for example, take the abstract description of a horse's strength and make it more concrete as follows: "Thor, the strongest draft horse in our stable, has pulled our Dodge 1500 pickup out of a mudhole." Effective writing employs concrete language.

Connotation—As opposed to the denotation, or dictionary meaning of a word, connotation refers to the nondictionary, associative meaning of a word. For instance, the term *red* denotes a color but may suggest or connote anger; the term *doubloon*, while denoting a Spanish gold coin, may conjure images of pirates, the high seas, and adventure.

Deduction—See **Syllogism.**

Denotation—As opposed to connotation, denotation refers to the dictionary meaning of a word. Thus, the term *doubloon*, according to the *Random House Dictionary*, denotes "a former gold coin of Spain and South America."

Description—The descriptive essay is the first of the four essay modes. In a description, the writer selects and arranges concrete details to convey an impression (or impressions) of the subject described. Description is also a pattern of development important to all writing: personal, academic, creative, vocational, or professional.

Development—Also known as detail, complexity, diversity, or density, development must be present for an essay to say something significant. It consists of facts, examples, descriptive passages—anything that allows the reader to share something of the writer's experience of an idea, not merely the bare idea stated abstractly. A writer cannot validate a thesis without proper development.

Diction—Diction refers to your choice of words when writing. Your word choice, in turn, will depend on your issue and your audience. Generally speaking, diction can be either formal or informal. See also **Style**.

Ellipsis—Ellipsis drops unneeded words in parallel structures so that sentences are more compact: "I went to the store; she, to the bank." The ellipsis dots (. . .) are frequently used in academic writing to indicate where words have been dropped from the original of a quoted source.

Epistrophe—Epistrophe is the repetition of a word or words at the end of consecutive word groups: "I scream, you scream, we all scream for ice cream."

Essay—If you learn nothing else from this text, you should learn what an essay is. Ways of organizing our impressions, thoughts, and experiences, essays may be broken into four modes: *description, narration, exposition,* and *argumentation* (count the literature essay as exposition). Regardless of the essay type, we must make sure that our essay has an introduction, a body, and a conclusion, all held together by a single dominant impression, in the case of description; a plot, in the case of narration; a central idea, in the case of exposition; or a central proposition, in the case of argumentation.

Ethos—*Ethos* is a term, based on Aristotle, for a method of persuasion relying on the character of the person making the argument.

For example, if the person presenting a case about the dangers of pesticides on cattle is a veterinarian with several years' experience in industrial agriculture, then her credentials will add weight to the argument; the audience is more likely to believe the validity of the argument based on the speaker's expertise and authority in the field. For this reason, when you introduce outside materials into your own essays, you should establish the credentials of your source. If for no other reason, an audience may base their judgment of the speaker's character simply on her appearance or on how she presents herself (how she dresses, what she looks like, etc.). Thus, even an inexperienced speaker may by these means establish the respect and trust of her audience.

Evidence—Evidence refers to the proof that supports your central claim, accusation, or proposition. Listerine, for instance, could cite no evidence to support its claim that its products helped cure dandruff. Similarly, before we find a man guilty of a crime, we must find proof or evidence—fingerprints, DNA tests, and eye-witnesses, among other forms—that indicate his guilt. In composition, evidence such as facts, statistics, quotes, and examples will be presented through the essay's development and support.

Exposition—The third mode of essay writing, the exposition, or expository essay, is intended to explain or inform. To do so, we may make use of one of the expository techniques covered in this text: example, comparison and contrast, process, cause and effect, and so on.

Figures of Speech—A departure from the literal meanings of words, figures of speech are used to convey even more vivid images or impressions of the topic about which we are writing. One kind of figure of speech, a *metaphor*, is a direct comparison between two objects not in the same category and states that one object is another. "The moon was a ghostly galleon" is a familiar metaphor in which the poet Alfred Noyes equates the moon with a ship. Two metaphors from Proverbs include "The mouth of the righteous is a fountain of life" and "Pleasant words are a honeycomb, / Sweet to the soul and healing to the bosom." A *simile* is another figure of speech comparing two objects not in the same category but making use of such terms as *like, as,* and *so.* Thus, "Bill was so skinny he looked like a snake that had frozen" is a simile comparing Bill with a frozen snake. Other similes include "All of our righteous acts are as filthy rags" and "Reckless words pierce like a sword." A third figure of speech worth noting is *personification,* the attributing of human qualities to nonhuman objects. The sentence "The trees marched up the hill in a straight line" is an example of personification because trees cannot literally march. Another example of personification is "Wisdom has built her house. / She has hewn her seven pillars"; on a literal level, wisdom cannot build or hew—these are human activities. Two more figures of speech are *synecdoche* and *metonymy,* both of which rely on substitution. Synecdoche means a part substitutes for the whole, or a whole for the part: "All hands on deck!" substitutes *hands* (part) for *sailors* (whole); "I bought a new set of wheels" substitutes *wheels* (part) for *car* (whole); "Los Angeles won the World Series" substitutes *Los Angeles* (the entire city) for the *Angels* or *Dodgers* (the baseball team). Metonymy means substituting a term closely associated with another: "The White House issued a statement" substitutes *White House* (residence) for *president* (resident; person making statement); "The fish rose from the deep" substitutes *deep* (attribute) for *ocean* (object with depth; home of fish); "All reports go to the corner office" substitutes *corner office* (workspace of important worker) for *boss* (important worker). Other, lesser-known figures of speech are defined elsewhere in this glossary.

Function Shift—Function shift (*anthimeria*) lets poets turn nouns into verbs, or verbs into adjectives, and so on, to create colorful descriptions that arrest the eyes: "Her family summers in the mountains and winters in Florida"; "This drink will hair your chin"; "The kids arted the walls with several drawings."

General—Referring to many individuals or individual objects, opposite of specific. Generality is a relative matter; a word that is general in one context may be specific in another. For example, the word *dog* is general in relation to *Weimaraner* but specific in relation to *mammal*. General statements in essays have the same effect on the reader as abstractions; without specific, concrete reference points, they sound vague. Thus, the statement, "I am proud of my car" is quite general and vague. The following, though still general, is more specific: "I am proud of my Toyota." And this statement is the most specific, and thus least general, of all: "I am proud of my 2018 Toyota Camry."

Illustration—Illustration is simply another word for example.

Image—A word or series of words appealing to the senses, an image is made of concrete detail and, at times, figures of speech. The following description from John Steinbeck's *Of Mice and Men* is filled with concrete images (italics added): "A few miles south of Soledad, the Salinas River drops in close to the *hillside bank* and runs *deep and green*. The *water is warm* too, for it has *slipped twinkling* over the *yellow sands* in the sunlight before reaching the *narrow pool*."

Induction—Induction is the process of arriving at a general conclusion/proposition on the basis of specific proof or evidence. If, for instance, after sampling twelve green apples and finding them sour we reach the conclusion that all green apples are sour, we would be using induction.

Introduction—The opening part of an essay, consisting of one or more paragraphs. In a descriptive essay, the introduction puts forward the subject to be described and establishes mood. In a narration, the introduction generally captures the reader's interest, sets out the main character(s), establishes point of view, and sometimes creates mood or tone. In expository and argumentative writing, the introduction captures reader interest, presents the topic, establishes tone, and generally but not always states the thesis. In a literary analysis, the introduction names the author and title of the work to which the writer is responding, states the work's premise, focuses on a literary element, and offers a thesis that explains how the element functions in the work. A boring introduction diminishes reader interest. It is often wise to write your introductory paragraph last, with a complete knowledge of the essay's contents.

Irony—Irony is a device often used for humorous or surprise effect. We may be acquainted with *verbal irony*, which can verge on sarcasm, when we say one thing but mean quite the opposite. If we say, "Boy, I really enjoyed that class" and mean just the opposite, we have employed verbal irony. Often we have seen *situational irony* at work. An ironic situation is one in which appearance and reality, expectation and fulfillment are at odds. Thus, in a murder mystery, all surface clues may point to the butler as the murderer; this is appearance, and we expect the butler to be found guilty. Irony enters in when it is revealed that the maid is, in reality, the guilty one. *Dramatic irony* means that the audience knows information that the characters do not: a wife disparages her husband to a friend on the phone when the audience sees the husband overhearing the conversation. *Cosmic irony* occurs when the universe seems to work against everything a character does: it rains every day that a woman plans a picnic for her family.

Issue—Issue denotes a narrowed-down topic, one that meets the subject matter and length requirements of an essay. To arrive at an issue, the writer must use multiple methods of prewriting and invention. For example, if your instructor asks you to write an essay on controversial legal decisions, you will need to spend a considerable amount of time brainstorming, clustering, free writing, and researching before you arrive at a workable issue. In this instance, you may have moved from controversial legal decisions to the not-guilty verdict for George Zimmerman in the Trayvon Martin murder trial. The relationship between writer, issue, audience, and purpose is essential to the development of a suitable thesis for an essay.

Kairos—*Kairos* is a form of persuasion based on opportunity. The speaker tries to persuade his audience that the present moment is the best for a particular course of action. The famous poetic idiom *carpe diem* ("seize the day") is based on this appeal.

Known-New Contract—This contract is a universal pattern of sentence construction that places information already known to the audience in the subject slot and new information in the predicate. Following this pattern creates cohesion among a group of sentences.

Litotes—Litotes is the use of understatement, again usually for emphasis or humor: "Her new yacht cost only three million dollars"; "She is the president of no small company"; "He feels not unlike a fool." Litotes can be signaled, as in the examples above, by the deliberate use of negatives (*no, not un-*) or an ironic use of qualifiers such as *only* or *just*.

Logical Fallacies—Logical fallacies are errors in reasoning and may most often appear in our argumentative essays. Below is a list of some of the most frequently occurring fallacies.

1. *False Analogy*—consists of comparing two things which, though seemingly alike, are really very different (e.g., We have pure food and drug laws, so why can't we have laws to keep moviemakers from giving us filth?).

2. *Argument in a Circle*—consists of offering a restatement of the main assertion as a reason for accepting that assertion (e.g., "There is only one argument that can be made to one who rejects the authority of the Bible, namely that the Bible is true." —William Jennings Bryan).

3. *Presumed Cause and Effect*, or *Post Hoc ergo Propter Hoc*—consists of citing two events and insisting that because one happened first, one caused the other (e.g., Young people joined the Bernie Sanders campaign because they were brought up in permissive households).

4. *Non Sequitur*—consists of asserting that one fact has led or must inevitably lead to a particular consequence; literally means "It does not follow" (e.g., If gay marriage becomes law, then more straight people will lose health benefits at work).

5. *Begging the Question*—consists of the writer's assuming to be true what it is his responsibility to prove, of building his

argument upon an undemonstrated claim (e.g., The stance that the president's socialist healthcare plan will cost the nation billions of dollars builds on the unproved claim that the plan is indeed socialistic).

6. *Argumentum ad Hominem*—consists of attacking the opposition rather than addressing the issue at hand (e.g., A critic attacks Tea Party members for being insensitive to the poor rather than examining their stance on reducing government spending).

7. *Argument by Extension* or *Red Herring*—consists of extending the issue in question, or adding distractions, until one is arguing a different subject altogether (e.g., Commissioner Sue Jones can't be convicted of embezzlement because the district attorney who is prosecuting her is a wife-beater and hates all women; he is therefore unqualified to handle this case).

8. *Either-Or*, or *False Dilemma*—consists of distorting the issue by insisting that only two alternatives exist (e.g., The abortion issue boils down to a simple choice between the American family and murder).

9. *Hasty Generalization*—consists of making a general assumption without considering enough facts (e.g., All Vroom-Vroom cars are worthless junk because one Vroom-Vroom car blew a tire).

10. *Argumentum ad Populum*, or *Argument by Consensus*—rests on the assumption that a statement is true because a majority of people believe it (e.g., We should watch *The Best TV Show Ever!* because it is the most popular show on television).

11. *Straw Man*—attributes a position or trait to a person that he or she does not actually hold (e.g., A newspaper accuses John Smith of sympathizing with terrorists when he has never taken such a position).

12. *Slippery Slope* or *"The Next Thing You Know . . ."* *Fallacy*—asserts than an action, usually harmless in itself, will invariably lead to other actions that will end in a dangerous consequence (e.g., If we allow sports betting in Calbrasia, then people will

spend more of their income on betting, which will lead to bankruptcies, and the next thing you know, the entire state of Calbrasia will fall into ruin).

13. *Tu Quoque* or *Whataboutism*—consists of deflecting an accusation by pointing out a similar or worse offense committed by one's accuser (e.g., You accuse me of cheating on my taxes, but what about how you skimmed money from the Hoying account?).

Logos—*Logos* is a term, based on Aristotle, for a method of persuasion based on an appeal to reason. The most basic forms of appeal are those of induction or deduction. This appeal also works when the writer can back up her assertions with statistics, research data, or other hard facts that are relevant to the subject matter at hand. For example, if the writer establishes a link between traffic fatalities and cellphone use while driving by finding supporting statistics from the National Transportation Safety Board, then she has a valid reason to assert a cause-and-effect relationship between the two. By using *logos*, the writer also burnishes her own standing with an audience by appearing knowledgeable about the issue under discussion.

Lyric Poetry—Poetry that centers on an image or series of images is called lyric poetry.

Metaphor—See **Figures of Speech**.

Monroe's Motivated Sequence—Developed by Alan H. Monroe at Purdue University in the 1930s, this sequence is a plan by which a speaker may alert the audience to a need, identify a solution to that need, and then convince the audience to adopt the solution. The sequence is both a process and an organizational blueprint and is a common strategy used in advertising. The first step of the sequence is *Attention*: your introduction should not only establish the thesis triangle but also grab the attention of your audience. The strategies of *pathos*—humor, a vivid story, an unusual or shocking fact—work best here. (In a commercial, an appealing or eye-catching image is often presented.) The second step is *Need*: you must alert your audience to a problem that needs their attention. The strategies of *logos*—statistics, data from credible sources—will work best to establish that this problem actually exists and that it truly affects the audience. (In a commercial, the actor is often stuck in some desperate, humorous, or humiliating situation.) The third step is *Satisfaction*: you must set out the solution to the problem. Again, the strategies of *logos*—credible testimony, solutions researched from authoritative sources, rebuttal of counterarguments—will work best here. (In a commercial, this is the step that introduces the product being sold.) The fourth step is *Visualization*: you must make the audience see either how the future will be worse if they do not take action (or do not buy the product), or how the future will be better if they adopt your solution (or buy the product). Emotional appeals to the audience's fears or optimism may work best here. The final step is *Actuation*: you must present a reasonable course of action that your audience can immediately take to enact your solution. (In a commercial, this is the step that tells the audience how and where to buy the product.) This sequence is persuasive in purpose and works best if the writer clearly presents the problem, offers a simple solution, and presents an easy method for adopting the solution.

Mood—An atmosphere created by a written work that evokes an emotion in the reader. Mood is usually created by a combination of setting and tone. See also **Tone**.

Mythos—*Mythos* is a form of persuasion based on a cultural or national tradition the speaker shares with her audience. If, for example, a speaker tries to persuade an audience to support legislation based on a common belief in "government of the people, by the people, for the people" (an allusion to Abraham Lincoln's famous Gettysburg Address), then she is appealing to a shared sense of patriotism. (Lincoln's own speech includes an allusion to Thomas Jefferson's Declaration of Independence—"the proposition that all men are created equal"—and thus also makes an appeal to *mythos*.)

Narration—(1) One of the modes of the essay, narration tells a story. However, narration may also be used to develop description, exposition, or argumentation. (2) In storytelling and literary analysis, narration is related to point of view. Asking what type of narration is used in a story is roughly equivalent to asking what point of view is used. Narration may include, therefore, raw exposition from the narrator—his or her perceptions of or commentary on events and characters and setting—or may simply record the action of the story, much like a camera, without any narratorial intrusions.

Narrative—A story told by a narrator, typically shaped to a plot and colored by the narrator's persona. The narrative can take many forms: a movie, a novel, a short story, an essay, a poem, a fable, and so on.

Narrative Poetry—Poetry that tells a story is called narrative poetry.

Narrator—A special persona adopted by an author or writer to be the voice of a story.

Open Form—Opposed to closed-form poems, open-form poetry does not strictly adhere to any patterns. Also known as *free verse*.

Paradox—Paradox is a statement containing a contradiction that is nevertheless true: "The deeper you go, the higher you fly / The higher you fly, the deeper you go" (The Beatles).

Paragraph—A series of sentences that form a unit within a larger prose work. Each new paragraph is set off by an indentation of the first line. In an essay, certain paragraphs perform specific functions: an introductory paragraph (or paragraphs) should capture reader attention, present the topic, establish tone, and state the thesis; body paragraphs should support the thesis, each paragraph containing a topic sentence supported by details; and a conclusion, made of one or more paragraphs, should summarize the main ideas of the body, state or restate the thesis, take a broader view of the topic, issue a call to action, or offer the writer's judgment of the issue at hand. The number of paragraphs in an essay is dictated by the scope of the thesis. A narrow thesis should limit the essay to fewer paragraphs, whereas a broad thesis will demand several paragraphs of development.

Parallelism—Parallelism is a stylistic device by which ideas of equal importance are expressed in similar grammatical form. The most famous example of parallel sentences may be Julius Caesar's statement, "I came, I saw, I conquered." The sentences are exactly parallel—or similar—in structure. Eighteenth-century English literary giant Samuel Johnson offers us some of the best examples of parallelism in the language: "We are all prompted by the same motives, all deceived by the same fallacies, all animated by hope, obstructed by danger, entangled by desire, and seduced by pleasure" (taken from *Rambler* essay #60).

Pathos—*Pathos* is a term, based on Aristotle, for a method of persuasion based on an appeal to emotion. The speaker has several methods of making such an appeal: vivid or engaging storytelling, striking figures of speech, and humor are three common devices. A speaker may try to elicit an audience's sense of optimism, or fear, or any emotion in between in order to establish an emotional connection between himself and his listeners. One goal of such an appeal is to make the audience believe that the speaker shares their views and their feelings. The *pathos* appeal, because of its power, should never be used to distract the audience from the real issues or to drive them into a rage or a panic.

Person—The term *person* refers to the pronoun case in which an essay is written. The author of the essay or narrative written in the first person will make frequent use of the pronouns *I, we, me, my, us, our.* An author who writes an essay or story in third person makes use of the pronouns *he, she, him, her, they, them,* and so on. Person is the basis of point of view in fiction and other narrative forms. See also **Point of View**.

Persona—Literally, a mask. Used now to mean an assumed personality separate from the personality of the writer. A persona is commonly used to produce an ironic effect. Horace Miner adopts the persona of an anthropologist from a superior civilization in his spoof of Americans and of his own profession in "Body Ritual among the Nacirema." Jonathan Swift pretends to be a man who approves of cannibalism in "A Modest Proposal," probably the most famous use of a persona in all English literature.

Personification—See **Figures of Speech**.

Plot—The structure of events in a story, a plot begins with an *inducer*, which brings conflict to the life of the story's *protagonist*, and ends when the protagonist somehow resolves that conflict. Following the Aristotelian model, the plot saves its most exciting or tension-building event for late in the story, usually the moment when the protagonist is closest to achieving or losing his goal.

Point of View—The perspective through which a story is told, point of view describes the narrator's distance from the story and the pronouns used to label the characters. Point of view is categorized as either *first person*, *second person*, or *third person*. See also **Person**.

Premise—(1) A premise is the basic assumption upon which a line of reasoning—or an entire argument for that matter—is based. One of the central premises of The Declaration of Independence, for instance, is that all men are created equal and entitled to life, liberty, and the pursuit of happiness. (2) A premise may also be the central conflict that drives a narrative's plot. The premise of the movie *Star Wars: A New Hope*, for example, is that a team of rebels is trying to destroy the Empire's Death Star before the Empire can use it to crush the rebellion.

Proposition—A proposition is the central claim—or thesis, if you will—around which an argument is based.

Protagonist—The main character in a story.

Purpose—Every piece of writing has a purpose—an intended outcome. Essays are typically written to achieve at least one of four outcomes: to teach, to inform, to entertain, or to persuade.

The essay's purpose is tied to the writer's relationship with her target audience and chosen issue.

Rhetorical Question—A rhetorical question is one that is invented to provoke thought but not to be answered. In our speech and writing, we make use of rhetorical questions such as the following: "Who wouldn't be proud of such a son?" or "How many pedestrian fatalities will be enough for us to revisit crosswalk and traffic laws?"

The Rule of Three—The Rule of Three, or *trebling*, is the deliberate use of three elements to give shape to a sentence, a passage, or an entire work of art. There are three types: (1) the *uniform three*, in which all things have similar value, as when Jonah is trapped in the belly of the whale for three days; (2) the *accumulative three*, in which each of the three things is increasingly better (or worse), and in which the sequence leads to a climax, as when Ebenezer Scrooge is visited by three increasingly scary Christmas ghosts; (3) the *contrasting* or *opposite three*, in which the last element overturns or counters the first two, as when the three stepsisters in Cinderella try on the slipper, or when Goldilocks encounters the chairs, the bowls of porridge, and the beds in the house of the Three Bears. In stories, when the Rule of Three appears (as in the Cinderella story), it often signifies that the hero is about to undergo a transformation.

Satire—Satire is a form of writing that pokes fun at people, institutions, and ideas. Horace Miner in "Body Ritual among the Nacirema" satirizes both the American obsession with hygiene and the scientific method of anthropological studies.

Setting—The setting of a story (or of a narrative essay) is the time and place in which the characters (including the narrator) act. The setting is not only a backdrop but also the boundary imposed on the characters: they cannot act in a way not suitable to the setting.

Simile—See **Figures of Speech**.

Speaker—(1) Like the narrator in fiction, the speaker is a persona, in this case adopted by a poet to be the voice of a poem. (2) The speaker is also someone who gives a speech, elegy, oration, or other form of live, public, oral address.

Stanza—A group of lines in a poem comparable to a paragraph in prose.

Story—A story is a sequence of events, usually shaped by a plot and told by a narrator.

Style—A style is the particular manner in which one writes. John Donne's style, for instance, is marked by archaic (to us) vocabulary and complex sentence structure:

Mark but this flea, and mark in this,
How little that which thou deniest me is. . . .

Alberto Ríos's style, on the other hand, is much more familiar:

The world on a map looks like the drawing of a cow
In a butcher's shop, all those lines showing
Where to cut.

Syllogism—The basic unit of logic used in deductive reasoning, a syllogism contains a major premise, a minor premise, and a conclusion, as in the following example:

Major premise: All men are mortal.
Minor premise: Mike is a man.
Conclusion: Mike is mortal.

For the syllogism to work, the premises must be valid and the conclusion must logically follow from them.

Symbol—An object used to stand for something else. A flag, for instance, symbolizes the country it represents, the dove symbolizes peace, and the Star of David symbolizes Judaism.

Theme—The main idea or message conveyed by a narrative, often what one can conclude based on the actions of the characters or the narrator. For instance, the theme of Frankie Mac's "Being

Good" is that peer pressure should not lower our self-esteem or prevent us from trying new things. Themes are not what the narrative is about, but what the essay says about a certain idea. For example, in Lisa Bailey's essay "Black and White and Blue All Over," media coverage is not the theme. What her essay says about media coverage—that a community can misapprehend a local newspaper's presentation of events—is the theme. Themes are created through repetition and emphasis. A good piece of writing may contain multiple themes.

Thesis—The most important part of an essay, the thesis expresses the main idea to which all other elements of the essay are subordinate. Embodied in the thesis are *issue, audience, writer's stance,* and *purpose.* An explicit thesis appears in one sentence, whereas in an implied thesis, a series of sentences conveys the essay's intent through images, anecdotes, observations, and other means.

Tone—The attitude that the writer takes toward her subject matter. Thus, the author's tone in an essay written to protest the dumping of nuclear waste just outside the city limits may be one of outrage. But the term *tone* can also refer to the writer's attitude toward and relationship with her reading audience.

Transitions—Transitions are devices used to connect sentences with sentences, paragraphs with paragraphs. We should be aware of two kinds of transitions: the repetition of a key word or idea (or a synonym or a pronoun substituting for that idea); and traditional expressions such as *furthermore, additionally, for instance, finally,* and so on. Transitions create important bridges between ideas within an essay, making the essay a whole entity rather than a series of disjointed statements and assertions.

Unity—Unity is a quality that should be a part of every essay and paragraph. In a tightly unified essay, every detail in that essay should in some way support the thesis. In a unified paragraph, every detail should support the topic sentence. Details that fail to support the thesis of an essay or the topic of a paragraph should be eliminated. See also **Coherence**.

Writer—The writer, the essay's author, can adopt any number of personas, serious or not, in order to establish a tone and present an issue to the audience. You have many roles to fill in your life, and you can use any of them as an essay writer. You could be a concerned parent, an angry taxpayer, or an avid football fan. You can also pretend to be someone else entirely. Whatever persona you adopt, it should have a vested interest in the issue being discussed in the essay and should show a credible understanding of that issue. In part, your essay's merit will be judged based upon how well you present your voice and how well you demonstrate your knowledge.

CPSIA information can be obtained
at www.ICGtesting.com
Printed in the USA
JSHW012137030722
27649JS00013B/164